What Has Christianity Ever Done for Us?

A MONASTERY ON MOUNT ATHOS, ONE OF THE HOLIEST SITES OF GREEK ORTHODOX CHRISTIANITY. MOUNT ATHOS IS A PENINSULA JUTTING OFF THE GREEK MAINLAND, WHERE THE MONKS OF TWENTY MONSTERIES KEEP ALIVE THE TRADITIONS OF OVER 1,000 YEARS OF SPIRITUALITY.

JONATHAN HILL

What Has Christianity Ever Done for Us?

LION

Copyright © 2005 Jonathan Hill
This edition copyright © 2005 Lion Hudson

The author asserts the moral right
to be identified as the author of this work

A Lion Book
an imprint of
Lion Hudson plc
Mayfield House, 256 Banbury Road,
Oxford OX2 7DH, England
www.lionhudson.com
ISBN 0 7459 5168 6

First edition 2005
10 9 8 7 6 5 4 3 2 1 0

Acknowledgments
pp. 21, 66, 80, 108, 109, 136, 139, 141, 153, 158
Scripture quotations are from the New Revised
Standard Version published by HarperCollins
Publishers, copyright © 1989 by the Division of
Christian Education of the National Council of
the Churches of Christ in the USA, and are used
by permission. All rights reserved.

p. 39 Extract from 'When Love Comes to Town'.
Words by Bono. Copyright © 1988 Blue Mountain
Music Ltd.

A catalogue record for this book is available
from the British Library

Typeset in 14/16 Modern 880 BT
Printed and bound in Singapore

CHARLEMAGNE, THE FRANKISH WARRIOR KING WHO
CARVED OUT A NEW EMPIRE IN WESTERN EUROPE IN
THE EIGHTH CENTURY. HE IS SHOWN HOLDING A
MODEL OF THE MINSTER HE ESTABLISHED AT HIS
CAPITAL, AACHEN. WING FROM THE FORMER APSE
ALTAR IN AACHEN CATHEDRAL, C. 1485.

Contents

Introduction

Why do we seal wine bottles with cork? Where did the Taj Mahal get its dome from? What has an eight-foot giant who spent his time bending iron bars got to do with free education for everyone? Who invented the limerick? Where did musical notation come from? Why was the world's first fully literate society not in Europe, Asia or North America? And what is the proper behaviour when using the public baths?

These are a few of the questions that will be answered in this book. All the answers are connected with Christianity and the mark it has left on our heritage. Christianity has had an enormous influence over every aspect of Western life, from what we drink to how we speak, from how we write to how we mark the seasons. That remains true even as Christianity struggles in the West. All of us, whether we know it or not, are the heirs of our Christian past.

In this book we look at some of the contributions that Christianity has made to the world. Today, Christianity is the largest religion in the world, and is followed by approximately a third of the planet's population. It has spread beyond its ancient heartlands in Europe and the Middle East to North and South America, Asia, central Africa and the Pacific. It is, by any standard, a significant element of modern culture. But it has played a major role in history too. Without Christianity, today's world would be very different in many ways, quite apart from the obvious 'religious' ones.

Most people would accept that Christianity has, of course, got many things wrong. It was Christians who engaged in the Crusades, for example – the series of wars against the Muslims in the Middle Ages. In 1996, 900 years after the first Crusade was launched, thousands of Protestant Christians took part in the Reconciliation Walk, retracing the route of the crusaders in order to apologize to the Middle Eastern countries they had attacked. Four years later, Pope John Paul II also issued an official apology from the Roman Catholic Church, urging, 'Let us confess... our responsibilities as Christians for the evils of today.'

These acts of contrition may have come a little late, but they have been no less sincere for all that. Certainly, Christians today are among the first to recognize that the church has done wrong in the past, and they are among the first to condemn not only the Crusades but the excesses of the Spanish Inquisition, the witch hunts and so on. And as we shall see in this book, there have always been voices within Christianity raised against the church itself when it steps out of line.

But our focus here is on the positive heritage of Christianity – the times when it has got something right. What debt do we owe the Christians of the past – whether we ourselves are Christians or not? This book isn't meant to be a defence of Christianity: I certainly don't try to argue that Christianity is true, for example, and I don't have an agenda of my own that I am trying to push. Rather, it aims to be an objective look at some of the positive contributions that Christianity has made to the world over the past 2,000 years.

The first chapter takes a look at how ingrained Christianity has become in Western culture, and how it has made an impact elsewhere too. In particular, the religion has deeply influenced how we speak, how we read and write, and how we mark the passage of time.

In the second chapter, we see some of the most obvious effects of Christianity on culture through the ages: Christian art and literature. Christianity has inspired some of the greatest and most famous art created in the past two millennia, and this goes beyond overtly 'religious' works. We look at how Christianity deals in myths – stories that are, at heart, about everyone – and how this gives it much of its power.

This theme is expanded on in the third chapter, which deals with Christian attitudes to the world around us. Christianity is not just about mythic stories, but about mythic places, and we find out how it connects with the landscape. It not only interprets that landscape but changes it too, and this is where we look at one of the most striking achievements of Christianity: the development of church architecture.

Next we look at how Christianity has influenced the way we think. Chapter 4 examines how the religion has promoted education and learning, in everything from the first universities to the first fully literate society. Chapter 5 focuses on the understanding of people and the world that Christianity has led to – both the interaction of individuals and the group, and the rise of science. Today, we often think of science and religion as intrinsically at odds, but that is a modern, relatively recent development.

To many people, religion is essentially about living a good life, and this is the subject of the next two chapters. In chapter 6 we look at one of the central problems tackled by philosophers and other thinkers over the centuries – what it actually means to lead a good life – and at some of the Christian answers to that question. Figures such as Francis of Assisi, Thomas Aquinas and Jesus himself have offered interesting and appealing lifestyles that continue to inspire. Some of that inspiration comes across in chapter 7, where we see some of the practical things Christians have done to improve the world when they have got stuck into politics – as both rulers and subversives.

What might Christianity do next? That is the subject of the final chapter, where we consider briefly the current situation of the religion and think about a few of the contributions it could make in years to come.

CHAPTER 1

Culture and Thought

'All Protestants,' declared Alexis Khomiakov, 'are crypto-papists.' Khomiakov, a prominent Russian poet, political thinker, inventor and (in what little spare time remained) dog breeder, was writing to a Western friend in 1846, and he was claiming that all Western Christians, whether they know it or not, are basically Roman Catholics. In fact, Khomiakov regarded Western culture itself as intrinsically Catholic. That's a statement I suspect not many readers will agree with, especially those who are neither Catholics nor any other kind of Christian. What Khomiakov meant, of course, was that over the centuries Catholicism had become so ingrained into the Western mindset that even those who rejected it were, in a sense, allowing it to define the way they thought.

Is it true? Today, the majority of people in the West are no longer Christian. In western Europe in particular, most people now inhabit a post-Christian society, where the outdated norms of Christianity are no more binding than the outdated norms of, say, the Vikings' religion, or that of the Romans. In eastern Europe, the heartland of the Orthodox Christianity that Khomiakov was passionately defending as an alternative to Western Catholicism, the legacy of Communism has left Christianity in an ambiguous position. And in the Middle East, the ancient home of Christianity, it has long been driven to a minority position by Islam.

Yet all these places and more are still deeply influenced by their Christian heritage. From the way we speak or write to the way we mark the seasons, Christianity still leaves its stamp on all of us.

Throwing ink at the devil – Christians and the roots of language

It was during the Reformation that Christianity left its clearest imprints on language. The Reformation was a movement of protest against the Catholic Church – at that time the only church in Europe – which swept over the continent in the sixteenth century. It was started by the German monk Martin Luther, who in 1517 published 'Ninety-Five Theses' criticizing certain elements of Catholic practice. To his own considerable surprise, he found himself the mouthpiece for a great groundswell of resentment that had been building up for centuries. One of the key beliefs of Luther and others like him was that individual Christians should have direct access to the Bible, which they believed was God's primary means of communicating with humanity, and they should not have to rely on some priest telling them what was in it. Translators appeared within the ranks of the 'Protestants', as the adherents to the Reformation movement were called, ready to turn the Bible into vernacular tongues so that the people could read it. And this happened at a critical period in the development of modern languages: authors were just starting to write in the everyday languages of normal people, rather than in the Latin of the educated classes, and this meant that these languages were changing and developing new forms at an incredible pace. This is why so many common phrases and sayings in use today come from the works of William Shakespeare: he and others like him were writing at just the time when modern English was, essentially, being invented. The impact of the Reformation and its Bibles for the masses on this already very fluid situation was immense.

Take William Tyndale, for example, a leading light of the Reformation in England. He made the first modern English translation of the Bible in the 1520s and 30s, for which, in addition to his Protestant views, he was burned at the stake in 1536. He had, however, left his mark on his language. Phrases we think of as biblical, such as 'let there be light' or 'ye of little faith', come from his translation of the Bible. But so do many more that have become common clichés, such as 'eat, drink and be merry', 'the powers that be', 'the salt of the earth', 'a man after his own heart' and 'the signs of the times'. These and many others found their way into the famous Authorized Version of the Bible, also known as the King James Bible, because it was commissioned by James I of England to replace the large numbers of English Bibles that had appeared in the decades since Tyndale. By this time, of course, England was officially Protestant, and translating the Bible had changed from being a capital crime to something the king himself sponsored; no doubt the spirit of Tyndale felt vindicated, if slightly aggrieved, by this. The King James Bible appeared in 1611 and was enormously successful: even today, it is still widely read, especially in America. Its language is old-fashioned by today's standards, but the fact that it is still largely intelligible is simply because of its innate clarity. Because modern English has been so influenced by this translation, the text remains readable even four centuries on.

Yet the efforts of Tyndale and the teams who worked on the King James Bible pale before those of the man who started the Reformation in the first place, Martin Luther himself. He not only translated the Bible into his own language of German, but he essentially had to create the modern form of that language to do so.

It all happened in the 1520s, after Luther's ideas had been condemned by the Holy Roman Emperor, Charles V. Fortunately, the monk was protected by his patron, Frederick the Wise of Saxony, who spirited him away to a lonely castle called the Wartburg. Here, completely secluded from the outside world, Luther grew a big beard as a disguise and set to work translating the scriptures into German. It was extremely difficult work: although a good scholar, Luther was only in his element when surrounded by other people. This big, loud, charismatic man found himself

MARTIN LUTHER — REFORMER, THEOLOGIAN, TRANSLATOR AND BEER CONNOISSEUR. PAINTING BY LUCAS CRANACH THE ELDER, 1532.

emotionally starved, spending day after day hunched over a desk in a tower room. He was plagued by ill health, especially chronic constipation. And he believed that even supernatural powers were conspiring to stop his work. On one famous occasion, it seemed to him that the devil appeared and tried to distract him. Luther was, in fact, rather obsessed with the devil, whom he held responsible for anything that went wrong, however minor; but he regarded him with contempt rather than fear. When he heard the devil stomping around at night, he would mutter, 'Oh, it's just you,' and go back to sleep. At other times, he would 'chase him away with a fart', as he charmingly put it. On this occasion, we are told, Luther hurled his ink pot at the apparition, causing it to vanish. However, when Luther said that he fought the devil with ink, he meant by his writings – a reflection of Luther's basic Christian belief that the best weapon against the devil was not physical violence but learning.

Despite all this, and in just eleven weeks, Luther produced the first draft of a complete German New Testament. Like Tyndale, Luther intended this to be read not by professional churchmen but by the ordinary man in the street. Since this was his aim, Luther needed a Bible that as many people as possible would be able to read – not an easy task, given that there was no one language that everyone spoke, even within Germany. The language spoken in the German states at this time is now known as Middle German, but it was in fact a bewildering variety of languages. The two main divisions of the language – High German (spoken in the south) and Low German (spoken in the north) – were each subdivided into an array of dialects, depending on where you were and what class you belonged to. Worse, the kind of German that appeared in books – when they were in German at all, rather than Latin – tended to be a special 'written' German that bore little resemblance to what people on the street spoke.

What Luther had to do was translate the idioms of everyday German into a written form comprehensible to people who spoke quite different dialects from each other – a tough challenge by anyone's standards. He answered the challenge by adapting the court language used in the state of Saxony, changing the style so that it sounded like normal, everyday speech. He was especially keen for the details of the text to make sense to the people of his time. So, for example, where the scriptures mention precious stones, Luther researched the kinds of jewels that were used in German courts. He went to slaughterhouses to check that he was getting the details of Old Testament sacrifices right. His overriding concern was to produce a text that would ring true to ordinary, working people.

Luther succeeded beyond his wildest dreams. The *September Testament* – so called after the month of publication in 1522 – sold 5,000 copies in two months, an

A RECONSTRUCTION OF THE
REVOLUTIONARY PRINTING PRESS INVENTED
BY JOHANNES GUTENBERG, WHICH
ALLOWED LUTHER AND OTHERS ACCESS TO
A HUGE AUDIENCE MORE QUICKLY THAN
ANYONE HAD MANAGED BEFORE.

astonishing run in an age when printing had only been possible for a few decades and most people couldn't read anyway. When Luther was writing, only about one in three people in the most sophisticated towns could read – a figure that dropped to one in twenty in the countryside, where most people lived. In fact, it was in large part the efforts of Luther and others like him that changed the situation dramatically.

The power of the press – Christians and literacy

Luther had, with his monumental translation, created a new standard of written German – what would become known as modern German, the standard spoken and written language of the country to this day. But more than this, he, together with others such as Tyndale, had helped give the power of the written word to the people. The printing press had been invented in 1436 by Johannes Gutenberg, who had piously chosen the Latin Bible as the first book to be published. The invention made the mass production of books relatively cheap and easy. As a result, by the time Luther was writing, nearly a century later, it was far easier for him to circulate his ideas. But this had a knock-on effect: not only was it easier for people to get reading material, but now there was something they actually *wanted* to read. Luther believed that every person should have direct access to the Bible, because he believed that it was the Bible, not the church or its priests, that should be the ultimate and sole authority in religion. And many people agreed with him. As Luther's movement spread rapidly across the German-speaking states, and even beyond, an instant demand was created for Bibles and other books. As that demand was filled, literacy levels rose, since people needed to be able to read the Bible for themselves, not simply listen to someone else's interpretation.

Thirty or forty years ago, it might have seemed that the written word was on its way out. The appearance of the telephone, then radio, television and computers meant that for many people the spoken word or the image were the primary means of communication, not the letter. Yet the incredibly swift rise of the Internet, together with the unprecedented convenience of email, means that the written word is still central to the modern world. The mass literacy that has enabled this to take place, together with the uniformity of language that underlies it, is to a large extent an heirloom of the Reformation and its Christian ideals.

In fact, writing and literacy were fostered by Christians long before Luther. In the Dark Ages, for example, as the Christian Roman empire crumbled and new powers arose throughout Europe and the Middle East, missionaries headed out to the new territories to bring the message of Christ. They quickly found that persuading people to accept that message was only the first hurdle that had to be cleared. If the new Christian population had no priests from their own people, the religion would never be really rooted in their culture – it would have to be imported to them, generation by generation. But in order to have a church and priests of their own, the people had to be able to hold church services in their own language. And for that, they had to have Bibles and other Christian writings in their own language. Yet general standards of literacy among the non-Roman peoples of the Dark Ages were considerably lower even than in western Europe in Luther's time. In fact, some countries didn't have writing at all. The missionaries therefore found themselves having to refine languages and writing systems so that it was possible to provide people with Bibles they could understand – and in extreme cases they had to invent alphabets from the ground up. It's sometimes easy to get the impression that European history from the sixth century to the ninth consisted almost entirely of these enterprising missionaries educating entire countries more or less single-handedly. That's an exaggeration, of course, but it was certainly a heroic age.

The most famous of these missionaries were Cyril and Methodius, two Greek brothers from the Orthodox Church, who in the ninth century brought Christianity to the Khazars, a Slavic nation living between the Black Sea and the Caspian Sea, and later to the Moravians in eastern Europe. In order to do this they had not only to learn the Slavic language but also to find a suitable writing system for it. Cyril adapted the Greek alphabet to suit Slavic, and this is why modern Russian is still written in an alphabet that looks a little like Greek, and which is called 'Cyrillic'.

An even more enterprising missionary, who lived some centuries earlier, rejoiced in the splendid name of Mesrob Mashtotes. He brought Christianity to Armenia, a mountainous country situated midway between the Roman and the Persian empires. Its location meant that, over the centuries, Armenia had seen a lot of Romans heading east to fight the Persians, and a lot of Persians going west to kill the Romans, but no one had paid much attention to the place they were marching through. Unlike Cyril and Methodius, who were Greeks who brought Christianity to other nations, Mesrob was actually Armenian himself, at a time when Christianity was a minority concern there. Like Cyril and Methodius, however, he recognized that a religion could never take root in a population unless it made sense in that population's language and culture. He therefore invented an alphabet for Armenia, which at that stage had none, and set about translating the Bible into it. We are told that he also invented an alphabet for the Georgians, who lived to the north, although this does not survive. Mesrob's efforts were enormously successful: the Armenians took Christianity to their hearts, and today the Armenian Church remains one of the most ancient national churches still in existence. The religion is an integral part of Armenian culture, and one of the things that allows Armenians to retain a strong sense of who they are and where they come from, wherever they may be – for today Armenians are among the most dispersed nationalities in the world, with communities in every country around the globe. Even more than this, however, Mesrob brought learning and scholarship to his people, and gave them the tools they needed to spread Armenian culture itself. In the generations after his death, Armenia went through something of a golden age of literature – something that would have been impossible without the literacy that came with Christianity.

And even in ancient times, Christians were experimenting with ways of bringing literacy to those for whom normal methods of reading and writing were impossible.

CYRIL AND METHODIUS. THEY PROBABLY DRESSED SLIGHTLY MORE PRACTICALLY FOR ACTUAL MISSIONARY WORK. WOOD ENGRAVING, ANONYMOUS, 1863.

Didymus the Blind sounds like the name of a blues singer, but it was in fact the name of a famous Christian teacher and writer who lived in fourth-century Alexandria. Despite losing his sight at the age of four, he succeeded in mastering all disciplines of learning, even geometry. Didymus managed this because he possessed an incredible memory, but evidently his disability caused him some frustration. There is a story of him complaining about it to the celebrated hermit Antony of Egypt, who rather unhelpfully replied that even rats could see, but Didymus was lucky enough to possess the spiritual senses of angels. Didymus tried to find ways to help blind people to read, and experimented with carved wooden letters with the idea that people could feel their shapes and 'read' by touch. This was, in fact, a precursor to the Braille systems used by blind people today, and is a graphic illustration of the extraordinarily close association that Christianity has always had with reading. Didymus was not the only Christian to be particularly concerned with those without sight. Basil of Caesarea, who lived a generation later, established special hospices and provided guides for blind people. In the fifth century, Limnaeus, a Syrian Christian hermit, preached to blind people and had houses built for them.

Christianity, of course, is not the only major religion to foster literacy. Islam has also had a profound effect on the areas where it has permeated. But there is one significant difference between the two: the issue of language. The Qur'an is written in Arabic, and Muslims believe that this is in itself significant: Arabic is the language of God, and although the Qur'an can be translated into other languages, you really need to learn it in Arabic. This has meant that Arabic has survived and flourished as a major language. Christianity, by contrast, has been less bothered about the language of the Bible: it is written in Hebrew and Greek, but that doesn't imply anything special about those languages. They are just the languages that the original authors happened to speak. So Christianity, more than Islam, has been happy to translate its scriptures into other languages, and this has had the effect not simply of transmitting its own history and culture but also of transforming it and bolstering the cultures to which it is transmitted. In this way, Christianity has had a more dynamic and complex role in the transformation of culture than Islam.

And if Christianity has permeated the way we speak and write, it has had an equally profound effect on our conception of time and the cycle of the year.

From Santa to the Easter Bunny – Christian festivals

It seems that our annual celebrations have become more and more extended, until there is no space between them. The moment Christmas finishes, Easter begins, pausing for Valentine's Day as a kind of interlude; then there's hardly a chance to draw breath before Halloween turns up. At least, that's the impression one might get from a stroll down the High Street. In today's Western world, our festivals have become increasingly commercialized, and retailers are desperate to ram them down our throats for as long as possible in order to maximize profits.

And yet annual festivals have always been a part of human life, perhaps for as long as people have looked forward to the return of spring or the gathering of the harvest. It may be fashionable today to complain bitterly about the commercialization of Christmas, Valentine's Day or whatever – but really the greetings card manufacturers and the rest are simply tapping into a basic human necessity: the necessity of marking the seasons.

In the past, in a more agrarian age, the changing of the seasons had an all-pervasive influence over people's lives. People celebrated the solstices and equinoxes, events which today pass most people by completely unawares. We are familiar with the great monuments that testify to the ancients' closeness to the cycle of the year and of the heavens. There is Stonehenge, for example, one of nearly 1,000 similar stone circles in England alone – some even bigger and more impressive, though less famous. The pyramids at Giza and the temples of Angkor Wat in Cambodia are also famous for the role that astronomical cycles play in their design – which does not, of course, entail that they were necessarily built by aliens or the scientists of Atlantis, as some people would have us believe! Newgrange, a striking monument in Ireland, older even than

'This is our present festival. This is what we are celebrating today – the coming of God to man... so that we might return to God... So let us keep the feast, not like a heathen festival, but in a godly way – not in the way of the world, but in a way above the world – not as if it were ours, but as it belongs to him who is ours, our Master's – not as of weakness, but as of healing – not as of creation, but of re-creation.'

Gregory of Nazianzus, *Oration* 38, on the birthday of Christ, AD 380

ANGKOR WAT (LITERALLY 'THE TEMPLE OF ANGKOR') AT ANGKOR, THE ANCIENT CAPITAL OF THE KHMER EMPIRE. THE TEMPLE WAS BUILT IN THE TWELFTH CENTURY BY KING SURYAVARMAN II AND DEDICATED TO THE HINDU GOD VISHNU, BUT IT LATER BECAME A BUDDHIST TEMPLE.

the pyramids, is designed so that the sun shines directly into its central chamber at dawn on the winter solstice.

And today, too, some cultures still celebrate the changing year. In Japan, television weather forecasts also feature information on what colour the leaves are or which kinds of blossom are currently out. The Japanese love of cherry blossom reflects a basic fascination with cyclical change. Cherry blossom is beautiful not only because of its appearance, but because it lasts only a short time, which gives its beauty an overtone of sadness. Yet it will pass to be replaced by something else, and in a year's time it will be back again.

In the West, meanwhile, the cycle of the year has taken on a Christian form. In fact, all the festivals mentioned at the start of this section are Christian in origin. Christmas celebrates the birth of Christ – hence the name, from the old word 'mass', meaning a celebration. (It is not, contrary to common belief, a reference to the Roman Catholic ceremony of the Mass, their name for the Eucharist.) Easter celebrates the resurrection of Christ on the third day after his crucifixion. Valentine's Day comes from the festival day of St Valentine, and Halloween is the day before All Hallows', also known as All Saints' Day, the day when all Christian saints are remembered. In the past, it was thought that all evil spirits would therefore make the most of the day that came before, since All Hallows' was clearly too holy for them to be out; and so Hallows' Evening – or *Hallowe'en* – became associated with ghosts, witches and the rest.

But are these really Christian festivals? After all, those pagans who built Stonehenge were celebrating the winter solstice at the end of December anyway. Isn't it a bit of a coincidence that the Christians then came along and stuck Christmas at exactly the same time? Similarly, didn't the Saxons celebrate the festival of their spring goddess – called 'Eostre' – at around the time that Christians would later celebrate the resurrection of Christ? Some people today therefore argue that to criticize modern society for the commercialization of these holidays is wrong. They were originally celebrations of the turning of the year, of fertility, the harvest and so on, and it is the Christians who have tried to hijack them with all this pious nonsense about Jesus!

In one way, of course, this is quite correct. Some Christian festivals did indeed have pagan forebears. Christmas, for example, is often associated with festivals such as Yule and Saturnalia. Saturnalia was the Roman celebration of the winter solstice, and involved serious parties and large quantities of alcohol; as such, it was the most popular holiday in the Roman calendar. Yule, meanwhile, was Scandinavian, and was correspondingly more dour, reflecting the grimmer climate of the north. At these times, plants such as holly, ivy and mistletoe were prized for their evergreen qualities – they represented the hope that all trees would regain their leaves in the spring. A tree would be chosen as the 'Yule log', to burn on the hearth throughout the festival as an offering to Thor, the Norse god of thunder. Sometimes this involved having an entire tree in the house, with one end in the fireplace; the trunk would be slowly fed into the fire as it was burned. And Yule was the time when the Wild Host would ride by on the winter skies, led by the god Odin himself, bringing the promise of fertility.

In fact, it seems that Christians chose to celebrate the birth of Christ not at the same time as Saturnalia, but halfway between that festival and another, the Calends of January. The idea was that the Christians (who celebrated neither of these pagan events) would have something of their own while everyone else was recovering from Saturnalia. That is why Christmas is on 25 December, rather than on 21 December, the date of the solstice. That, at least, was the explanation given by John Chrysostom, who lived at the end of the fourth century – the century when this date was fixed for good. There was, of course, no reason to suppose that this was actually the date of Jesus' birthday, something that can never be known. But if Jesus had been born on 25 December, he would have been circumcised on 1 January, because the Old Testament specifies that this should be done on the eighth day. Dionysius Exiguus, the sixth-century monk who established the modern system of dating the years from Christ's birth, actually chose to date from his circumcision, not his birth, because it coincided so usefully with the start of the year.

As Christianity spread throughout Europe in the centuries following the collapse of the Roman empire, and the old festivals began to be displaced by the new, it was

AN EIGHTH-CENTURY VIKING STELE, OR STONE MONUMENT. IN THIS SCENE, THE GOD ODIN IS SHOWN ON THE RIGHT RIDING SLEIPNIR, THE FATHER OF ALL HORSES (ALTHOUGH UNLIKE SLEIPNIR, OTHER HORSES DO NOT HAVE EIGHT LEGS). ON THE LEFT IS THE GATE OF VALHALLA, THE HALL OF THE DEAD, COMPLETE WITH VALKYRIES — WARRIOR WOMEN WHO TOOK THE SOULS OF THOSE WHO FELL IN BATTLE TO VALHALLA. CONTRARY TO THE POPULAR IMAGE, THESE VALKYRIES ARE NOT ENORMOUSLY FAT WITH PIGTAILS, AND THEY DO NOT APPEAR TO BE SINGING.

inevitable that many of the old customs would remain, but be Christianized. For example, holly lost its significance as an evergreen, and instead its red berries were interpreted as signifying the blood of Christ. New customs evolved, such as the staging of plays, something that came about in the Middle Ages. These plays would retell the story of the fall and salvation of humanity, and a central feature would therefore be the Tree of Knowledge from the story of Adam and Eve – a new role for the old Yule log. In fact, the Christmas tree in its modern form is said to have been invented by none other than Martin Luther himself. According to the story, he was walking home one winter night when he saw the stars shining through the branches of a fir tree. He thought the sight so beautiful that he cut the tree down and took it home, where he decorated it with candles so that his family could enjoy the sight too. Clearly, Luther's credentials as a family man were better than those as an environmentalist.

THE SCARIEST TOY EVER? THE CUT-OUT SHEET FOR A RUPRECHT PUPPET, C. 1850. ONE SHUDDERS TO THINK HOW MANY CHILDREN WERE PSYCHOLOGICALLY SCARRED FOR LIFE BY THIS THING.

So did the Christians simply steal pre-existing festivals? It seems the answer isn't that straightforward. Much of what we know as part of Christmas comes from Yule and other celebrations of the solstice, but Christmas itself was not based on those older festivals. Similarly, Easter coincides with the festival of Eostre, even taking its name from her (although most languages call it something similar to Pâche, the French version, which derives from a word referring to the suffering of Christ). Hares played an important role in the pagan festival, and it was a misunderstanding of these that turned them into rabbits and then into the American Easter Bunny. But little in the modern celebration of Easter comes from that festival. Indeed, we wouldn't know about that pagan festival at all if it weren't for the fact that the eighth-century Christian scholar Bede thought it worth recording – together with other pagan gods, festivals and names. So the Christians may have taken over parts of the pagan past, but we know this, in part, because they told us so themselves.

This complex situation is perhaps best summed up by the enigmatic figure associated with Christmas, who is known variously as Father Christmas and Santa Claus. He is, in fact, an amalgamation of two different characters. The Germanic Father Christmas is pagan in origin, going all the way back to the Wild Hunt of Yule and the gods Odin and Thor. In Germany, he is still accompanied by a sinister figure named Ruprecht, and while Father Christmas rewards the good children, Ruprecht takes care of the rest with his stick. Yet somewhere along the line this pagan and rather scary character became mixed up with St Nicholas of Myra, who lived in the fourth century (when the date for Christmas was being established!) and who died for his faith. He is remembered on 6 December, which in most of Europe is also a time for giving presents, because of a story about St Nicholas throwing money through a window to help the poor. It has been suggested that the Dutch settlers in America, in the city of New Amsterdam, had to wait weeks for their St Nicholas presents to reach them from Europe, and this is why the tradition there got mixed up with Christmas. When the British took the city and renamed it New York in 1664, they brought the Germanic Father Christmas with them, and he got confused with St Nicholas – or, in Dutch, Sinter Klass. The American Santa Claus was duly born. Like so much of our modern culture, he is a perfect amalgamation of paganism and Christianity, the product of a complex history – a history greatly influenced, but not completely determined, by Christianity.

Rhythms and cycles – the Christian year

What, then, is the Christian year? The big festivals such as Christmas and Easter are just the tip of the iceberg. As the centuries have passed, Christians have found more and more dates to mark, until today almost every day in the year has something to commemorate – indeed, some have more, so that two or more very different saints are forced, as it were, to timeshare the same day.

Different Christian churches have slightly different calendars – which is only natural, given that they disagree, at least, over who counts as a saint. But the calendar of the Roman Catholic Church is typical. For them, as for all Christians, the Christian year starts with the first Sunday in Advent, the period before Christmas. The Catholic Church commemorates the Virgin Mary on 8 December, and Christmas, of course, follows on 25 December. Mary gets another day on 1 January, and then on 6 January most churches celebrate Epiphany, when the Wise Men from the East presented their gifts to Jesus. The Christmas season rounds off with the commemoration of Jesus' baptism. After this follows a period known as 'ordinary time', which ends with the start of Lent on Ash Wednesday. Lent is a period of forty days during which Christians are meant to fast in commemoration of the forty days that Jesus spent fasting in the desert after his baptism and before the start of his public ministry. When Lent was generally observed, people would try to use up 'luxury' foods such as eggs and sugar on the day before Lent began – which is why pancakes were invented, and why that day is now known in Britain as Pancake Day. The idea of using up all the luxuries before the fast also gave rise to Carnival (in Venice, Rio de Janeiro and elsewhere) and Mardi Gras (in America, especially New Orleans – literally, 'Fat Tuesday'), which happen at the same time – although, naturally, both are far more exuberant than the British equivalent!

The last week of Lent is Holy Week, the high point of the church's calendar. It begins with Palm Sunday, which marks Jesus' entry into Jerusalem for the festival of

Passover. After this is Good Friday, which marks his crucifixion, and finally Easter Sunday, which marks his resurrection. The date of Easter varies from year to year because, like the Jewish festival of Passover on which it is based, it is calculated according to the lunar months, which do not coincide with the calendar months. Six weeks after Easter, Christians remember the Ascension, when, according to Luke's Gospel, the risen Christ left his disciples and returned to heaven. The church then reverts to ordinary time again until Trinity Sunday, when its members must contemplate the threeness of God – a day dreaded by priests, who must find some way to preach an interesting sermon on this most rarefied of topics. Next comes Corpus Christi (Latin for 'body of Christ'), when Catholics contemplate the miracle of the Eucharist. After more weeks of ordinary time comes the feast of the Transfiguration, which marks the occasion when Jesus allowed three of his disciples to glimpse his divinity. All Saints' Day is 1 November (the day after Halloween), and before you know it, it is Advent again. All of this is quite apart from the myriad of saints and minor festivals that are commemorated throughout the year. Every day has particular readings from the Bible or from other writings appointed to it, so that as the year goes by the whole of the Bible will have been read or heard in the church.

This cycle of the year is just the wider arc of a series of other cycles, too. The week is a year in miniature: every Friday is a small version of Good Friday, which is why it is traditionally a day of fasting – meaning that Catholics would not eat meat on this day. And every Sunday is a small version of Easter. Contrary to popular belief, Sunday is not the Sabbath. Jews rest on the Sabbath, the seventh day of the week, because according to Genesis, God created the world in six days and rested on the seventh. So the Sabbath is Saturday. Early in Christian history, however, it was decided that Christians would celebrate not the Jewish Sabbath but 'the Lord's day' – the day that Christ rose from the dead, Sunday. Sunday therefore came to have a similar meaning for Christians as Saturday did for the Jews, and at times it has even been called the Sabbath. The modern weekend, where both Saturday and Sunday are a holiday, is a combination of both – definitely having your cake and eating it, too.

Even within each day, there is a cycle, although for most Christians today it passes almost invisibly. In the Middle Ages, however, when churches and the religious life were everywhere, it was more evident. Monks would feel it the most, as their day began with the service of Matins and was subsequently punctuated by Lauds, Prime, Terce, Sext, None, Vespers and finally Compline. Each of these services consisted mainly of a set of prayers specially designed for the hour of the day at which they came. In this way, the natural rhythms of the day found expression in a religious form, to match the rhythms of the week and the year, which all went on at the same time.

And indeed, the observance of these cycles gave the church an important role in medieval science. Many monks became adept at astronomy, an essential skill in establishing the precise time of day so they would know when to pray. The development of astronomy matched that in the Muslim territories, because Muslims needed to know which direction to face when praying (towards Mecca). Both Christians and Muslims therefore became expert in the use of astronomical instruments such as the astrolabe, an instrument that was apparently in use in the eastern Mediterranean by late antiquity and which was introduced to the Muslims by the Christians they conquered in the seventh century. When the Muslims subsequently conquered most of Spain, the Christian monks in neighbouring territories learned about the astrolabe from them, and so the Christians relearned what they had once known centuries before.

Living with the past – Christians and history

Where did the Christian understanding of the cycle of the year come from? Perhaps its most important element is the recognition that history is important – a recognition that it inherits from Judaism. The Jewish year, just like the Christian year, revolves around a number of festivals that commemorate past events – indeed, some of the Christian festivals are based, in part, upon these old Jewish ones. For example, the Jewish festival of Purim celebrates the events described in the Old Testament book of Esther, which tells the story of the dastardly Haman, vizier to the king, whose evil plot to destroy the Jews is foiled by Queen Esther and her adopted father, Mordecai. Today, children dress up, go to the synagogue and listen to the story being retold, spinning noisy rattles every time Haman is mentioned, as if booing a pantomime villain!

Festivals like that help a community to remember some great event of the past – although, over time, the memory may fade but the festival remain. But there is another kind of festival that is more central to both Jewish and Christian celebrations, and that is where a past event is remembered but also, in a way that is hard to describe, re-enacted or made real once more for people today. In Judaism, this is what happens at the Passover, the annual festival that remembers the single most important defining event in Jewish history: the time when, led by Moses and pursued by Pharaoh, the Hebrews fled Egypt. This is the central event of the book of Exodus in the Old Testament, and it took place more than 3,000 years ago. The celebration of Passover today mirrors what happened then. For example, on the eve of the Exodus, the Jews did not bother to leaven their bread, since it would take too long. Similarly, Jews today eat unleavened bread at Passover. It is not simply a way of learning and remembering what happened then – it is a way of making it real. When the story of the Exodus is retold at Passover, the speaker uses the word 'we' to refer to the Hebrews who fled Egypt: this is something their distant ancestors did that they can partake in today.

This fundamental belief – that our history is part of who we are – is central to the Christian calendar too. At most church services, Christians of all denominations recite the Apostles' Creed, a universal statement of faith which, according to legend, was written by Jesus' followers themselves after his resurrection – although it actually developed over the following few centuries. One of the final items on the list of beliefs in the creed is 'the communion of saints', something that doesn't mean very much the first time you hear it. What it refers to is that all Christians are, in a sense, united: the

'When Haman saw that Mordecai did not bow down or do obeisance to him, Haman was infuriated. But he thought it beneath him to lay hands on Mordecai alone. So, having been told who Mordecai's people were, Haman plotted to destroy all the Jews, the people of Mordecai, throughout the whole kingdom of Ahasuerus.'

Esther 3:5–6

fact that they are Christians, and members of the same church, overrides all else – even the divisions of time, life and death. Traditionally, Christians distinguish between 'the church militant', which is the sum of all living Christians, and 'the church triumphant', which is all those who have died in the faith. Although their conditions are different, they are all members of the one church, and there is a fundamental communion between them.

Thus, the history of the church is very important to its current members, because the figures of the past are not simply people who died a long time ago, but they remain united to Christians today. This is one reason why every day in the calendar has its assigned saint or saints to be remembered on that day: by listening to and remembering their stories, the hearer can, to some degree, share in their achievements. And some Christian traditions take this idea of closeness to figures of the past even further. Ever since the first centuries of Christianity, the church has valued the relics of saints, believing that God's power can work through them. The practice of the early Christians

THE GOLDEN DOMES OF THE
KIEV-PECHERSK LAVRA BUILDINGS —
BUILT OVER THE ORIGINAL CAVES — TOWER
OVER KIEV. THE MONASTERY COMPLEX IS
ALMOST A CITY WITHIN A CITY, GROWING
ITS OWN CROPS AND EMPLOYING ITS OWN
ARCHITECTS, BUILDERS, TAILORS,
GARDENERS, COOKS AND BAKERS.

of laying their dead to rest in the catacombs of Rome, and holding services there to celebrate the martyrs, started a close connection between Christian worship and burial. That is why so many churches stand in graveyards. And many Eastern churches still preserve the bodies of saints. In Greece, churches sometimes bring out their local saint for a parade, when the people celebrate that saint's story and continued presence with them.

Perhaps the most striking example of this reverence for the saints is the Kiev-Pechersk Lavra, one of the holiest sites in Orthodox Christianity. As the Byzantine empire, the traditional stronghold of Christianity in the Middle East and Eastern Europe, dwindled in the Middle Ages, the faith took hold in the lands that would become Russia. After the fall of the Byzantine capital, Constantinople, in 1453, the new Russian capital of Moscow took its place; but the Russians retained a special place in their hearts for their old capital, Kiev, now the capital of Ukraine. For centuries it was, in a sense, the Russian Orthodox Rome. Here, in 1051, the Kiev-Pechersk Lavra was founded in the dramatic setting of a series of caves, hence the name ('Kiev Cave Monastery'). The holy caves became a major centre for pilgrimage, and they retained their aura even after the rise of Moscow and the decline of Kiev as a political power. The monastery is still there: miles of labyrinthine tunnels connecting different churches, towers, museums and ecclesiastic and cultural treasures beyond price. But threaded through the tunnels are numerous crypts. The cool, dry air of the crypts quickly mummified the bodies of those who died, and the monks, interpreting this as a sign from God, took to keeping the bodies of their predecessors in full view in the crypts. Today, these open tombs still line the tunnels, and the saints of the past – dressed in their robes, although with their faces covered – remain on view. They are not there simply as rather grotesque curiosities: on the contrary, the faithful who visit the monastery today show them respect and reverence, even lifting their children to get a better look.

This sort of behaviour strikes most Westerners today as unhealthily morbid. All the same, other cultures also recognize the value in trying to keep the dead as a living presence today. In Japan, for example, the families of those who have died keep a small shrine to the dead relative in the house. Graves are regularly tended and kept neat – indeed, the typical Japanese reaction to a picturesque, overgrown English country churchyard would be to wonder why nobody seems to care about the graves there. From an Asian point of view, Westerners are terrified of death and indecently keen to forget those who have died. But practices like those of the Kiev-Pechersk Lavra suggest that the Christian tradition has retained a strong sense of closeness to those who have gone before. It is a sense that remains even in those churches that do not preserve relics, as is shown by the importance of the church calendar.

Yet more than this, the Christian church regards itself as intimately joined to its founder, Jesus himself. The most important festivals of the Christian year celebrate key moments in his life. Just as with the Jewish celebrations, these dates in the calendar are not simply memorials of events that happened many centuries ago. They are ways of making those events real today, of, in a sense, participating in them. It is the same basic idea that is central to the Eucharist, the most important Christian ceremony. In the service, the priest says over the bread and wine the words that Jesus used at the Last Supper, the night before he was executed. By taking part in the service and consuming the bread and wine, the congregation and the priest not only re-enact the Last Supper but make it present to themselves. That is, they don't simply remember that it happened nor do they just repeat it, as if there were nothing special about the first time it took place. Instead, they use the service as a way of tapping into that first time, jumping over the intervening centuries.

The cycle of the year, then, illustrates an essential element of Christianity, something that distinguishes it from many other religions, and something that has a valuable influence on our culture: the importance of *history*. Buddhism, for example, revolves around the teachings of the Buddha, but it is the teachings that matter, rather than the fact that the Buddha delivered them, and their authority is based on their truth, not on him. But Christianity revolves around the historical person of Jesus, and it is rooted in the historical events of his life. The doctrine that God has become man – possibly the most central doctrine of the Christian faith – is a celebration of particularity: God became a particular man in a particular place at a particular time.

Plato, Confucius and a good argument – Christians in minority

It might be thought that all this is very well, but it doesn't say much about those parts of the world where Christianity has generally been a minority concern – which, indeed, make up most of the globe. After all, countries such as Japan or China seem to have done fairly well without many Christians. Isn't there an unreasonably Western bias here?

On the one hand, this is true. If we're looking at the ways in which Christianity has influenced aspects of life such as culture and learning, then obviously it will have exercised greatest influence on those countries and continents where it has existed for the most time and achieved the greatest infiltration into common culture. But it can also be interesting to see what happens when Christianity engages with cultures where it is new, or has only recently been introduced. We shall see various examples

> 6
> *'I must repeat to you the words of Isaiah... "Bread shall be given to him, and his water shall be sure."... Now it is evident that in this prophecy allusion is made to the bread which our Christ gave us to eat, in remembrance of his being made flesh for the sake of his believers, for whom also he suffered, and to the cup which he gave us to drink, in remembrance of his own blood, with giving of thanks.'*
>
> Justin Martyr,
> *Dialogue with Trypho* 70,
> c. AD 150

of this in the coming chapters, but a general theme is this: when Christianity (or, indeed, any other belief system) exists as a minority concern, it is well placed to act as a critical influence on the majority viewpoint. Indeed, it can be positively subversive.

Often this tendency can involve opening up a striking new dialogue within a society's culture, providing fresh ideas or a new view of old ones. This happened, for example, in the early centuries of Christianity, when it was still a minority religion within the Roman empire, alternately tolerated and proscribed by the authorities. It thrived and spread, however, and some of the more intellectually inclined Christians started to reinterpret the common ideas of philosophers and other thinkers in a Christian light. This was the beginning of Christian theology. Some non-Christian philosophers resented this, however, and in the second century one of them, a Platonic philosopher named Celsus, wrote a book entitled (presumably with a hint of sarcasm) *The True Doctrine*, which represented a trenchant attack on what he regarded as these barbaric idiots who were twisting ancient and noble doctrines into a debased form, suitable only for the intellectually inadequate and the socially inferior. (Christianity, at this time, was often considered a religion for the lower classes.) For example, the Christians believed that, at the end of time, Christ would return and everyone would be resurrected to face judgment. Celsus said that this was simply a crude misunderstanding of the Platonists' doctrine of the immortality of the soul, which stated that upon the death of the body the soul survives to face eternal bliss or damnation, depending on the life that it lived.

A century after Celsus lived, however, his book was answered by a man whose philosophical credentials were at least as weighty as his own: Origen Adamantius, 'Origen the Unbreakable', a towering figure of the third century. Origen was a dedicated Christian of almost frightening severity, whose devotion to a frugal lifestyle had, it was alleged, led him to castrate himself at an early age. But he was a man of great courage too, whose bravery in guiding the church of Alexandria through a period of persecution led to a life on the run from the authorities. Origen was educated by some of the leading intellectuals of the day, and indeed in his later years he became famous as a wise man even among pagans. No less a figure than the mother of the emperor would seek his company, at a time when Christianity was still officially proscribed. And one of Origen's most important books was entitled simply *Against Celsus* – a line-by-line examination and refutation of Celsus's attack on the Christians.

The striking thing about Origen's response to Celsus was that he didn't simply present Christian doctrines and try to defend them. He recognized that the heart of Celsus's argument lay in his claim that Christians had essentially stolen all their ideas from Plato, but misunderstood them. With considerable audacity, therefore, Origen turned the argument back against Celsus, claiming that the Christians had in fact understood Plato very well, that Plato had even been a kind of crypto-Christian living 400 years before Christ, and that it was the pagan Platonists such as Celsus who had been mistaken all along! For example, Origen examined the descriptions of God that were found in Plato's works and compared them to the Bible. He concluded that if Celsus and those like him were really interested in understanding

Plato and seeking the truth, they would have been better off coming to the church.

The debate between Celsus and Origen is, of course, of only antiquarian interest today; there are probably few people who will base their assessment of Christianity upon a consideration of how similar it is to Platonism. But it shows the willingness of Christian thinkers, when in the minority, not simply to go on the defensive but to take the argument to the opposition. In this way, Christianity can seize upon ideas from the cultural mainstream and make them its own; but at the same time there is a corresponding influence the other way, as those ideas and the cultural mainstream itself are affected by this new line of thinking. In the case of this example, Platonism survived for centuries after Origen, largely in a Christianized form – something due in no small part to the efforts of Origen himself.

Another example of Christianity offering a new view of existing culture comes from the Far East, and concerns one of the most striking Christian books of modern times. It was written by Matteo Ricci, an Italian missionary of the sixteenth century. Ricci was one of the most brilliant men of his and every age, and a supremely important figure in history. Indeed, if you had to choose someone to be the first ambassador between East and West, you could hardly pick anyone better. He was something of a Renaissance man, of the kind remarkably common at this time: educated by the Jesuits in Rome, he became a master of astronomy and mathematics as well as theology. One of the keys to Ricci's vast learning was his invention of the 'memory palace', a mental aid to memorizing. He would sort everything he learned and mentally place it in its appropriate room in the 'memory palace' for easy retrieval later.

At this time the Jesuits were sending missionaries to every corner of the globe, and Ricci felt the call of China. He accordingly arrived in the new Portuguese settlement of Macao, a trading post on the Chinese coast near Canton, in 1582. Here, Ricci and the other Jesuit missionaries could meet the Chinese people who made up most of the population, and they could learn their language and culture before moving into China itself.

Christianity had been introduced to China as long ago as the seventh century, and it had apparently flourished for a time across the country, but it had since died out. In fact, by the seventeenth century, neither the European missionaries nor the Chinese themselves had the faintest idea that there had once been a Christian church in the country. The new missionaries who arrived with the Portuguese were having little success: aggression on the part of the Portuguese authorities had made the Chinese extremely suspicious of Westerners, and any found within their borders were liable to be arrested as spies. However, one missionary, a charismatic Italian named Alessandro Valignano, recognized that the key to success lay not in marching in and declaring that they had a new religion that was better than what the Chinese had already. This would never work. That approach had, essentially, been tried in South America by the conquistadors – and the result, as we shall see in chapter 7, had been disastrous. Instead, Valignano believed, the missionaries should rely on the fact that the Chinese respected learning and tolerance, and loved religious debate. The missionaries should therefore learn Chinese – an audacious undertaking, never before attempted – and

MATTEO RICCI, IN CHINESE CLOTHING. CONTEMPORARY CHINESE COPPER ENGRAVING.

study Chinese culture. If they could show that they respected the Chinese, and offered their religious ideas as a contribution to a debate instead of seeking to impose them, they might have some success.

Valignano and his missionaries, including Ricci, therefore adopted the language and customs of the Chinese, shaving their heads and dressing as Buddhist monks, and even taking Chinese names. They then allowed their hosts' curiosity to do their work for them – although they naturally gave this a helping hand with a display of maps, clocks and other remarkable objects from the West. The advanced scientific learning of Jesuits such as Matteo Ricci – or Li Matou, as he now called himself – was also a cause of considerable wonder among the Chinese scientists, who were fascinated by the gaps in their own knowledge that the foreigners could fill. Ricci was better at predicting eclipses than their own astronomers. They were puzzled by the translation of the Greek mathematician Euclid that Ricci wrote for them, since the methods were so different from those of Chinese mathematics. Ricci also produced an impressive map, one of the most detailed maps of anywhere at this time, which showed China's true position in the world – something that amazed and rather annoyed the Chinese, who had had no idea of the extent of the rest of the world. Somehow, Ricci also found time to make a name for himself as a painter of Chinese landscapes. All of this meant that he and his small band of colleagues succeeded in getting themselves regarded as interesting cultural ambassadors, rather than the idiotic barbarians whom most Chinese generally assumed inhabited other countries.

At the same time the missionaries wrote, in Chinese, a series of pamphlets designed to explain their religion in terms that made cultural sense. Ricci also used music to spread the ideas of Christianity – needless to say, he was an accomplished musician, although he did not like Chinese music. Instead, he composed new songs in the European style, which became very popular. The outcome of all this was Ricci's remarkable *The True Doctrine of the Lord of Heaven*. In it, Ricci took on the unenviable task of translating Catholic doctrine not only into a completely alien tongue but into an equally alien thought system. He knew that if Christianity was to make sense to his readers, let alone appeal to them, he had to make it relevant to them. This meant ensuring that it dealt with the intellectual and religious issues that they were used to. Thus, in his book, Ricci focused on philosophy and metaphysics: the existence of God and the nature of creation and the human soul, and he sought to teach the basic Christian doctrine of the Incarnation of Christ for the salvation of humanity. His treatment was influenced by the writings of Ignatius Loyola, the founder of the Jesuits, but he translated the terms into Chinese, effectively creating a new theological language. Ricci also avoided topics such as the Trinity and the nature of revelation which he did not think would prove palatable to the Chinese. The book was a success, as Chinese philosophers were intrigued by this new approach to their own tradition, and even Emperor Kien-Long, who persecuted Christians, had it put in his library of great Chinese books.

And the dialogue went the other way too. In Ricci's day, Europeans knew hardly anything about China. There were no dictionaries of the country's language, and no

> 'The learning I shall now discuss is a learning entirely to do with the inner life and which is for oneself – in a word, it is that learning by which a man is made whole.'
>
> Matteo Ricci,
> *The True Doctrine of the Lord of Heaven*

one really knew exactly where it was or how big it was. Ricci, with his brilliant maps and dictionaries of Chinese, changed that. He was the first to devise a system of transliterating Chinese words into Latin script, a project that led to the translation of Confucius into Latin and the introduction of Chinese cultural ideas into Europe.

To this day, Ricci is one of the best-known figures from European history in China, and his role in advancing Chinese knowledge and disseminating it to the West is widely recognized and celebrated. Yet strangely, he might have been even more pleased with his success in a country he never visited – Korea. The churches that he and his colleagues planted in China survived and continue to grow, but Christians have always been a small minority in the country. Korea, by contrast, is the only Asian country to have a really significant Christian population, and the situation is all the more striking for the fact that the Koreans essentially converted themselves. Like China, Korea had a long tradition of Confucianism and Buddhism, both of which were firmly ensconced throughout the country. In around 1770, however, an ambassador to China named Chong Tu-Won returned home with a copy of Matteo Ricci's *True Doctrine*. He and his friends recognized it as an intriguing new approach to their traditions, and they sought out further information about Western religion and culture. Christianity became enormously popular among intellectuals. Without the aid of any foreign missionaries, the growing circle of Christians essentially ordained themselves as priests and started performing the sacraments. By the start of the nineteenth century, there were 10,000 of them. Despite clampdowns from the authorities, the numbers continued to grow. Today, approximately a third of the 45 million inhabitants of South Korea are Christians, and the Central Full Gospel Church in Seoul has the largest congregation in the world, with fully half a million worshippers.

CHAPTER 2
The Arts

One of the most momentous dates in British history was 21 October 1805. On that day a British naval fleet, commanded by the brilliant Lord Horatio Nelson, defeated a combined French and Spanish war fleet almost twice its size at the Battle of Trafalgar. Lord Nelson's courage and daring saved Britain from invasion by the mighty armies of Napoleon Bonaparte – but Nelson himself was mortally wounded in the battle and died onboard his ship, the *Victory*.

Little wonder that the British chose to commemorate this event and its hero at the centre of their greatest city. In the 1830s, the great space of Trafalgar Square was laid out at the heart of London, just down the road from the Houses of Parliament. At the centre was Nelson's Column, 56.4 metres (185 feet) high, with a 5.2 metre (17 foot) statue of Nelson himself on top. The square, surrounded by neoclassical buildings and filled with monuments to Britain's heroes, was a fitting centrepiece to the city that ruled the greatest empire of all time.

But one of the plinths of the square never had a monument put on it, because there was not enough money for the planned statue of William IV on a horse. For a century and a half the plinth remained vacant, until in 1999 the first of a series of temporary artworks was put on it. Made by the English artist Mark Wallinger, it was entitled *Ecce Homo* – 'Behold the Man'. The title is a quotation from John 19:5, and it is what Pontius Pilate said to the crowd when he presented Jesus to them before his crucifixion. The statue depicted Jesus, naked except for a loincloth and crown of thorns, standing helplessly on the plinth as though being exhibited to the crowds of tourists who thronged to the square every day.

Like all the other works of art that have since been displayed on this plinth in Trafalgar Square, *Ecce Homo* proved controversial. For one thing, instead of the usual beard and long hair, this Jesus had no hair at all. He looked utterly ordinary. In fact, surrounded by the trappings of nineteenth-century imperialist Britain, he looked insignificant. The nearby statues, of forgotten imperialist icons such as General Napier and Major General Sir Henry Havelock, are huge and magnificent; but this Jesus was life-sized, almost dwarfed by the plinth on which he stood. To some, the statue represented the ailing Church of England, increasingly marginalized in an ever-more secular Western society. But to others, it represented an important statement of Christian values. This Jesus rejected the trappings of power exemplified in his surroundings and appeared weak and helpless. But the presence of such weakness here, at the heart of power, was itself a kind of strength. It seemed a powerful and moving representation of the topsy-turvy values that Jesus himself preached. This Jesus – presented simply as 'the man' – had a lot to say to modern society, whether they were Christian or not.

The creation and installation of *Ecce Homo* – by an artist who was himself not a Christian – and the debate that surrounded it demonstrate the power that Christianity retains even today in the world of art.

The plump Jesus and Leonardo's uglies – Christianity and the visual arts

Ecce Homo confounded many people's images of Jesus. But what did Jesus look like? Virtually every portrayal you see today – from Orthodox icons to Mel Gibson's *The Passion of the Christ* – shows us a thin Jesus with long, dark hair and a beard. In fact, the earliest known picture of Jesus, from the middle of the second century, is in the Capella Greca in Rome, and it portrays a young, short-haired, clean-shaven man in a Roman toga. All the early pictures of Jesus look like this, often making him rather podgy into the bargain, and it was only in the fourth century that Jesus acquired a beard and centre parting. It was then, too, that the tradition arose of Jesus having beautiful fair hair – the ancestor of the blue-eyed, blond Jesus of Victorian sentimentality, typified by William Holman Hunt's painting *The Light of the World*. Of course, as a first-century Jew, Jesus probably *did* have a beard (although long, straight hair was not fashionable at the time). What all this goes to show is how each age tends to remake Jesus in its own image.

A PICTURE THAT DIVIDES VIEWERS – IT'S EITHER DEEPLY MOVING OR VILELY SENTIMENTAL. **THE LIGHT OF THE WORLD** BY WILLIAM HOLMAN HUNT, 1853.

There was, incidentally, an early tradition that Jesus was ugly. This seems to have been based not on historical memories but on Isaiah 53, an Old Testament passage about a 'suffering servant' that the Christians interpreted as a prophecy about Jesus, and which describes the servant as plain to look at. By the fourth century, however, it was assumed that Jesus, being God, would naturally be extraordinarily good-looking, and that became the dominant tradition for many centuries.

The changing face of Jesus over the ages illustrates how central the visual arts have always been to Christianity – to expressing the Christian message, but also to influencing and spreading it. The art it has inspired has helped Christianity not only to become rooted in some cultures, but to survive when the authorities have turned against it. The classic example is the years of Communist rule in Eastern Europe and the Soviet Union. In these countries, the Orthodox Church had been deeply entrenched in society and culture for a millennium. But the Bolsheviks, after coming to power in Russia in 1917, set about trying systematically to eradicate Orthodoxy from the country. Officially, neither Orthodoxy nor any other major religion was forbidden, but ideologically it was incompatible with atheistic Communism, and the authorities hoped to wipe it out as much as possible. Churches were closed and seized by the state, clergy were harassed, imprisoned or executed, and the dissemination of most religious literature was prohibited. The Orthodox Church had a brief respite during the Second World War, when Stalin re-established it in order to use it to rally the people against Nazi Germany; but Kruschev later clamped down on the religion more harshly than ever. At the same time, other Christian denominations were attacked, to such an extent that the 1,200 Roman Catholic churches that had been there in 1917 were whittled down to two in under thirty years. It is often said that there were more Christian martyrs in the twentieth century than in all the previous nineteen centuries put together, and a good proportion of those who died were killed in the Soviet Union. Little wonder that, as early as 1918, Patriarch Tikhon of Moscow condemned the new Soviet government and oversaw the setting up of the underground Catacomb Church, which operated secretly throughout the Soviet period.

Yet through all this, the values of Russian Orthodoxy survived. The church buildings and monasteries may have been largely empty, but they remained as silent witnesses to the faith that had built them. The great novels of Dostoevsky, Tolstoy and others were read, and the religious questions with which they grappled continued to exercise people. And the icons survived too. Icons are among the most distinctive elements of Orthodox Christianity – not simply beautiful expressions of the faith, but central to it. They were first painted in the Byzantine empire in the sixth and seventh centuries, and they soon became the subject of controversy as some theologians and emperors believed that their use was idolatrous. After the eighth century, however, they ceased to be controversial.

An icon is a painting, usually of Christ or a saint, but it is not meant to be a realistic portrayal like a photograph. Instead, the picture is intended as an aid to worship, and so the artist strives to convey the spiritual nature of the subject. This means that icons have a very stylized appearance, but they are also instantly recognizable. A modern Russian icon, for example, looks much like a medieval Middle Eastern one. Orthodox Christians believe that beauty plays a central role in religion. There is a story that in the tenth century, Prince Vladimir of Kiev decided that his nation needed a religion, and so he sent ambassadors to the Muslims, the Byzantines and the Catholics to decide which religion was best. Those who visited the great cathedral of Hagia Sophia in Constantinople reported that they did not know whether they were in heaven or earth, since they could not believe that such beauty could exist on earth. God clearly dwelt there with the Orthodox, and so Vladimir converted and Russia has been Orthodox ever since.

So it's not surprising that icons are also intended to be objects of great beauty. They are usually painted on wood, and artists traditionally use layers upon layers of paint – up to thirty – to create the glowing colours that often prove remarkably durable through the centuries. Orthodox Christians believe that the use of icons in worship reflects a central Christian belief – that in Christ, God became part of the physical world and sanctified it. If the glory of God can be contained within a normal human body, then the holiness of God and his saints can also be accessed through a beautiful image. The Orthodox do not worship the icons, of course, but they do believe that they offer an authentic medium by which we can come into contact with the spiritual world. John of Damascus, an eighth-century Orthodox theologian who strongly supported the use of icons in worship, wrote, 'The beauty of the images moves me to contemplation, as a meadow delights the eyes and subtly infuses the soul with the glory of God.'

But quite apart from being a remarkable aesthetic tradition in its own right, the tradition of icons has played an essential role in preserving and transmitting Christian

'Just like the holy and life-giving cross, so too the holy and precious icons, painted with colours, made with little stones or any other materials for this purpose, should be placed in the holy churches of God, on vases and sacred vestments, on walls and boards, in houses and on roads... For each time that we see their representation in an image, each time, while gazing upon them, we are made to remember the originals, we grow to love them more, and we are more induced to worship them.'

The declaration of the Second Council of Nicea, AD 787

'Christ acheiropoietos' — literally, 'Christ not made by hand'. According to legend, King Abgar of Edessa, an independent state halfway between the Roman and Persian empires, asked Jesus to visit him. Jesus wrote back explaining that he was unable to do so, but also sent a cloth which he had pressed to his face, leaving a miraculous imprint. This relic, the 'Mandylion', was supposed to have miraculous properties, and to have inspired icons like this sixteenth-century example from Russia.

culture. Icons convey spiritual ideas to those unable to read them in theological tomes; they are a spirituality for the people, not for academics or other specialists. Gregory the Great, a much-loved pope of the sixth century, once said that 'the picture is to the illiterate what the written word is to the educated'. A good example of this principle in Catholicism is the Stations of the Cross, a series of meditations on the death of Christ, which is often represented in churches by a series of pictures, each one showing a stage in Christ's Passion. In many churches, the pictures are found at intervals around the walls, allowing people to physically walk from one station to the next and contemplate each scene as they come to it.

Similarly, icons preserved the spirit and the teaching of Orthodox Christianity, and with it the spirit of holy Russia, throughout the Soviet period. The people remained in touch with their past and their heritage in the form of the saints the icons depicted. Ironically, the persecutions of the Communists led to a greater interest in Orthodoxy throughout the world. Many church properties were looted and later sold to foreigners, while many private individuals, driven to poverty, were forced to sell their own icons. As a result, an unexpected market in Russian icons arose overseas, especially in America. Many Americans and others found themselves buying icons at art shops or antique dealers, and they became quite fashionable throughout the 1920s and 30s.

It would be possible to fill a book with examples of remarkable Christian art; indeed, many books have been filled in just this way. Orthodox icons are only one example of beautiful ecclesiastical artwork. Another well-known one is the tradition of manuscript illumination, which we shall see again in chapter 4. The most famous illuminated Bibles and other Christian works of the Middle Ages, such as the Book of Kells and the Lindisfarne Gospels, rank with the most stunning works of art in history. They also testify to the traditional Christian emphasis on writing – not simply as a means of recording and transmitting information, but also in the creation of objects that are worthwhile in their own right. Christians have, as a rule, not extended to the Bible quite the same reverence that Muslims have for the Qur'an: there is no rule in Christianity that says the Bible must never be placed on the floor, or lower than any other books in the room, for example. But traditionally, Christians have seen Bibles as important *objects*. In nineteenth-century America, each family had a 'family Bible', which was passed from generation to generation and also served as a record of the family, with marriages, births and so on being noted on the blank pages. The medieval illuminated manuscripts bear testimony to a similar concern to make the Bible not just a handy book of religious instruction, but an important *thing* in its own right – an interplay of words and art that brought beauty to instruction. This was also the origin of what is today called 'concrete poetry', where a poem is written with regard to how the words look on the page, as well as how they sound when spoken. Acrostics – poems where the first letters of each line spell out a word or phrase – have been around since ancient times, but the ninth-century monk and writer Rabanus Maurus gave them a new spin with his *In Praise of the Holy Cross*. This featured pages of apparently random letters, like a modern wordsearch, superimposed over pictures of figures. If you looked only at the letters within the figures, they would spell out a poem. Here, then, the visual and the instructional blended in a work intended to enlighten the mind and the heart together. This work also enhanced the canny Rabanus's standing with the authorities, since the figures who bore these edifying verses represented none other than Emperor Louis the Pious.

Medieval art was, like most medieval creative pursuits, intended to teach a moral or spiritual lesson rather than just entertain. We will see some examples of this approach in the next chapter, looking at medieval church architecture and stained glass. But perhaps the last and greatest flowering of medieval Christian art was the work of Hieronymus Bosch, a rather peculiar character of the fifteenth century who lived near Antwerp. Bosch – who adapted his splendid name from that of his town, Hertogenbosch, also known as den Bosch – was a devoted Catholic. He belonged to an organization called the Brotherhood of Our Lady, which commissioned artworks to adorn its chapel in the town. His colleagues must have been pretty bemused by what Bosch produced, though, since his paintings testify to a decidedly overstrained religious imagination. They are populated by terrifying demons, covered with spikes and teeth, and scenes of peculiarly unpleasant tortures, such as people sliding down knife blades or being forced to carry demons on their backs. Weird creatures with staring eyes stomp their way through Bosch's surreal landscapes. His work has been prized in modern times as a forerunner of the surrealism of Salvador Dali, as an exploration of the stranger reaches of the subconscious or as a dark warning of the dangers of experimenting too freely with recreational drugs; but Bosch intended it as religious instruction. For example, his portrayal of St Antony in the desert, surrounded by men with pigs' snouts for noses, creatures consisting solely of heads with legs, and bizarre crosses between fish and boats, is meant to illustrate the spiritual torments through which the saint passed as he was tempted.

So Christianity has developed a large and rich tradition – indeed, a number of different traditions – of religious art. But equally striking has been the influence of Christianity on art in general, beyond obviously devotional works. It was in the Renaissance, in particular, that modern Western art came into being, and Christianity had a great impact on the process. As we shall see in chapter 5, a strong streak of mysticism ran through the Renaissance. People believed in the essential

interconnectedness of all things, in the mysteries of the human soul and in the spiritual value of beauty. This new approach was partly because the Renaissance saw a revival of interest in ancient, pagan ideals and especially in the philosophy of Plato; these pagan ideals were combined with the Christian world view that these new philosophers inherited from the Middle Ages.

Possibly the greatest of these philosophers was Marsilio Ficino, a man for whom voyaging within the depths of the soul was clearly sufficient, since he appears never to have left Florence in northern Italy at any point in his life. He was a figure who left a huge mark on his time, being perhaps the most brilliant scholar and thinker in a century that abounded in such characters; his Academy, founded in imitation of Plato's, was one of the foremost intellectual establishments in the world. Ficino was a Catholic priest, but he also believed that spiritual and divine truth could be found in Plato – to such an extent that he kept a candle burning before a statue of Plato, and said that the works of the great philosopher should be read in church. Ficino was a classic Renaissance man, a philosopher and scholar, and also one of the best doctors and musicians of the age. The ruling Medicis of Florence would allow no one else to treat them, and Ficino never charged them a fee, being not only a man of principle but sufficiently rich to put his principles into action.

Ficino believed that the visual arts were a spiritual endeavour. He argued that contemplation of beauty necessarily brings us closer to God, because God himself is the ultimate Beauty. This kind of idea had originated with Plato, but took the form that Ficino knew in the works of later Christian Platonists such as Gregory of Nyssa and Augustine. So whereas painting had earlier been thought of as a rather workmanlike activity, Ficino regarded it as equal to poetry. Such was his influence that painting rapidly increased in social standing in Italy and became regarded as an intrinsically religious art form – even when the subject matter was not in itself Christian. By framing beauty, artists could bring the soul of the viewer back to its divine origins in God, the ultimate Beauty.

The result was the extraordinary flowering of art in Renaissance Italy. Artists such as Sandro Botticelli devoted themselves to portraying images from classical pagan mythology, but their work was intended to lead the viewers to contemplate the teaching of Christian Neoplatonists such as Ficino. For example, when Botticelli painted the Roman gods Venus and Mars, he did so to make a statement about the superiority of love over war. Michelangelo, arguably the greatest Renaissance artist, believed that spiritual value could be found in all natural beauty, and he sought to depict this in works such as his towering statue of *David*. Michelangelo's most famous work, the decoration of the ceiling of the Sistine Chapel in Rome, combined this

devotion to beauty with the Christian ideals with which, to a Renaissance Neoplatonist like himself, it was inextricably intertwined. Interestingly, however, Michelangelo later lost his faith in Neoplatonism and the intrinsic value of beauty. He came to believe that, paradoxically, ugliness could convey spiritual truth more profoundly than beauty – and so, over the years during which he worked on the Sistine Chapel, the figures he painted became ever more anguished, culminating in his depiction of the Last Judgment. Another painter who rebelled against the emphasis on beauty was Leonardo da Vinci, who believed that spiritual value could be found in all nature – and so he tried to paint his subjects as accurately as possible, taking a particular interest in depicting ugly people.

It was the emphasis on the intrinsic spirituality of nature that helped to lead Western art, during and after the Renaissance, to the pursuit of realism which has been a central feature of art ever since. In Asia, the visual arts remained more stylized – which is why the Chinese were so astounded by a picture of the Virgin Mary that Matteo Ricci showed them. They had never seen truly representational art before, and they thought the image must be somehow real. The laws of perspective, for example, were unknown to the Chinese, who simply depicted more distant objects above closer ones. But in Renaissance Europe, these laws and other aids to accuracy were discovered, allowing artists to achieve far more realistic images. Moreover, the interest in accuracy spurred artists and others to investigate the human body in more detail, providing an incentive to the study of anatomy and medicine.

Probably the zenith of Western representational art was the work of the Dutch masters in the sixteenth and seventeenth centuries. These artists rarely depicted religious subjects, though this itself was a result of religious views. The Netherlands were at this time strongly Calvinist, and Calvinists disapproved of religious art, thinking it bordered on idolatry. Artists such as Rembrandt van Rijn therefore concentrated on depicting still lifes or scenes from normal, secular, everyday life. His contemporary, the poverty-stricken Jan Vermeer, painted views of his home town, and

THE FALL OF MAN AND THE EXPULSION FROM PARADISE BY MICHELANGELO BUONAROTTI, FROM THE SISTINE CHAPEL, 1510. THIS IS MICHELANGELO'S FAMOUS DEPICTION OF THE STORY OF GENESIS CHAPTER 3, WHERE ADAM AND EVE FALL PREY TO THE SERPENT'S TEMPTATION AND ARE SHAMEFULLY CAST OUT OF EDEN.

Jan Steen specialized in witty depictions of taverns or excessively messy homes. Indeed, 'a Jan Steen household' still means a chaotic mess in Dutch today. Yet some artists could combine this emphasis on realism with an infusion of the passion and emotion of the older, more overtly Christian art. One such artist was Peter Rubens, a devoted Roman Catholic who essentially revitalized the art traditions he inherited. He often worked with his friend Frans Snyders, a brilliant still life artist. Together, these two represented the epitome of the Flemish tradition, among the most subtly brilliant styles of painting ever developed. The techniques used by some of these master painters were incredibly painstaking, involving the use of seven layers of paint, sometimes requiring the painting to be set aside for long periods of time between applications. Little wonder that some of these still lifes are remarkably small – but they still glow as beautifully as a Russian Orthodox icon.

Stadium rock and 'Do-Re-Mi' – Christianity and music

I was there when they crucified my Lord,
I held the scabbard when the soldier drew his sword.
I threw the dice when they pierced his side,
But I saw love conquer the great divide.

> **6**
> '*I don't believe I'd sing the way I do if God hadn't wanted me to.*'
>
> Elvis Presley

An evangelical hymn from the eighteenth century? No – 'When Love Comes to Town' by U2 and B.B. King. Since their formation in the 1970s, U2 have remained, in the words of *Time* magazine, 'rock's hottest ticket'; but the band members have never hidden their Christianity. On the contrary, they have used it to inform songs like the one quoted above. Lead vocalist Bono, meanwhile, spends much of his time campaigning for good causes, such as ending Third World debt, projects that come very much from his Christian faith.

Whether the music of U2 or other Christian bands is better or worse for their faith is a moot point. The fact remains that Christianity has a remarkably powerful influence over modern music. One of the more unexpected music successes of recent years, for example, was when EMI Classics Spain reissued an old recording of a Gregorian chant, sung by the Benedictine monks of Santo Domingo de Silos. It was a runaway worldwide hit, selling 3 million copies in the United States alone and spending eight weeks in *Billboard*'s international top ten.

Music certainly has been an integral part of Christianity ever since its inception. The Gregorian chant that was such an unlikely bestseller in the 1990s, for example, dates back to the sixth century, but it evolved out of earlier musical traditions that go back, in part, to Jewish hymns from the time of Jesus and before. It's striking to think that the hymn that, according to Matthew's Gospel, Jesus and his friends sang after the Last Supper was perhaps something a bit like Gregorian chant. The chant is a kind of plainsong, the predominant musical form in the early church, which consists of only one melody line, with no descants or counterpoints. It is a simple form of music, one that pretty much anyone could join in; but its simplicity is also deliberate, part of its meditative nature. The songs were intended to set the texts, biblical and otherwise, that were being sung, and to focus the mind on their meaning. In other words, this kind of singing was central to the liturgy, the services that were held in Christian churches; and the singing was an integral element in the creation of the beautiful, spiritual atmosphere that Christians sought.

Different regions developed their own chants, but in about the sixth or seventh centuries a new tradition, the Gregorian chant, came about after they were compiled together and developed. Traditionally, Pope Gregory I was the man responsible for this. Gregory was an enormously energetic pope, one of the key figures of the early Middle Ages.

Over the centuries, though, the liturgy became increasingly complex. We shall see in the next chapter how churches and cathedrals became bigger and more complicated in their design in the Middle Ages, with the development of the Romanesque and then the Gothic styles of architecture. In the same way, the music became more elaborate to match. To start with, this was just a proliferation of more and more chants, which were impossible to remember. The church developed ways of writing them down. The Greeks and Romans had named notes after letters, but now church musicians invented new symbols to represent the notes, based on Latin punctuation signs, and drew them at different heights on the page to indicate pitch. The notes used became standardized – Gregory the Great, again, is (probably apocryphally) credited with the invention of the eight-note octave. By the tenth century, the idea had arisen of drawing a long horizontal line through the note signs, to indicate a 'fixed' pitch to act as the basis for the others, which with the addition of other lines became what we would recognize as a musical stave. As this was happening, the tunes themselves were becoming more complex, as plainsong began to give way to polyphonic hymns, where different singers sang different melody lines at the same time. The new methods of writing music meant that different melodies could be indicated on the same line of text, allowing more complicated compositions to be recorded.

At the same time, some enterprising churchmen invented new ways to help people learn to sing all this stuff. One was an Italian monk called Guido d'Arezzo, who lived in the eleventh century and was a key figure in the design of the musical stave. It was he who first hit on the idea of having several horizontal lines and using the spaces between them to 'sit' the notes in, providing a clear way of showing pitch, while still using the old symbols to indicate the duration of the notes. Guido seems to have been rather a controversial character who spent much of his time being kicked out of monasteries. Evidently people were very attached to the traditional ways of doing things and didn't like all this newfangled nonsense he was coming up with for writing music. He invented innovative ways of teaching people to sing – for example, he assigned different notes to different parts of the hand, and trained his students to sing by pointing to different fingers. More interesting though was his 'system of solmization', known more familiarly as the 'Guido System'. Guido took a Latin hymn to John the Baptist that had been written in the eighth century, which began with the words, '*Ut queant laxis, Resonare fibris, Mira gestorum, Famuli tuorum, Solve polluti, Labii reatum.*' ('So that your servants may sing at the tops of their voices the wonders of your deeds, absolve the sin from their stained lips.') Then he took the first syllables of each of the song's lines – *Ut, Re, Mi, Fa, Sol, La* – and assigned them to the six tones of the octave. This helped students to memorize the notes in the form of what was called a 'mode' – the ancestor of the modern scale. Later, *Ut* turned into *Do*, and an extra syllable, *Ti*, was added to the end, so that the system could be used for learning the whole octave. And that is where 'Do-Re-Mi' comes from, the song famously featured in the musical *The Sound of Music*. Evidently, the child in that film who complains that the syllables are meaningless was not very well informed about medieval church music!

All of this was of course choral music, which has always been central to Christian worship. Today, some church traditions, notably the Orthodox Church, still use only choral music, unaccompanied by instruments, in their services. In the West, however, even plain choral music became sometimes extremely complicated, a prime example being the famous 'Spem in Alium' by the sixteenth-century English composer Thomas Tallis, which has forty parts.

At the same time, instrumental accompaniments developed. The sophisticated notation systems invented during the Middle Ages for church singing allowed composers to produce pieces for a number of instruments playing together. By the late sixteenth century, composers were writing music for large groups of instruments, and the ancestor of the modern orchestra was born. These first orchestras were basically strings only, but by the eighteenth century the other sections, such as brass and woodwind, had been added. And as composers became more ambitious with their settings, the orchestras expanded. The nineteenth century saw a fashion for improbably vast orchestras, such as the one conducted by Johann Strauss the younger, which had nearly 1,000 instruments. To date, the largest orchestra ever assembled was made up of musicians from across Canada and played in Vancouver in May 2000. It had 6,452 musicians, a truly scary thought.

Yet some of the greatest names in Western composition were devoted, to varying degrees, to Christian music. The obvious example is Johann Sebastian Bach, who in the first half of the eighteenth century produced a dizzying quantity of music, especially for the church organ, an instrument on which he excelled as a performer. His output was truly astonishing: for one three-year period, Bach composed, set and rehearsed with his choir a brand new cantata every week! Bach is especially remembered for his use of contrapuntal techniques – where different melodies, playing at the same time, set off and interplay with each other. It was a remarkably complex and mathematically precise development of the polyphonic sounds that first emerged in medieval church

'*This is how we arrange the notes in the scale. First we put the Greek letter gamma. After that we use seven letters of the alphabet in capitals to indicate the notes: A, B, C, D, E, F, G. After that, we repeat the same seven letters, but we put them in lower case.*'

Guido d'Arezzo, *Micrologus*

singing, and Bach's refinement of it has led to his being called possibly the greatest composer, or even one of the foremost geniuses in any field, in European history. But Bach did not simply write music to sound nice: on the contrary, all his work was dedicated to God. That was clear enough from the ecclesiastical genres with which he worked, setting innumerable biblical or other church texts to music. But he also believed that the intricacy and beauty of his scores bore witness to the glory of God. They were intended to draw the mind of the listener not to the cleverness of the composer but to the divine Beauty itself. In Bach, the Neoplatonic ideals of Marsilio Ficino and the Renaissance took on a new form, the form of the Enlightenment, when beauty was found in order and God was the supreme mathematician.

Furry feet and crumpled macs – Christianity and the literature of the soul

But art does not have to be explicitly religious to be deeply influenced by Christian values. One of the most prominent examples of subtly Christian art in recent times is J.R.R. Tolkien's *The Lord of the Rings*, arguably the most popular book of the twentieth century. Many readers have been awed by the sheer detail of the mythical world that Tolkien invented, with its different races, geography, history and languages; but it is striking that none of the characters and races of *The Lord of the Rings* or his other books appears to follow a religion. There are supernatural beings in Tolkien's world, but they are not worshipped by anyone; and nobody goes to church, prays or does anything of the kind. All the more puzzling, given that Tolkien himself was a devoted Roman Catholic and claimed that his story was an intrinsically Christian – indeed, Catholic – one.

The reason for his claim is that *The Lord of the Rings*, although it takes the form of an adventure story, tackles some of the deepest issues of human nature that Tolkien believed were illuminated by Christianity. The main narrative revolves around Frodo, a diminutive hobbit, who finds himself in possession of the One Ring. The Ring was created by the Dark Lord Sauron in ages past, and it is the source of his power and malice. To defeat the Dark Lord, Frodo must destroy the Ring – which, unfortunately, can be achieved only by travelling to Mordor, the land of Sauron, and throwing it into the volcano where it was forged.

The catch is that the Ring, being intrinsically evil, gradually corrupts whoever carries it. The Ring represents the temptation of power: it whispers to its bearer that, if he chooses, he can use it himself to fight Sauron and usurp his power. As Frodo travels closer to Mordor, the power of the Ring grows, and he must increasingly fight the temptation. Some of his companions are weaker and are driven to madness and treachery by the Ring. Most pathetic of all is Gollum, who was once a hobbit, but found the Ring and was warped by it into a wretched creature eaten up with malice and avarice for his 'Precious'. In the end, at the volcano, Frodo is overcome by the Ring and announces that instead of destroying it he will claim it for himself. The world is saved when Gollum appears, attacks Frodo, seizes

GOLLUM BROODS ON HIS 'PRECIOUS'. FROM THE FILM **THE LORD OF THE RINGS: THE TWO TOWERS**.

WHAT HAS CHRISTIANITY EVER DONE FOR US?

the Ring and in his jubilation stumbles over the cliff and into the fire.

Tolkien stated that he hated allegory, and his work was not intended to be a sort of restatement of the Christian message in a new story, as his friend C.S. Lewis did with *The Lion, the Witch and the Wardrobe*. But much of it reflects Christian ideas and values. When Frodo inherits the ring from his uncle Bilbo, for example, he says to Gandalf that it is a pity that Bilbo did not kill the malicious Gollum when he had the chance. Gandalf is described as a 'wizard', but despite this and his standard wizard garb – long cloak and pointy hat – he never seems to do any magic and instead derives his authority from his personal charisma and the advice he offers. In fact, Gandalf is more like an Old Testament prophet, and he replies to Frodo's complaint:

Pity? It was Pity that stayed his hand. Pity, and Mercy: not to strike without need. And he has been well rewarded, Frodo. Be sure that he took so little hurt from the evil, and escaped in the end, because he began his ownership of the Ring so. With Pity... do not be too eager to deal out death in judgement. For even the very wise cannot see all ends. I have not much hope that Gollum can be cured before he dies, but there is a chance of it. And he is bound up with the fate of the Ring. My heart tells me that he has some part to play yet, for good or ill, before the end; and when that comes, the pity of Bilbo may rule the fate of many – yours not least.

The teaching that pity can be stronger than judgment, that mercy can bring only good, most of all to the one who is merciful, is central to Christianity. And so too is the faith that, somehow, the course of events is being managed. No one in *The Lord of the Rings* ever mentions God, but that does not mean he is not there, under the surface. You could compare it to the book of Esther, one of only two books in the Bible that do not mention God (the other is Song of Songs). Esther tells the story of a plot against the Jews at the court of the mighty King Ahasuerus and the clever way in which the plot is foiled and the villain brought to justice. At no point is God referred to, but Jews and Christians alike have always interpreted the story as implying his presence – things work out as they should because God is guiding everything behind the scenes. In the same way, the mercy shown by Bilbo to Gollum does, in the end, reap its reward – for without Gollum, Frodo could not have destroyed the Ring.

Despite its enormous popularity, few people, perhaps, will argue that *The Lord of the Rings* ranks with the greatest literature that the world has produced, and the equally popular film trilogy directed by Peter Jackson and based on the book is not quite up there with *Citizen Kane*, entertaining and well made though it certainly is. Yet it does share themes and concerns with some works that are commonly ranked with the best. The journey motif, for example, is reminiscent of *Pilgrim's Progress*, the great work of John Bunyan. Bunyan was a rather disreputable character, a foul-mouthed youth from a poor English family in the early seventeenth century. However, while serving in the Civil War, he became convinced that he was cut out for something better. He was called from his post, and the soldier who replaced him was promptly shot by the enemy. Bunyan concluded that God had spared his life for some great purpose;

what he thought God was doing with the unfortunate man who took the shot is unrecorded. Subsequently, Bunyan became deeply interested in the kind of Christianity preached by Martin Luther and other Protestants. He became a Puritan, a vocal minority in the Church of England who focused on the well-being and salvation of the individual's soul, and who called on people to live more ethical, holier lives. Bunyan's preaching, however, proved too extreme for the more Anglo-Catholic authorities who returned to power in 1660 with the restoration of King Charles II, and he was imprisoned for twelve years. It was during this time that he wrote *Pilgrim's Progress*. The whole book is an extended allegory, following the journey of a character named Christian from the City of Destruction to the Celestial City. Along the way he passes through places such as Vanity Fair and encounters characters with names such as Prudence, Mr Stand-Fast and Worldly-Wise Man. There's no subtlety about the allegory here, but Bunyan's genius lay largely in the way he combined this overtly religious and instructional material with a concern for everyday life and the ability to tell a gripping story. Bunyan's decision to place this allegory of the spiritual journey within a recognizable landscape, with an insight into what it represented for ordinary people, ensured that his work would become an undisputed classic. It has been called the most successful book ever written, after the Bible, and its earthy spirituality was very influential in both England and America.

While Bunyan was languishing in jail, another Englishman was producing a very different classic of Christian literature. John Milton had enjoyed a rather more promising upbringing than Bunyan, having been educated at Cambridge and landing a cushy job as a tutor, as well as going on a cultural trip to Europe, where he met the famous lawyer and theologian Hugo Grotius and old, blind Galileo himself. But like Bunyan, Milton was a Puritan, and he became increasingly prominent as an opponent of the bishops of the Church of England, and of King Charles I. After the Civil War and the execution of Charles in 1649, Milton wrote in defence of the Parliamentarians who had done it, arguing that it is the people's right to oppose or even kill the king if he is a tyrant. Like Bunyan, he did not do very well when Charles's son, Charles II, returned to the throne in 1660 – although he escaped harsh punishment and simply retired from public life. Milton had, in any case, gone completely blind in the meantime.

Milton spent his retirement writing poetry, which he would compose in his head at night and then dictate in the morning. In 1667, he published *Paradise Lost*. Like most authors at the time, he did this by making an agreement directly with the printer, since modern publishing houses did not really exist. The printer Samuel Simmons paid him £5 when the contract was signed, and a further £5 for each of the three impressions that were printed of the poem – £20 in all. This was quite a bargain, given that *Paradise*

Lost is generally considered the greatest long poem ever written in English and among the best works of poetry of all time. The poem is an epic retelling of the fall of Adam and Eve, but it focuses not on the human characters but on the devils, and above all Satan, the leader of the fallen angels who plans to wreck God's new creation, Earth. The striking thing about Milton's treatment of the story is that he makes Satan almost a sympathetic character. Satan is evil, of course, and his plan of opposing God is wicked; but Milton begins the poem by describing a sort of committee meeting in the chief city of hell, Pandemonium, where the devils discuss what to do. By putting different arguments in the mouths of the devils, Milton explores their characters and motivations for opposing God. So although Satan is condemned, Milton intends his readers to understand why he acts as he does. The poem therefore revolves around a complex approach to sin and pride, and how potentially noble qualities such as self-belief and power can be warped. Milton takes a Christian story and turns it on its head – by concentrating on the 'bad guys' – but then reinvigorates it with the Christian concern for motivation, for what drives people to behave as they do.

A similar concern, coming out in a very different way, can be found in the work of Fyodor Dostoevsky, one of the greatest of the nineteenth-century Russian novelists. Dostoevsky had, to begin with, something of a charmed life: the son of a wealthy doctor, his independent income allowed him to write full time at his leisure. However, he was not allowed to enjoy it in peace. His left-wing activism brought him several years' imprisonment and hard labour in Siberia, followed by military service. Afterwards, Dostoevsky was always a haunted man. Despite a growing reputation as a novelist, he was plagued by a gambling addiction, constant debts and epilepsy throughout his life.

Of course, if the cliché is true, then great art can only be produced by great suffering, and that seems to have been the case with Dostoevsky. His novels explore great religious and philosophical themes such as the nature of God or the purpose of evil, all seen from the viewpoints of his characters, who represent different approaches to life. Their stories revolve around themes of sin and redemption, the great issues of the human soul, at least as Dostoevsky saw it. Throughout his work, he was deeply influenced by the Russian Orthodox Church, to which he was devoted.

Possibly Dostoevsky's most famous book was *Crime and Punishment*, written in 1866. The hero – or anti-hero – of the novel, an impoverished student, murders a horrible old moneylender. His rationale is that he needs her money more than she does, and in any case she is so loathsome that killing her is a service to society. The bulk of the novel follows his state of mind in the following months, as he wrestles with his guilt and increasingly feeble-sounding justification, and as he is dogged by the police inspector, who evidently knows his guilt but is waiting for him to give in and

FYODOR DOSTOEVSKY, IN AN UNCHARACTERISTICALLY CALM MOMENT.

confess. In the end, that is precisely what the murderer does, and in his harsh sentence of imprisonment in Siberia he finds himself paradoxically freed. Confronting his sin has led to redemption. A slightly surprising reworking of the book's format led to the TV detective series *Columbo*, the gimmick of which is that the viewer sees the murder at the start of the show and then follows the shabbily dressed detective as, like Dostoevsky's police inspector, he dogs the murderer until they are trapped.

Why are novels such as *Crime and Punishment* considered great art? There is no pat answer to that. But one of the things that characterizes great literature is that it deals with the most fundamental issues facing human beings. Who are we? What is the world and what is our place in it? How can we find happiness in an uncertain world? How do we deal with the choices that confront us and what happens as a result? These are the kinds of questions that Dostoevsky deals with – and so, too, does Tolkien. His characters may be rather silly creatures such as elves and furry-footed hobbits, but the issues of temptation, good and evil they confront are not so different from those within us all. The difference is that in fantasy the author can externalize some of these elements – by representing them in the object of a Ring, for example – rather than spend much of the time in the characters' internal worlds, dissecting their thoughts and motivations, as Dostoevsky does.

There is nothing necessarily Christian about such concerns. Non-Christian writers such as Albert Camus and Jean-Paul Sartre have dealt with such things in their works too, just as profoundly. But Christianity does have its own distinctive voice in the discussion and its own answer to those problems. Much of the power of Christianity comes from the fact that it does deal with these issues. Christianity is, in a way, not just concerned with what happened in the past: it is concerned with people today. This is true of all the great religions, but one of the striking things about the way Christianity speaks to people is its use of stories. Dostoevsky chose to cast his musings on human nature in the form of stories, and in so doing he was deeply influenced by his Orthodox Christian heritage. In Christianity, the use of stories to illuminate human nature comes across most clearly in its reliance on myths.

Selling your soul and finding the grail – Christianity and myths

Most of the Bible consists of stories of one kind or another, and many theologians today try to get away from the very 'doctrinal' approach to theology that dominated for much of the modern period. According to that approach, Christian faith is a matter of believing a certain set of statements to be true, and theology is the study of those

> 'If it were not for Christ's Church, indeed there would be no restraint on the criminal in his evildoing, and no punishment for it later, real punishment, that is, not a mechanical one… which only chafes the heart in most cases, but a real punishment, the only real, the only frightening and appeasing punishment, which lies in the acknowledgement of one's own conscience.'
>
> Speech of the Elder Zosima, *The Brothers Karamazov*, Fyodor Dostoevsky,

statements and how they relate to each other. But according to the 'narrative theologians', Christianity is faith not in a set of statements but in a person, Jesus, who lived a certain life and did certain things. That is not to say that the doctrinal and narrative approaches are incompatible, and many theologians seek to find a way to balance them and take the best of both. For example, doctrines are often based upon narratives. Take the Nicene Creed, the basic statement of faith for most Christians. Much of the creed consists of a brief retelling of the story of Jesus: 'For our sake he was crucified under Pontius Pilate; he suffered death and was buried. On the third day he rose again in accordance with the Scriptures; he ascended into heaven and is seated at the right hand of the Father.'

Christianity draws much of its power from this story and others. They are told and retold, not simply as statements of fact, but as things that happened in the past. Stories have an extremely powerful effect on people, whether they are religious or not: just think of the widespread popularity of TV dramas of every kind, whether ongoing soap operas or short drama series. A glance through the TV schedules of any evening, in most countries, will reveal a fair selection of genres: for example, factual documentaries, comedies or game shows. But a disproportionate amount of time will be given over to the telling of stories. People want to hear stories, and they always have done, because stories affect us at such a deep level.

The stories that affect us most deeply and timelessly are often called myths. The word 'myth' is often used to mean something that never happened – as when people say that the tale of King Arthur is 'just a myth'. But it can also have a wider meaning, to refer to a story of some kind that is told and retold because it expresses some deep truth about human nature or the world. Such a story can be a myth whether the events happened or not. A good example might be the story of Achilles at the siege of Troy, the subject matter of Homer's *Iliad*. The tale of the rage of Achilles and its tragic consequences speaks deeply to the human condition. Did it happen? Well, Troy was a real place, but beyond that no one really knows. However, that is only incidental to the deeper truth of the myth.

To take a modern example, consider the story of Robert Johnson, one of the enduring myths of the twentieth century. Johnson, a casual labourer who lived in Mississippi in the 1930s, wanted to be a musician – but every time he picked up a guitar, he was booed off stage. Ostracized by his community, Johnson left home and became a drifter, moving from town to town, sleeping in railway yards and jumping on trains as they passed in the night. On his return some years later, he sat down, produced a guitar and began to play – at which everyone was amazed. Somehow, Johnson had transformed himself from mediocrity into the greatest guitar player anyone had ever heard. And they said that he had sold his soul to do it. At some lonely Mississippi Delta crossroads, on a moonless night at midnight, Johnson had met the devil and struck the terrible bargain: mastery of the guitar in exchange for his immortal soul. From that moment, Johnson could not escape his fate. His songs, recorded in a hotel room in 1936 and again the following year, testify to a man on the run from internal demons – there was, as he put it, 'a hellhound on [his] trail'. And within a couple of years he was dead, killed by a poisoned bottle of whisky while playing at a juke joint – the victim, it was said, of a jealous husband. Dead before the age of thirty, the location of his grave has been lost.

Did it really happen? Robert Johnson was a real person, who did record in the 1930s and who perished in mysterious circumstances in 1938; and his recordings were indeed of uncommon quality. In fact, he is usually cited as the greatest blues singer of all time, a major figure in the evolution of twentieth-century music and a key influence on Muddy Waters, Eric Clapton, The Rolling Stones, Jimi Hendrix and a host of others. His music is the elevation of relatively simple folk music into an art form that itself speaks powerfully to the human condition. For this reason alone, irrespective of the legends surrounding its maker's life, it will endure. But as to whether he really sold his soul to the devil – no one knows the truth of that. His namesake, the blues singer Tommy Johnson, actually claimed to have done this, but Robert made no such claim. Apart from songs such as 'Hellhound on My Trail', 'Me and the Devil Blues' and the famous 'Crossroad Blues', there is little evidence either way. He never acknowledged any outside source for his phenomenal playing, although he is known to have been taught by a mysterious figure called Ike Zimmerman, who is said to have practised the guitar at night while sitting on gravestones. But the point is that, rooted in reality as it is, the story has a power of its own. Robert Johnson, the faceless drifter determined to make a name for himself, made the terrible mistake of invoking supernatural forces that would eat him up from within and take his life. Or was it a mistake? For the music of Robert Johnson lives on today, winning Grammys fifty years after it was recorded. Some might say that the price he paid, however terrible, was worth it.

A story like that is a myth. It speaks to us because it tells us something about the human condition. In the case of Robert Johnson, it is a myth that is based to some degree on reality, and which feeds in part off the remarkably powerful recordings that the real Robert Johnson made, which continue to inspire. Another classic myth is the story of King Arthur, the noble king who was betrayed by his wife, Guinevere, and his most trusted knight, Sir Lancelot, and was slain by his wicked son, Mordred. This is an example of a myth that is utterly untrue. Perhaps Arthur did really exist as some kind of warlord in Dark Ages Britain, but the stories of his court, the Round Table and the search for the Holy Grail are a medieval invention. Although not true in the sense of having actually happened, stories like this have another kind of truth, because they say something true about life, something that cannot be put into words except by telling the story itself, because human beings are fundamentally story-telling animals: we respond to stories on a level beyond normal understanding. For this reason, the really great stories, the stories of King Arthur, of Achilles fighting Hector at Troy, of

Peter denying Jesus at cockcrow, of Augustine racked with anguish in the garden of Milan, endure. They are not just about the characters in the story; they are, at some deeper level, about all of us.

And the Christian myths, perhaps more than any others, tackle the heart of the human condition: who we are, who we are meant to be, what limits us and how we are saved. For this reason alone, the Christian myths – primarily the story of Jesus – are among the most powerful and enduring stories that humanity possesses. C.S. Lewis commented that the Christian stories are exactly like the myths of any other culture, with the added bonus that they happen to be true; but many would say that they are also more inspiring. Compare one of the most ancient myths of all, the Sumerian tale of King Gilgamesh, two-thirds god and one-third man, who set out on a fruitless quest for immortality. The story of Gilgamesh is moving and profound, dealing with issues that go to the heart of concerns both modern and ancient, and for that reason it has been consistently popular since it was rediscovered in the nineteenth century. But Gilgamesh as a character is arguably a lot less sympathetic and comprehensible than his parallel in the Christian myths, Jesus, who was fully God and fully man, weighed down with the cares of both, but ultimately triumphant. In the end, such conclusions must come down to individual taste – but there could be a strong argument for the success of Christianity being largely due to the appeal of its myths. And, as we shall see later, Christianity managed to combine the mythic qualities of ancient religion with the scientific concerns of philosophy, giving its myths a dimension that those of other religions lacked.

Just as Tolkien externalized the concerns of the soul by creating concrete representations of the temptation of power, such as the Ring, or of the charismatic authority of wisdom, such as Gandalf's staff, so too myth can externalize the conflicts of the soul creating a narrative on a potentially cosmic scale. This has certainly been the case in Christianity. One of the most famous Christian myth-makers was Valentinus, who lived in the early second century. He was part of the 'Gnostic' movement, a religious trend that existed both inside and outside Christianity, and revolved around the notion that the physical world is intrinsically evil. Valentinus taught a remarkably complicated mythology to explain how this evil world came about in the first place. He believed that within God there was a large hierarchy of divine beings. The lowest on the ladder, Sophia (or Wisdom), became jealous of those above her; fortunately, Sophia managed to remain inside the divinity, but only by casting off her jealousy, which sank and turned into physical matter. It also turned into a sort of minor, inferior god, who, unaware of the existence of the true God above him, proceeded to create the physical world out of the remnants of Sophia's emotions. That is certainly a peculiar story, and it's one that more orthodox Christians have had a lot of fun mocking ever since – for Gnosticism, including the teaching of Valentinus, was condemned by the church. But Valentinus was not just trying to explain where the world comes from. He was trying to explain the conflict that rages within the human soul, where good and evil war with each other. Valentinus believed that his mythology helped to show that human beings are mired in sin and darkness – since the world was

> '*Christ Jesus...*
> *though he was in*
> *the form of God,*
> *did not regard equality*
> *with God as something*
> *to be exploited,*
> *but emptied himself,*
> *taking the form*
> *of a slave,*
> *being born in*
> *human likeness.*
> *And being found*
> *in human form,*
> *he humbled himself*
> *and became obedient*
> *to the point of death –*
> *even death on a cross.*'
>
> Philippians 2:6–8

created from sinful passion by an ignorant god – but that they can ultimately hope to be restored to the spiritual realm above, since that is where the raw materials from which they were made originally came. The passion of Sophia is, in a way, the story of all human beings, projected onto the cosmic stage of myth.

Valentinus, like many Gnostics, also loved mysterious names and words that hinted at deep knowledge. For example, one of his names for the highest part of God is 'Abraxas'. This is a magical word, because if you give each of the letters a number, based on where they fall in the Greek alphabet, the sum of those numbers is 365 – the number of days in a year and also the number of heavens that Valentinus believed emanated from the god Abraxas. In fact, the name 'Abraxas' may well be the origin of the later 'magical' word 'abracadabra'.

Yet the greatest Christian myth-maker was also one of the great figures in world literature – Dante Alighieri. Dante was born in Florence in the late thirteenth century and later settled in Ravenna, where he died; he was therefore living on the eve of the Renaissance. He wrote a number of books, including some on politics, which he was deeply involved in; but by far his most famous was the cycle called *The Comedy*. This extraordinary work – made up of the *Inferno*, *Purgatory* and *Paradise* – was an extended account of a vision that Dante claimed to have had in 1300, in which he apparently travelled through hell, purgatory and heaven. In writing this epic, Dante was joining in a long tradition of medieval literature about the afterlife, one that went back to a ninth-century poet with the marvellous name of Walafrid Strabo. Walafrid – whose surname means 'squinty' and was apparently a nickname – wrote an influential poem called *The Vision of Wetti*, describing a vision that one of his tutors at the monastery had had of the punishments awaiting those who died in sin. Walafrid was clearly something of a radical reformer, since most of those hanging from chains or being stretched on the rack were apparently priests who had abused their position; evidently, this was Walafrid's way of trying to improve the general quality of the priesthood.

Dante used the same genre more ambitiously – to try to provide a description of the medieval world that had been so perfectly produced by philosophers such as Thomas Aquinas. Aquinas, whom we shall meet again later in this book, had created a remarkable Christian philosophy by blending the Christian tradition with the recently rediscovered theories of Aristotle. In this world, everything was ordered and had its place, and this was what Dante hoped to reflect in his poem. Hell, purgatory and heaven, according to Dante, were clearly divided up into different regions and categories, and all souls were carefully allocated to the appropriate place. And, like Walafrid Strabo, Dante had no compunction about putting the religious authorities in their place: most of the popes of his time are found languishing in hell.

There is much in Dante's work that is strange to modern readers. For example, purgatory – the place where Christians go before moving on to heaven, because they must first do penance for their sins – is described as a huge mountain, rising up out of the ocean in the southern hemisphere, with the Garden of Eden at the top. Walafrid Strabo, incidentally, had been the first to describe purgatory as a mountain, five centuries earlier. Clearly, we are dealing once again with myth – as we are when we encounter, in the innermost circle of hell, a monstrous Satan, encased in ice, munching eternally on the broken bodies of Brutus, Cassius and Judas Iscariot. To Dante, betrayal – either of Julius Caesar or of Christ – was clearly the most pernicious sin. But again, this mythology, cast in the grandest terms, is simply a reflection of what happens to the individual. The journey that Dante goes on in the poem reflects the journey that every Christian goes on in their spiritual life. It is this concern for individual spirituality, together with its remarkable imagery and poetry, that makes Dante's *Comedy* one of the most important works of literature ever written. It certainly proved enormously popular: within a century, twelve commentaries had appeared on it. By the middle of the sixteenth century, it had been renamed *The Divine Comedy*, reflecting not just its subject matter but its brilliance. The work's style had just as much influence as its content too: Dante was a champion of vernacular languages, and he wrote in Italian. The great popularity of *The Divine Comedy* meant that it played a central role in establishing modern Italian, just as Luther's Bible translation would later do for German.

Thomas Aquinas, by the way, although not normally considered much of a poet, did make a small but important contribution to the history of poetry. He wrote a number of prayers and hymns, among which occur the following lines, to be recited by a priest after saying Mass:

Sit vitiorum meorum evacuatio
Concupiscentae et libidinis exterminatio,
Caritatis et patientiae,
Humilitatis et obedientiae,
Omniumque virtutum augmentatio.

It is, of course, a limerick. I regret to report that this verse is all about imploring God to remove the speaker's sins and replace them with virtues, and nowhere mentions either a man from Nantucket or a bus bound for Ealing; but at least Aquinas had begun the noble tradition that would later lead to the likes of Edward Lear.

The galactic railroad and the ill-fitting suit – Jesus, Japan and rejection

Myths like these, Christian and otherwise, are deeply embedded in the culture of a particular society. So what happens when a religion is transplanted to a new culture? We will see some examples of that in this book, but it certainly has fascinating ramifications in art. Take Japan, a country that, when it first received the Christian message from Jesuit missionaries in the late sixteenth century, seemed a very hopeful prospect, with 300,000 converts by the end of the century. However, the authorities banned the religion and inflicted terrible tortures and executions on the faithful. Christianity was driven underground. Even in today's more tolerant times,

'Through me the way is to the city dolent;
Through me the way is to eternal dole;
Through me the way among the people lost…
Before me there were no created things,
Only eterne, and I eternal last.
All hope abandon, ye who enter in!'

Inscription on the door to hell, Dante Alighieri, *Divine Comedy*, 'Inferno III', tr. Henry Wadsworth Longfellow

fussy about what you ate or where you lived, it was an intrinsically hostile environment. As far as the third-century world was concerned, the desert might as well have been outer space. To go there was to make a powerful statement: it was to turn one's back, figuratively and literally, on the world.

There was already a strong tradition of thinking of the desert as a place to try to atone for one's sins or to find God. In the Old Testament, for example, after the Israelites escaped from the Egyptians, they travelled through the desert of Sinai to reach the Promised Land. However, when they got there, they didn't much like the look of it, since it was full of decidedly fierce-looking people already. According to Numbers 14, God, annoyed at this petulance, decreed that the Israelites would therefore spend the next forty years wandering the desert before they would be allowed to enter the Promised Land. The story establishes well the association of the desert with penance: it is a place to go as a punishment, or to contemplate one's sins. But that makes it a place to win a victory too. In 1 Samuel 23–24, we read the story of the hero David, on the run from King Saul. Saul was not exactly a bad man, but in the story, he was weak and he feared the young, strong David, who had managed to kill the giant Goliath of Gath, and who seemed ready to take over the kingdom from him. David swore his loyalty to Saul, but Saul tried to kill him. David escaped and hid in the desert of the Holy Land – not really a sandy desert like that of Egypt, but a sort of desiccated scrubland. Here, as David hid in a cave with his men, Saul, out hunting him, went into the cave 'to cover his feet', as the Hebrew has it – a modest euphemism for relieving himself. ('Feet', whenever written in the Old Testament, is generally a euphemism for another part of the body!) As he did so, David secretly cut a corner off Saul's cloak. As Saul left with his men, David appeared and showed him the fragment. It proved that David could have killed Saul when he was in the cave, but he had chosen not to. Saul, in tears, swore that David would be king after him and gave up the chase. It is a moving story that is perfectly set in the desert – a place that, in its uncompromising harshness, represents the emotional and spiritual journey that the characters undergo.

Little wonder that Antony and others like him sought out the same kind of environment as a place in which to purge themselves and find God too. In fact, in so doing they were following the example of Jesus himself. According to Matthew 4, after being baptized by John the Baptist (another desert dweller), Jesus also retreated to the desert. There, we are told, he fasted for forty days and nights, after which the devil appeared and tempted him. Only after undergoing all this did Jesus embark on his public ministry.

Yet this recurring understanding of the desert is just part of a complex understanding of the power of *landscape* within Christianity. Take, as another example, mountains. Many religions have a special place for mountains: in China, for example, Buddhists and Confucianists alike regard mountains as holy places, and they are a favourite place for shrines, temples and monasteries. In Christian literature, where deserts represent finding God through self-denial or emotional crisis, mountains represent a more direct route. After the Israelites fled the Egyptians and before becoming lost in the desert, they camped around Mount Sinai. Moses went up the mountain to meet with God and receive the Law. In Matthew's Gospel, one of the first things Jesus did after coming out of the desert was to go up a mountain and deliver the Sermon on the Mount. (This account may partly come from Matthew's tendency to try to draw parallels between the life of Moses and that of Jesus; in Luke's Gospel, Jesus delivered much of the same teaching on a flat plain.) Many of those who followed in the footsteps of Antony of Egypt congregated on a hill in the desert, the holy mountain of Nitria, thereby combining the two traditions; and to this day one of the holiest sites of the Greek Orthodox Church is Mount Athos, a rocky and spectacular peninsula off the Greek mainland, covered in monasteries.

Symbolic landscapes, symbolic stories

Why do these same ideas crop up again and again, and why is it important? They are a way of tapping into a notion as ancient as religion itself: that of spiritual landscape. We saw earlier how ancient folk religions revolved, to a large extent, around the changing of the seasons and the skies throughout the year. These things were an integral part of the lives of those first worshippers. But so too were the landscapes in which they lived. For example, the ancient Egyptians venerated the Nile river along which they lived, and upon whose annual flooding they depended for their livelihood.

Christians have always retained this sense that particular places are important. Sometimes this has been of necessity. In the early years of Christianity, the church at Rome was especially significant, because Rome was the most important city in the world. It was, moreover, the place where Peter and Paul, two of the key leaders of the first generation of Christians, had been executed. Before his death, Paul himself, in his letter to the Romans, had adopted an uncharacteristically humble attitude to them. In most of his letters, Paul tended to write in a decidedly strident way, laying down the law to his readers, and it was obviously hard for him to avoid doing so in this one. In the first chapter, he says, 'I am longing to see you so that I may share with you some spiritual gift to strengthen you – or rather so that we may be mutually encouraged by each other's faith, both yours and mine.' For Paul, who was dictating this letter,

'Who will follow someone who makes his way through such places and elevates his mind to such heights, who, as though he were passing from one peak to another, comes ever higher than he was through his ascent to the heights? First, he leaves behind the base of the mountain and is separated from all those too weak for the ascent. Then as he rises higher in his ascent he hears the sounds of the trumpets. Thereupon, he slips into the inner sanctuary of divine knowledge.'

Gregory of Nyssa,
The Life of Moses II 167,
c. AD 390

humility clearly came as an afterthought, but at least he was making the effort.

Several decades later, the church at Rome received another letter from a Christian leader who was doomed to die there. Ignatius was bishop of Antioch when, in about 107, he was sentenced to be taken to Rome and thrown to the lions. While travelling there, he wrote a number of letters, including one to the Roman church, urging them not to try to intercede on his behalf. Ignatius believed that it was God's will that he should die for his sake, and for his own part, he actually looked forward to his death, because it meant he would soon see God. Every sentence of his letter testifies to the psychological strain under which it was written, and the peculiar excitement of its author. Ignatius believed that Rome, which lay far to the west of Antioch, was an appropriate place to die for Christ's sake. As he put it, 'How good it is to be sinking down below the world's horizon towards God, to rise again later into the dawn of his presence!'

Rome would, of course, later become the central city of Catholic Christianity. Its bishop would gradually increase in both spiritual and worldly power to become the pope. Yet the importance of Rome to Christians pales before that of Jerusalem, the city where Jesus was crucified and where he was raised from the dead. Peter and Paul were associated with Rome because they were both believed to have been martyred there, but Jerusalem also had James, who was not only one of the most important leaders of the church in the first generation but Jesus' own brother.

Today, there is particular interest in James, following the discovery in Jerusalem, in late 2002, of an ossuary – a box for the burial of bones – with his name on it. The Aramaic inscription on the box, which dates from AD 63, describes the bones as belonging to 'James, son of Joseph, brother of Jesus'. There are considerable doubts about the ossuary's authenticity, however: it seems that, though the 'James, son of Joseph' part of the inscription does come from the first century, the 'brother of Jesus' part was added later. A Christian forgery, clumsily done on a genuinely antique box, perhaps? Or perhaps, as others have suggested, the ossuary really was that of Jesus' brother, but the original inscription did not make that clear, and someone thought it would be useful to alter it in order to match what was genuinely believed.

While the media picked up on the box as controversial evidence for Jesus' existence, more interesting, really, is the putative link to James himself. James, who might in some ways be considered the founder of Christianity, was rather painted out of the story by later generations, including some of those who wrote the New Testament. His Jewish understanding of Christianity was supplanted by the more inclusive approach of Paul, and the figure of James himself slipped into the background. The arguments over what may have been his ossuary help to redress the balance, even if only a little bit.

Jerusalem, however, has never been out of the spotlight. Indeed, in the Middle Ages the city was considered the centre of the world. Medieval thinkers were, of course, well aware that the world is a sphere, something that had been known since ancient times; but the known world extended only from Britain in the west to India in the east, and from Scandinavia in the north to the Sahara in the south. Anything else was pretty much guesswork. However, this meant two things. First, it was possible to map the known world on a neat circle, representing just one side of the globe; what was on the other side was unknown. Second, Jerusalem came nicely in the middle of such an arrangement. The Romans had generally drawn maps with Rome at the centre, but the Christians now subverted that tradition to put Jerusalem in the same position.

Moreover, the further east you went, the holier you got. In the Middle Ages it was believed that the Garden of Eden, where Adam and Eve lived in bliss before the Fall, was somewhere in Mesopotamia, in modern-day Iraq. Further east than that, people let their imaginations run riot: fabled lands such as China and Cathay could contain pretty much anything, as could the lands to the south of Ethiopia. All of this is illustrated beautifully in the famous 'Mappa Mundi', or 'Map of the World', which was made in England in the thirteenth century. The map, which has Jerusalem at the centre and east, not north, at the top, is intended to be a depiction of the world (including a lot of highly imaginative pictures of some of the inhabitants of its more exotic regions) – but more important than that, it is meant to show what the world *means*. It is a work of religious cartography. Jerusalem is at the centre of the world not simply as a matter of geography, but as a matter of importance: the world revolves around the life, death and resurrection of Jesus. And just in case anyone failed to appreciate this, the artist depicts Christ sitting in glory at the top of the map, overseeing the whole world. The continents and seas, the mountains and rivers are all alike under the providence of God. He has set everything in its place, and everything derives its significance from him.

The Mappa Mundi was partly based upon a description of the world in the works of a man with the strange name of Orosius of Braga. Orosius was from Portugal but lived in Africa in the fifth century, where he became friends with Augustine of Hippo, probably the most famous theologian of all time. Augustine was, at this time, working on a massive book that would change the course of Western thought: his famous *City of God*, which set out his understanding of history and the political world. Augustine believed that the world was the stage for an incredible drama that was played out within human history, the story of God's dealings with humanity. Since he was busy working out the theological implications of this, he suggested to Orosius that he might back it up with a historical study. Orosius therefore produced his *History Against the*

'The earth is placed in the middle region of the universe, being situated like a centre at an equal interval from all parts of heaven... The circle of lands is so-called from its roundness, which is like that of a wheel... For the ocean flowing about on all sides encircles its boundaries. It is divided into three parts; of which the first is called Asia; the second, Europe; the third, Africa... Europe and Africa occupy one half, and Asia alone the other. But the former were made into two parts because the great sea enters from the ocean between them and cuts them apart.'

Isidore of Seville,
Etymologies XIII 1-2,
c. AD 600

WHAT HAS CHRISTIANITY EVER DONE FOR US?

Pagans, a book of decidedly dubious literary merits but important as the first real attempt at a Christian history of the world. He divided the history of the world into the story of four great empires – Babylon, Greece, Carthage and Rome – and told their story with an emphasis on the role of God throughout. For Orosius, these great empires, and the world whose geography he described in such detail, were the stage upon which the story of God and his people unfolds.

Orosius's work was very popular in later centuries: no less a person than King Alfred the Great made a rather free translation of it into English. Its popularity testifies to the importance within Christianity of history, and indeed stories in general – like those we saw in the last chapter. For if the landscape is heavy with symbolism, it makes sense only within the context of stories that flesh out and create that symbolism. Mountains represent coming close to God only because there are stories of people such as Moses and Jesus climbing them, while the desert represents the facing of temptation and other inner demons only because there are the stories of David and Saul, Antony of Egypt and the rest. Together, the stories and the landscapes act to create a kind of symbolic language. This is the language of myth, the kind of myths we saw in the last chapter. It is a powerful language because it connects us to a greater reality – to the world around us and the history that came before us. It recognizes that we cannot understand ourselves in isolation. We are part of a wider world – not simply dropped within it, but intimately involved in it, inevitably interacting with other parts, and determined by those who came before. The Christian use of symbols and stories is a reflection of an organic kind of world view, one that seeks to link human beings to the wider world, rather than leave them disconnected and isolated. That, by contrast, is the tendency of modern living. In this respect, Christianity shares the best elements of the old, pagan religions. It seeks to place human beings within the greater context of the stories and histories that surround us, and within the greater world of which we form a part.

The numinous and the sublime

This sense of myth, of symbolic places and stories, is common to many religions. But Christianity goes rather deeper than most, because a close link between God and the world is hard-coded, as it were, into its most central doctrines. On the one hand, there is the doctrine of Creation – the idea that the universe was created by God. In fact, Christians have traditionally believed not simply that God made the world, as we might make an object and then leave it, but that he sustains it from moment to moment. That is, if God were to relax his attention for an instant, the world would cease to exist. A Christian writer who expressed this in a particularly striking way was Irenaeus, a theologian who came from what is now Turkey but was bishop of Lyons, in modern-day France, in the second century. He described the universe as being held in the hand of God. As he put it:

Who understands his hand – that hand which measures immensity; that hand which, by its own measure, spreads out the measure of the heavens, and which holds in its hollow the earth with the abysses; which contains in itself the breadth, and length, and the deep below, and the height above the whole creation; which is seen, which is heard and understood, and which is invisible?

It was a way of thinking that would prove very pervasive throughout the centuries. Thomas Aquinas, the greatest Christian thinker of the Middle Ages, argued that God simply is existence itself: so for something to exist is, in a way, for it to partake of God. Quite what that means is a bit unclear – it certainly supports Aquinas's other contention that God is intrinsically incomprehensible. But it does mean that God is therefore immeasurably greater than the world – for he is the only thing that exists in its own right, as it were – but at the same time he is closely linked to his creation, for he supports it at all times. In the fourteenth century, Irenaeus's imagery was reused by one of the most popular writers of the period, Julian of Norwich. Despite the name, Julian was actually a woman, an 'anchoress' – someone who, like Antony of Egypt, aimed to live alone leading a life of contemplation of God, but who instead of going out to a wilderness remained in the town. Anchoresses lived in sealed houses in the middle of the town and took a vow never to leave; but people could visit them and talk through the window. They were, in other words, 'anchored' in the community. It was considered a very good idea to have a local anchoress, who could pray for the townsfolk – it was an essential institution in any decent town. Mother Julian – who was presumably named after the saint to whom her church was dedicated, and whose own name therefore remains unknown – was an enormously popular anchoress. We can see why if we read her *Revelations of Divine Love*, a description of a series of visions of Christ she experienced as a young woman, and her thoughts about them. Her book is shot through with a warm common sense and essentially cheerful outlook on life, however bad things may seem; it was Mother Julian who said that God assures us that 'All shall be well, and all shall be well, and all manner of things shall be well.' And she also described one of her visions, in which she was shown how God relates to the world:

> 'It is clear, therefore, that the intelligences... have existence from the first being, which is existence alone, and this is the first cause, which is God.'
>
> Thomas Aquinas,
> *On Being and Essence 4*

He showed me a little thing, the size of a hazelnut, in the palm of my hand; and it was as round as a ball. I looked at it with the eye of my understanding, and thought, 'What may this be?' And I was answered, 'It is all that is made.' I marvelled how it might survive, for it seemed to me it might suddenly have fallen to nothing, it was so small. And I was answered in my understanding, 'It survives, and will do for ever, because God loves it.' And so everything exists through the love of God.

Perhaps the most striking statement of this basic idea comes in the work of Jonathan Edwards, who was one of the most important theologians of the eighteenth century, and probably the most significant American theologian of all time. Unfortunately, he died in 1758 of an over-strong smallpox vaccination before he had a chance to write what he planned as his greatest work. Edwards is interesting because he represented the Calvinist tradition, which at the time was quite a doctrinaire tradition of Christianity – that is, there was a generally accepted account of what Calvinist Christian doctrines were, which left little room for originality. Edwards, however, managed the difficult task of sticking closely to Calvinist orthodoxy while developing interesting new approaches within that tradition. He argued that creation is not some once-for-all thing that happened at the start of time, as if God created the world and then sat back to let it get on with its own devices. On the contrary, creation is ongoing. At every instant, God creates the world again and again; the original act of creation, described in Genesis, was simply the beginning of a continuous process. Just as a film is really not a moving image at all, but a succession of still images that pass so quickly the illusion of movement is created, so too the world does not really persist from moment to moment, as it may appear, but is a succession of new creations.

Yet if the doctrine of Creation suggests a close involvement of God with the world, an even closer one is suggested by the doctrine of the Incarnation. In its classical form, this doctrine states that God became man. Jesus was God and man at the same time, not simply a sort of crossbreed, like *Star Trek*'s Mr Spock who was half human and half Vulcan. Neither was he a human being acting as if he were God, or God pretending to be human – an idea illustrated in a rather wacky document from the early church called the Acts of John. The Acts of John is one of a number of extra-canonical Gospels, works that, like the Gospels of Matthew, Mark, Luke and John in the New Testament, purport to describe what Jesus did. They are, however, decidedly improbable to varying degrees; and the Acts of John is one of the more enjoyably silly, since one of its aims is to teach that Jesus was really a divine being who was just pretending to be human. Jesus, we are told, would change appearance all the time, sometimes being an old, bearded man and sometimes a youth. He never left footprints, never needed to eat or

'Now you ask me, 'How shall I think of him, and what is he?' and to this I can only answer, 'I don't know!' Because with that question you have brought me into that same darkness, and that same cloud of unknowing, where I want you to be. For all other created things and their works, yes, and the works of God himself, a man can, though grace, have full knowledge, and can think about them; but of God himself can no man think. So I would leave everything that I can think of, and choose to love the thing that I cannot think of. Why? Because he can well be loved, but not thought. By love may he be found and held, but by thought never… Strike upon that thick cloud of unknowing with a sharp dart of longing love, and do not leave it, whatever happens.'

The Cloud of Unknowing 6

go to the toilet, and, most worryingly, had no private parts at all! Still, enjoyable as this kind of thing was, the church ruled at an early stage that it was extremely heretical. The orthodox belief is that Jesus was fully human and fully divine, with neither nature predominating over the other.

The ramifications of this doctrine influence every other part of Christian belief and practice. If God could become man, what does that tell us about God? But equally, what does it tell us about human nature, and about the world? We can think of the doctrine more widely, and think of God becoming a material thing, an inhabitant of the material world that we live in. When Christianity first developed, such a doctrine was distasteful to many. Greek philosophers in the tradition of Plato were increasingly stressing the immaterial nature of God: they believed that God was utterly unlike the world, incomprehensible to human minds and that he existed at a great distance from the world. To know God, one had to turn one's back on the world. How could Christians claim to know God in a human being?

Ideas like those of the Platonists did have a major influence on Christianity. There have been many great Christian mystics who have taught that God is beyond the ability of human beings to understand him at all, and that understanding this fact is, paradoxically, the first step to coming to know him. One of the best-known texts expressing this teaching is a small book called *The Cloud of Unknowing*, which was written in England in the middle of the fourteenth century. The author, whose name is unknown, but who was a contemporary of Julian of Norwich, tells his readers that God is hidden from us by a 'cloud of unknowing', which symbolizes the fact that we cannot understand him. But he is still accessible to us - not by knowledge, but by love. If we forget all other things apart from the cloud in which God is hidden, if we put the world and everything within it under another cloud, the 'cloud of forgetting', and focus on the cloud above us – not with the power of the intellect, but with the power of love – then we may hope to come close to God.

Strikingly, these ideas tie in with what we saw earlier about the symbolism of the landscape. The first Christian writer to explore the idea of the unknowability of God, and how we can nevertheless know him, was Gregory of Nyssa, who was writing in the fourth century. Gregory believed that, although most of the stories in the Bible were true, most of them were also intended to convey some deeper, spiritual meaning. One was the story, in Exodus 24, of Moses climbing Mount Sinai to meet with God. According to the text, as Moses climbed, he passed first through cloud and then into the darkness where God was. As usual, Gregory takes the mountain to symbolize the journey of every Christian who comes to know God. And for him, the cloud signifies the fact that God cannot be seen or heard physically, while the darkness signifies the fact that he cannot be grasped by the mind either. Only by passing through these realizations, just as Moses passed through the cloud and darkness of the mountain, can we come to meet God for ourselves. And indeed, it is ultimately from this very story that the author of *The Cloud of Unknowing* took the idea of the 'cloud' itself.

Nevertheless, the mysticism of the cloud and the darkness, though powerful and poetic, is only half the story. Christianity has also cherished a rather earthier kind of spirituality, one that does not look for God by turning its back on the world, but finds God *in* the world. The first way of thinking comes from the doctrine that God is greater than the world, but the second comes from the doctrine that, in the Incarnation, for better or for worse, God actually lived in the world and became part of it. Irenaeus, whom we encountered earlier, put this idea at the centre of his theology. He believed that if we can talk about God becoming human, then we can turn around and talk, at the same time, of humanity becoming divine. And not just humanity, but the world itself. The world, through the Incarnation, has become 'infected' with divinity, and is pulled up to the level of God.

There has therefore been a strong Christian tradition of seeking God in nature. Look once again at Jonathan Edwards. Edwards was fascinated by the natural world: one of his earliest writings is a short scientific paper describing how spiders can fly through the air by using their own silk as parachutes. In his journals, he described how he became increasingly aware of the beauty of nature, and, at the same time, how he saw this beauty as coming directly from God. He would sit and gaze at the moon for hours, admiring the work of God. As he put it:

God's excellence, his wisdom, his purity and love, seemed to appear in everything; in the sun, moon, and stars; in the clouds, and blue sky; in the grass, flowers, trees; in the water, and all nature; which used greatly to fix my mind.

Edwards believed, in fact, that beauty was the key to understanding God and the world alike. He suggested that the beauty we see in the world is, on the one hand, deliberately put there by God – so he has designed the sky and the landscape, and the relations between living things, as a work of art. Nature, for Edwards, is essentially happy: he believed that birds sang for joy, and indeed that those spiders that fly through the air on silk do so for sport. But more profoundly, the beauty of the created world is a reflection of the beauty of God, who created and continues to create it. God is the most beautiful thing there is, and the beauty of the relations between created things is a reflection of the beauty of the Trinity, the one God existing as a loving community of three persons. Edwards likened the beauty of God to music, a form of elegance and beauty that transcends the understanding.

This idea didn't start with Jonathan Edwards, of course. In fact, the notion that God is Beauty, and that we can find God if we start by seeking out the beauty around us, predated Christianity itself. In Plato's *Symposium* (or 'Drinking Party'), written 400 years before Christ, Socrates urges his rather drunk listeners to seek true beauty not in the things they see around them but in spiritual things, and by becoming lovers of beauty in the abstract to grasp the life of the gods and to live a life of virtue. The Platonic philosopher Plotinus, who lived in the third century AD, developed ideas like this to speak of mystical experiences in which the soul becomes united with the divine and comes to exist in a spiritual realm of pure beauty. Plotinus believed that the physical world is a kind of reflection of the higher, spiritual, intellectual realm, and if something is beautiful, that simply means it reflects that higher realm more perfectly. God therefore is Beauty itself, in its highest and purest form.

Christians, recognizing much of value in these Platonic ideas, incorporated them into their own philosophy and spirituality. They combined them with the Jewish ideas they learned from their long meditations upon the Bible. They felt that they read the teachings of people such as Plato and Plotinus in Psalm 27, verse 4:

One thing I asked of the Lord, that I will seek after:
to live in the house of the Lord all the days of my life,
to behold the beauty of the Lord, and to inquire in his temple.

But the Christians did come to temper these ideas with another approach too. It is significant that Edwards claimed to feel the presence of God not just in rainbows and moonrises, but in the rain and thunder too. His contemporary, the Irish philosopher Edmund Burke, expressed this idea in his famous essay, *A Philosophical Inquiry into the Origin of Our Ideas of the Sublime and Beautiful*, which was published in 1756. Burke was a lawyer-turned-philosopher and sometime member of Parliament, and indeed played an important role in the history of British politics by helping to form the notion of a political party – essential when opposing the policies of King George III, which Burke spent some considerable time doing. It has to be said, however, that Burke was perhaps not the most sparkling speaker the House of Commons has ever seen. Some of his speeches lasted for eight hours, and his audience would have vanished long before Burke finally sat down.

Despite all that, however, Burke was also deeply concerned with religious matters, and he is remembered above all for his aesthetic philosophy. He distinguished between two qualities that things can have – being *beautiful* and being *sublime*. If something is beautiful, that means there is something about it that we like, which makes it attractive and pleasant to look at, listen to or think about. The emotion that beauty causes in us in love. But if something is sublime, that means it is awesome or terrifying. If we are faced with something sublime, it fills our mind completely and we are unable to think of anything else. But at the same time, Burke suggests, there is a sort of delight when we encounter the sublime – not pleasure, exactly, because the sublime is always unsettling, but something good nevertheless. There is something thrilling about size, majesty and power, especially if we do not fully understand it, or it is in some way hidden from us. That is why we may exult in a thunderstorm, even though it terrifies us at the same time.

So what is the most sublime thing of all? As we might expect, for Burke, it is God. Burke suggests that, although we know God is loving, wise and so on, the divine quality that strikes us most forcibly is his *power*. God is omnipotent, all-powerful, capable of doing anything; and while we may admire or love his other qualities, it's this almighty power that really causes a gut reaction in us. Indeed, Burke suggests that, when human beings first came to have an idea of God, it was this notion of raw power that was uppermost in their minds; and it was only when Christianity appeared that the idea of love and benevolence was added. Whether or not that is an accurate account of the historical development of religion is debatable, but what is important is that we have here an explanation of how the presence of God can be detected in the world around us. Where Jonathan Edwards sees the beauty of God in the natural world, Edmund Burke sees the sublimity of God: powerful, awesome, terrifying, but also mysterious, moving and inspiring. It is a notion that is often expressed in the word *numinous*, which means something powerful, mysterious and supernatural.

All this is terribly edifying, but what does it mean for us today? Why should we thank the Christians for these ideas? They are important because they express the belief, which is fundamental to Christianity perhaps more than any other major religion, that *the world matters*. This means that places matter. The desert, as a general idea, matters because it represents trials and spiritual strife – but more than that, the desert of Sinai matters because the Jews encountered God there; the desert of Judea matters because Jesus was tempted there; the desert of Egypt matters because St Antony battled and conquered his personal demons there. The God of the Christians is not some remote, spiritual reality to be discovered by turning away from the world. That was the God of the Platonists. The God of the Christians, by contrast, acts in time and space: his power and his love are encountered by particular people at particular times in particular places, and those times and places retain a special significance and power over us because of that. The Christian belief in the presence of God in the world, which he created and which he became part of, and in which he continues to act as a presence in history, is just part of a general Christian interest in the physical world which we shall see recurring in the following chapters.

Saving worms and drinking the stars – Christians and the environment

Because Christianity holds the physical world to be so important, it's perhaps not surprising to find a tradition of love for the natural world in the religion. Bernard of Clairvaux, for example, one of the most influential spiritual writers in the Middle Ages, stated that trees and stones could teach you more than books could, and he attributed his wisdom and spiritual insight to the amount of time he devoted to meditating in woods. Columba, the great Irish saint who brought Christianity to Scotland, managed to build his famous monastery on the island of Iona without cutting down a single tree. Of course, there aren't many trees on Iona anyway, but Columba made a virtue out of necessity, commenting, in reference to a nearby forest, 'Though there is fear in me of death and of hell... I have more fear for the sound of an axe over in Doire.'

Perhaps the most famous Christian saint associated with a love for nature is Francis of Assisi, whom we shall see in more detail in chapter 6. Francis's *Canticle of the Sun*, the first known work to be written in Italian, is an ode of praise to the natural world, beginning with the sun and ending, perhaps ominously, with death. In the course of it, Francis declares, 'Praise to you, Lord, for our sister, mother earth, who sustains us and governs, and produces different fruits with coloured flowers and green

> 'This life must not be prematurely written off; in this the Old and New Testaments are at one... Christ takes hold of a man at the centre of his life.'
>
> Dietrich Bonhoeffer,
> *Letters and Papers from Prison*

plants.' According to legend, Francis could speak to the animals and would preach to birds; it is, however, true that he was in the habit of picking worms off the road and carrying them to safety. Francis had a very strong sense of the natural world's status as God's creation, and he therefore believed that God could be encountered within it. By revering and caring for the world, one honoured God.

While Francis is often taken as a sort of unofficial patron saint of the environmental movement, perhaps a better figure would be a more modern saint who was the Orthodox Church's answer to the American figure of legend, Johnny Appleseed. Nicephorus was a monk on the Greek island of Chios in the late eighteenth and early nineteenth centuries, and he made trees something of a speciality. He was in charge of the tree nursery at his monastery, and he came to appreciate his trees especially since Chios is a rocky island without much large-scale vegetation. Nicephorus made it his business to try to reforest the island, taking his young trees and planting them all over the place, as well as giving them away for others to plant. He prayed for farmers and other people who looked after trees, and he gave them money from his inheritance to help their work; and when people confessed their sins to him, he would even make the penance planting trees – the more sins, the more trees! 'If you don't love trees, you don't love God,' Nicephorus said, summing up his view of life.

Of course, it would be anachronistic to identify all these figures with modern environmentalists. The notion that the natural world is a fragile thing that must be protected is a modern one, and people such as Francis of Assisi or Bernard of Clairvaux did not have to contend with the threat to the environment that exists now. Today, however, Christians are increasingly aware of the responsibility towards the environment that their religion entails, and there is a rapidly growing movement within Christianity to become ecologically sensitive and try to preserve the natural world. Some environmentalists regard the Christian tradition as part of the problem, rather than the solution: it is sometimes said that Christianity's human-centred view of life, with human beings as the focus of God's attention, necessarily marginalizes the rest of the natural world. Moreover, the creation story of Genesis, with the notorious command in Genesis 1:28 that man is to have 'dominion' over all things, has been essentially a blank cheque for people to do what they like to the natural world. Certainly these charges have historically had some weight. But many Christians point out that the word for 'dominion' in that verse means something like 'benevolent stewardship', suggesting that the role of human beings is to look after the world, not tyrannically exploit it. An authentically Christian viewpoint – one that appreciates that the physical world is the creation and expression of God, and that it is the stage in which God's saving actions are performed – shies away from the notion that the world exists only for the good of humanity and that humanity has a carte blanche to exploit it.

There is, incidentally, one rather striking area in which Christians have made the very most of the goodness of the natural world – alcohol. Today, some Christians, especially Protestants, believe that it is wrong to drink alcohol; but such scruples were rare in the past. Wine was, after all, central to the most important Christian rite, the celebration of the Eucharist – for Jesus had blessed the wine at the Last Supper, an act that was repeated every time the Eucharist was performed. In the Middle Ages, therefore, when monks went to church several times a day, an enormous quantity of wine was required. The monasteries therefore grew their own vineyards, selling the excess wine to raise money for themselves or for the poor. Many monasteries also had beehives, because they needed a constant supply of wax to make candles for the services. Naturally, this meant that they had large quantities of honey lying around, so they turned it into mead – a sort of honey-based wine that was popular in the Middle Ages.

There was also the matter of beer, which had been a staple drink in Europe for centuries. Beer then was rather more nutritious than most beer today, and it was brewed daily by village women. But the monasteries became increasingly involved in beer production. Ever since its invention in ancient Sumeria, beer had been associated with religion; but a more immediate reason for the monks' interest in it was the fact that they spent much of their time fasting, eating decidedly meagre meals. The nutritional value of beer made it an excellent choice for a drink to accompany those meals, and the monks became good at making it – so much so that many monasteries went into commercial production and sold the beer on, often in their own pubs. Little wonder that

> 'We old folks have to find our cushions and pillows in our tankards. Strong beer is the milk of the old.'
>
> Martin Luther

the caricature of the medieval monk developed as a jolly, fat man with a red nose! There is even a patron saint of beer, Gambrinus, a Belgian king of the early fifteenth century, who is supposed to have invented the method of flavouring beer with hops.

Some monks, however, were a little more refined in their tastes, and they developed drinks that are still enjoyed today. The early sixteenth century saw the invention of Benedictine at the monastery of Fecamp in France, while a century later the Carthusian monastery of La Grand Chartreuse gave its name to a liqueur that was first distilled by the monks as a life-giving elixir. Meanwhile, whiskey was becoming increasingly refined: no one knows quite where it was invented, but its distillation was well established among the monks of Ireland by the early Middle Ages. Irish monks later took the drink to Scotland together with Christianity. One of the earliest known brewers of Scotch whiskey was one Friar John Cor, who in 1494, according to the records, purchased 14,500 pounds of malt for making 'aqua vitae' – the water of life, or whisky. Since that would have made well over a thousand bottles, the good friar was clearly not distilling it solely for his own consumption.

In America, of course, whiskey became bourbon – invented by the Reverend Elijah Craig, a Baptist minister, in the eighteenth century. Craig was something of a disreputable character, who spent some time in prison for causing disturbances with his sermons. But his distillery, it is said, pioneered the techniques needed to turn the 'white lightning' hooch of Kentucky into something a little more drinkable.

But perhaps the greatest contribution of Christianity to the world of alcohol took place in 1662, when Dom Perignon, the winemaster at the abbey of Hautvillers, made the first bottle cork. In so doing he invented champagne – which, after he first tasted it, led him to cry, 'I am drinking the stars!'

Domes, glass and a bare ceiling – Christian architecture

Christians have not only interpreted the landscape, they have also changed it – sometimes dramatically. The development of church architecture is one of the most obvious and lasting contributions of Christianity to the world. Indeed, in some of the heartlands of Christianity, there are towns that seem to consist of churches and little else. One such place is Ochrid in Macedonia, where it seems Byzantine civilization has never really ended. Historically, this was a major centre of Christianity in the Balkans, with a thriving and very influential tradition of Christian art. And today, by governmental decree, all new buildings in Ochrid must be in the old, Byzantine style, influenced by the church architecture. This town is striking testimony to the influence of Christianity, not only over the history of the area, but over its very appearance.

A church is, when you think about it, quite a peculiar thing. On the one hand, it is a building that is designed for a particular function. It is built for people to meet in, so it needs walls and a roof to protect them from the elements; it needs to have doors, windows and furniture, just like any other building. But on the other hand, its function is not practical but religious. It is built, ultimately, to praise God. So its design must also express ideas about God and the way he is worshipped. A church, in other words, is both a functional thing and a work of art.

It's the same paradox that we have already been looking at in this chapter – the paradox, central to Christian faith, that God is hidden and revealed, invisible and visible, beyond the world and within it, all at the same time. Only now we are talking not of the natural world but of the purely human, social world. In the last chapter we looked at how art, in its different forms, has expressed the Christian faith through the centuries. It might be said that the history of church-building is even more important, because it combines the purpose of Christian art with that of Christian function, a dual role that reflects the duality of how Christians see God.

At first, Christian churches were decidedly modest, as might be expected from a religion that was officially banned. The earliest known church is at Dura-Europos in Syria, dating from the third century, and it is simply a normal (if large) house that has been converted for ecclesiastical use.

All this changed about a century after that first-known Middle Eastern church was converted, when the emperor Constantine became a Christian in the early fourth century. Churches were now to be purpose-built, and they were to make a statement. These buildings were built along the same lines as Roman temples of the past, and they were also influenced by the 'basilica', a building found in many Roman cities and used for civil and legal administration – a sort of town hall and courthouse rolled into one. The general idea was to combine two basic designs. The first is that of the basilica, a long building where the congregation sits facing the priest at one end; the other is that of a round building, where everyone surrounds a central focal point. Because Christian worship revolved around the liturgy, and particularly processions of the priests and also of the congregation, the basilicas naturally took on a long sort of shape to provide the best setting. The body of the church in this scheme is called the nave and is where the congregation sits. The Roman churches took from the civic basilicas the idea of having columns down either side of the nave, which helped not only to support the roof and allow a wider building but also to demarcate areas, aisles, within the nave for processing up and down.

From the earliest times, even when Christians were meeting in private rooms, it seems likely that there would have been at least a conceptual distinction between the part of the building where the congregation was and the part where the priests were. By the fourth century this latter part had become the sanctuary, where the altar is located. But this was not right at the end of the building. Instead, it was *near* the far end, with a further, small part called the apse beyond it, where the bishop's throne was set (the word 'cathedral' comes from the Greek word for 'seat'). The other clergy were seated around the sides of the apse. In this way, the altar, where the Eucharist was celebrated, was kept *within* the people, midway between the bishop in the apse and the congregation in the nave. It was a dramatic illustration of the doctrine, so vital to those early Christians, that God had entered the world as one of them. Moreover, there might well be the relics of a saint buried under the altar – so that the Eucharist was celebrated in the midst of the living church and the dead church too, keeping that link with the past that we saw in the first chapter. Today, one of the best-known churches to survive in this Roman-basilica style is that of St Maria Maggiore in Rome.

In addition to the basilicas, the first state-sponsored Christians built baptisteries, for baptizing new believers, and martyrions, small chapels dedicated to saints. Both were normally round buildings, taking over the circular idea of earlier, non-Christian temples, and they often had a dome on top. In the later centuries of the Roman empire, the basilicas too were invariably topped off with a dome over the centre, something that helped to emphasize the round element of the design and the sense that the divine was at the centre of the life of the church. The first churches in this style were built in Italy, at Ravenna, in the early sixth century, and they are basically round with bits sticking out in various directions, depending on where the architects wanted the building to point. The most important thing, however, was the dome. In fact, the Byzantine architects had something of a fixation with domes. The most famous was the one on the great cathedral of Hagia Sophia at Constantinople, built in the 530s. The dome, larger than any that had been erected before, was 31.4 metres (103 feet) across and reached a height of 49.7 metres (163 feet); to those who gaped in awe from below, it seemed as if this vast quantity of stone was floating ethereally above their heads, supported by nothing more than a miracle. In fact, of course, it was supported by innovative vaulting and column designs that held the great weight more securely than any before – although it was done very simply, with four arches around the central square of the church and the dome supported on top. Such was the majesty of this incredible church that the basic design was copied throughout the Middle East in the centuries that were to come. Indeed, it went further than this. When, in the fifteenth century, Constantinople fell to the Turks, the heart of Orthodox Christianity moved north to the emerging power of Russia based in Kiev and, increasingly, Moscow.

In both cities, new cathedrals were built in the Byzantine style, topped with domes. In fact, they expanded the dome up and out, creating the novel 'onion' look that the Kremlin, the seat of power in Moscow, retains to this day.

The style also influenced Muslim architecture. When the Muslims conquered most of the eastern Mediterranean and Mesopotamia, they turned many of the churches they found there into mosques – mainly by the simple addition of a minaret, a thin tower from which the muezzin calls the faithful to prayer and an essential part of any mosque. Hagia Sophia itself, by the addition of minarets at its corners, became a great mosque, with all its Christian imagery removed from the interior. When new mosques were built, they often featured domes, especially in Turkey, Persia and India – a sort of combination of the Christian church dome with an echo of the dome-shaped tents that the Turks had once inhabited. Baghdad, for example, is full of remarkable domed mosques – some very ancient, some more recent, including some huge ones built by Saddam Hussein in a not-very-convincing display of piety. Yet perhaps the most remarkable example of the

THE MAGNIFICENT APSE OF THE BASILICA SANTA MARIA MAGGIORE IN ROME, FOUNDED IN THE EARLY FIFTH CENTURY. THE SPLENDID MOSAIC ON THE CEILING, SHOWING CHRIST IN GLORY TOGETHER WITH HIS MOTHER, WAS DESIGNED BY A FRANCISCAN FRIAR NAMED JACOPO TORRITI IN 1295.

THE GREAT DOME OF HAGIA SOPHIA. THE CATHEDRAL WAS CONVERTED INTO A MOSQUE AFTER THE FALL OF BYZANTIUM TO THE TURKS IN 1453, AND MOST OF THE CHRISTIAN MOSAICS WERE PLASTERED OVER AND REPLACED BY ARABIC TEXTS. IT IS NOW A MUSEUM, AND THE OLD MOSAICS ARE BEING UNCOVERED AND DISPLAYED AGAIN.

Byzantine dome transplanted to Islam is the Taj Mahal, built at Agra in India in the seventeenth century and, despite its minarets, not a mosque at all but a tomb, built by Shah Jehan for his beloved wife, Arjumand Banu.

In the West, meanwhile, a different style of church architecture evolved. It was partly inspired by the monastic movement. Early medieval monasteries were actually like little villages, where everyone lived in different huts or cells and shared some communal buildings such as the church or the dining hall. But later on the institutions became more integrated and evolved into large, single-building complexes, divided into a number of different rooms and sections of various kinds. So there developed the idea that a religious building could be divided up into parts, creating a sort of fortress of larger and smaller parts, an idea that influenced the design of churches and cathedrals. To the basic idea of the Roman-style basilica, therefore, was added a profusion of towers, side chapels, vaults and crypts. One common feature was to extend the side aisles of the nave right around the whole church, including around the back of the apse, so that you could walk all the way around without disturbing any service that was going on in the main body of the church. Sticking out from this ambulatory, as the continuous aisle was called, there could be large numbers

of side chapels, each with its own altar and seating area. These chapels would radiate out from the apse, forming an extension known as the corona, or crown. This style, now known as Romanesque, was used for the important abbey church at Cluny in France in the eleventh century. And it was further altered by the development of new architectural techniques, which allowed for soaring columns and arches. Where the Roman architects had sought to lead the eye *down* the church, the medievals sought to lead it *up*.

There was also the matter of the transept. This was an area that came in between the nave and the apse – in other words, where the sanctuary was traditionally located – but it actually stuck out on either side. This meant that if you looked at a plan of the building it would look like a cross. There was obvious symbolism here, and a transept of some kind had been common back in Roman times. However, the Middle Ages saw the new idea of making the two wings of the transept and the apse all the same size and shape (in this case, the apse is called the chancel, just to complicate things unnecessarily). This meant that the central part of the church where they crossed was a square, and that in turn meant that a tower could be built on top of it. In ninth-century Britain, the Anglo-Saxons put this to practical purposes, building towers on their churches to act as look-outs for marauding Viking raiders. Here, then, is the origin of the traditional European church, basically cross-shaped in plan, with a tower pointing to heaven. The transept also provided a vital liturgical function, by housing the choir. This kept the choir separate from both the priests and the congregation, which was clearly something to be desired. By the eleventh century, this kind of church design had become standard throughout Europe.

In chapter 5 we shall see the importance that the notion of harmony and order had for the medieval mind. This was reflected in church designs. A harmonious design, where different elements embodied various perfect ratios, reflected the harmony of God and the natural order of the world. God, after all, was the perfect architect; and those who designed churches were consciously imitating him.

Creating harmonious designs became easier as new techniques developed. In the later Middle Ages and early modern period, the Romanesque style gave way to Gothic, which was much lighter and more ethereal. The basic idea of Gothic architecture is to replace solid stone structures with a kind of latticework. So, for example, ceilings are supported by ribbed vaulting, and instead of massive walls holding the whole thing up, flying buttresses support the walls from the sides. This was done at the cathedral of Chartres, rebuilt after a fire in the late twelfth century, which was the first large building to make full use of flying buttresses. This allowed for far more space within the building, since there was no longer any need for great thick walls and pillars. One important result of this was that the walls, since they were supporting less weight, could have more windows in them.

Increasingly, these windows were glazed with stained glass. The technique had been developed by the ninth or tenth centuries, but only came into its own with the emergence of the Gothic style and the great scope it provided for larger and more numerous windows. Churches and cathedrals became covered in huge windows depicting scenes from the Bible or the lives of the saints, all done in the most vibrant, glowing colours. Like the icons we saw in the last chapter, these windows were intended, in part, to be a form of instruction for the unlettered. Those who could not read the Bible could learn and remember its stories from the windows. But the stained glass was also a thing of beauty, filling the building with colours of every shade as the sun shone through it. Stained glass was used together with architecture to create an atmosphere of beauty and holiness, one that would catch up the viewer into the spiritual world. Architects and artists designed and placed the windows with care, knowing where the sun would be at different times of day, so that the colours they used were appropriate to the location. They understood that the secret to good stained glass lay not in the windows themselves so much as in the effect the light had on the whole church interior. For the first time, light became an important feature of ecclesiastical design.

The abbey church of St Denis was one of the outstanding examples of the new style: its abbot, Suger, who rebuilt much of it in the twelfth century and wrote a convenient account of how he did it, was convinced that a beautiful place of worship would help to bring worshippers to God. Appropriately, Suger himself was immortalized by being depicted in one of the windows in his church, shown worshipping the infant Jesus. It's a little incongruous, given that Suger doesn't seem to have been an enormously pleasant man: in 1129, he successfully gained control of a nunnery at Argenteuil (having forged the deeds) and expelled all the nuns. The incident is famous because one of those nuns happened to be Heloise, the former lover of the famous philosopher, theologian, hymn-writer and controversial celebrity Peter Abelard. Fortunately Abelard happened to own an empty monastery that he wasn't using at the time, and he let the nuns live there instead. In fact, he looked after them so well that tongues wagged – despite the fact that his romance with Heloise had ended years earlier when her angry relatives had had him attacked and castrated!

Later church styles have been more varied. The movement of Martin Luther, John Calvin and others had seen the creation of the Protestant churches, which hoped to sweep away what they regarded as the elaborate superstition of medieval Catholicism. Their churches therefore tended to be plain and unadorned. Many abandoned the profusion of chapels and screens that had developed in the Middle Ages and made

their churches into single rooms – reflecting their belief that there was no fundamental difference between priests and people, so they should all occupy the same space. Many Protestant traditions retain the same approach today, so that a Baptist or a United Reformed church is likely to be a single, large room, little different in basic plan from a hall or lecture theatre.

The Catholics, feeling that all this missed the point of expressing beauty and mystery in church architecture, responded with increasingly elaborate churches, covered with fancy stone carvings. This baroque style was meant to play a similar role to the stained glass of the Gothic period, expressing Christian beliefs and stories in a visual form. In this way, the church was not simply a place to worship – it was itself used in that worship. At the same time, architects were increasingly bold in combining styles of the past. Perhaps the most famous example is St Paul's Cathedral in London, built to replace the old cathedral which burned down in 1666. Sir Christopher Wren produced an audacious design with a massive dome on top – something considered extremely controversial at the time, since it looked just like the Catholic cathedral of St Peter's in Rome, and no Anglican wanted a cathedral that looked Catholic. Still, Wren successfully

St Paul's
cathedral — the
only cathedral
in London to be
designed by a
single architect
— looms over the
city like an
enormous ship.

connived to get his cathedral built the way he wanted it, and today the dome of St Paul's still rises above the London skyline – a clever combination of the rectangular and circular church designs that had influenced Christian architecture right from the start.

Stained glass became fashionable again, although some of the techniques used in the Middle Ages had been lost. The images on the glass tended to be more representational, more concerned with depicting things accurately rather than creating an atmosphere of beauty – and they were often painted onto the glass, rather than stained. However, the style spread outside churches, so that by the eighteenth century it had become rather fashionable for aristocratic homes and other buildings to have stained glass. Fortunately, the nineteenth century saw innovations in stained glass that recaptured the beauty of its medieval form. Two Americans, John LaFarge and Louis Comfort Tiffany, invented opalescent glass in the nineteenth century, leading to the famous Tiffany lamps and other beautiful objects of the art nouveau style in the early twentieth century.

Sometimes, a church can express interesting ideas quite by accident. A wonderful example is the Roman Catholic Westminster Cathedral in London. Work began on the cathedral in 1895, only a few decades after the Catholic hierarchy was re-established in Britain. This was to be a fabulous statement of the glory of the church and of God, and it was designed in an exotic style, more like the early Byzantine churches than anything normally seen in Britain or in Catholic countries. Indeed, the architect, John Francis Bentley, travelled around the eastern Mediterranean when planning the church, seeking inspiration from the Orthodox style. Within the red-brick towers and domes, the cathedral was sumptuously decorated with mosaics and marbles, creating a dazzling display to rival St Mark's in Venice. Unfortunately, the design was enormously ambitious and there was not enough money to complete the decorations. Instead, it was envisaged that the completion of the interior of the church would take decades, even centuries.

Today, the cathedral's interior presents a bizarre appearance. The lower half of the walls is fabulously decorated with the rich mosaics and marbles – over a hundred different kinds of marble – but the upper half remains bare, black brick. The programme of decoration continues, with new art being installed every so often, and one day the cathedral will be complete. Then it will, undoubtedly, be one of the most dazzling church interiors in the world. But many people say that it should be left as it is. By day, the contrast between the richness of the lower half and the poverty of the upper is a richly symbolic sight – suggesting, perhaps, the humanity and the divinity of Christ, or the value of poverty over material wealth. By night, the lower levels glow like a treasure house, as dozens of lights reflect from the gold and other decorations, but the upper levels are hidden in darkness, overshadowing them. It looks like a profound theological statement about the visibility and the hiddenness of God. The cathedral seems to teach that we can easily come to know the richness and treasures of the revealed God, but beyond this there is the hidden God who is encountered only in the darkness of the 'cloud of unknowing'. All this from a building that was never intended to look like this and will probably be quite different in a few decades!

A city on a hill – mountain monasteries and citadels of rock

Designing and building a church is one thing. But any architect will tell you that a good building will be designed with its surrounding environment in mind. The architect should devote some thought to how it will look next to the other buildings nearby, or as part of the existing landscape. That consideration takes on special significance with a church, if we think of what we saw earlier about the importance of the landscape, both as symbol and as part of the world that reveals God.

Some of the most spectacular churches in the world are those that make use of dramatic landscapes. That is only to be expected: after all, human beings naturally attach special significance to beautiful or striking locations, and they are more likely to want to build something of importance there. But there is more to it than that. If the landscape has symbolic value – if the world is, as it were, a text written in the language of myth, if God can be encountered there, and if, conversely, the human society of the church is the place where God works, if church buildings are in some way special – then how appropriate it is if the church and the landscape can complement each other.

This needn't be anything extravagant. One charming example is the Church of the Good Shepherd in New Zealand. This little Anglican church was built in 1931 on the shore of Lake Tekapo in the heart of the Southern Alps. The startlingly blue lake is surrounded by the snow-covered mountains, and if the weather is clear, anyone standing by the church can look across to Mount Cook, the highest mountain in New Zealand. It's hardly the highest mountain in the world, but its dramatic peak looks like Everest. The striking thing about this church is that there is a big window directly behind the altar – something practically unheard of in conventional church design. The little congregation, as they face the priest, can see past him to the awe-inspiring scenery of the lake and the mountains. It is a simple but eloquent statement about the religious value of that scenery, and about the place of the church and God's people within it.

In other parts of the world, Christians have achieved a far more spectacular symbiosis with the landscape. A famous example is the Meteora region of Greece. Here, monks of the Middle Ages decided to emulate St Antony and escape the world – not by going *out* into the desert, but by going *up* the mountains. The Meteora is an extraordinary region, where the Pindus Mountains give way to the plains of Thessaly. Here, carved by the wind, mighty towers of rock rise from the landscape, dominating the plains beneath. The monks built their monasteries on the tops of these. It was a striking decision – on the one hand, they were escaping the outside world very successfully. Some of the monasteries could be reached only by a long and arduous climb – up the rock itself, since there were no stairs. Others were even more inaccessible, and supplies would have to be pulled up by rope, while the monks would be lowered by nets in order to work the lands around the rock pillars. But on the other hand, the monasteries were highly visible from ground level. According to Matthew 5:14, Jesus said, 'You are the light of the world. A city built on a hill cannot be hidden.' In other words, Christians are to set an example for those around them of how to live. The monks of the Meteora certainly took the teaching literally: they could not have hidden their cities if they had wanted to. Today, the monasteries still perch in their

fantastic and beautiful landscape, although only four of them are now inhabited.

A less well-known but equally striking use of the natural landscape is in Ethiopia. Many people might be surprised to learn that Ethiopia has one of the oldest and proudest Christian traditions in the world; it is often supposed that Christianity was first introduced to Africa by Western missionaries in relatively recent times. But while those missionaries were important, Africa already had its own ancient and thriving Christian traditions. Ethiopia was evangelized by a man named Frumentius, who was shipwrecked there in the fourth century. Clearly not someone to let misfortune keep him down for long, Frumentius led a successful new career in the strange, mountainous country where he found himself, rising to become secretary to the king. Ethiopia already had a strong Jewish tradition – it was believed that the royal family was descended from Solomon and the Queen of Sheba. Frumentius therefore felt that the country was a promising place for a Christian mission, and he later left for Egypt, part of the Roman empire and therefore Christian, to ask for a mission there to be arranged. He was duly sent back himself to be Ethiopia's first bishop.

The Ethiopians may have received Christianity from outside, but they soon made it their own. In subsequent centuries, Islam reached North Africa and swept across it.

THE SAN GIORGIO CHURCH AT LALIBELA IN ETHIOPIA. NEARLY 800 YEARS AFTER IT WAS CARVED FROM THE ROCK OF THE PLATEAU, THE CHURCH IS STILL IN USE.

The Christian populations of countries such as Egypt dwindled. In the mountains of Ethiopia, however, the people stood firm and the country survived as a kind of island of Christianity in a sea of Islam. It was almost cut off from Christians elsewhere, except for the old mother church of Egypt. The head of the Ethiopian church, the Abuna, was always sent over from Egypt – a situation that lasted until 1955. But the Ethiopians developed strong and individual traditions in religious art and the liturgy. Most striking was the appearance of their churches and also their monasteries – for the Ethiopian church, like the other churches of the Middle East and the surrounding area, has always had an extremely strong monastic tradition. Most of this developed in the mountains in the west of the country – for while Europe was going through the Middle Ages, the Ethiopians retreated to the great plateau, where the Blue Nile rises, to defend themselves against the Muslims. They largely abandoned the ancient capital of Axum, which lay to the east, more exposed to attacks from the Red Sea.

In the mountains, in the twelfth century, King Lalibela of Ethiopia founded a new ruling dynasty of the country – one that, controversially, was not descended from Solomon. It was therefore partly to establish his own credentials as a valid defender of the proud Ethiopian Christian tradition that Lalibela commissioned an incredible architectural project: the carving of a set of churches directly out of the rock at Roha, his new capital. These churches are one of the most extraordinary sights in Africa, often hailed as the eighth wonder of the world. Lalibela's masons dug down into the rock of the mountainous plateau, creating great wells or courtyards that surround the churches themselves. Some of the churches jut out from the walls of these courtyards, while others are free-standing in the centre. Perhaps the most famous is the church of St George, a perfect cross, the roof of which is roughly level with the surrounding ground. To enter the church, one must climb down into the courtyard – more like a well – that surrounds the rock church on all sides.

King Lalibela conceived Roha as a new Jerusalem. Even the river that runs near the churches is known as the Jordan. He chose his medium well: the rock churches have proved essentially indestructible and still stand, even though the town has dwindled to virtually nothing. It is now known as Lalibela, after the man who dreamed it up in the first place.

'Having become king, he meditated on the things which would please God, and he made many gifts to the poor and needy. And when God saw the strength of his love, the angel of God appeared to him in a dream and showed him how he was to build ten churches together, but each different from the other. And he did as God showed him, and when he had finished building these churches, he made his brother's son inherit the kingdom. Salutation to Lalibela, the builder of churches.'

The Ethiopic Synaxarium 12, Sanê

CHAPTER 4

Education, Education, Education

We saw in the first chapter how Christianity has always had a close association with the written word. That is partly, of course, because Christians of all traditions have always regarded the Bible as the single most important authority for their faith. Even if they do not all think of the Bible as infallible, or as literally God's word, they still think in terms of its ideas and imagery. And the Bible, of course, is a written text. That's not to say you have to read it yourself – one of its main uses has always been liturgical, which means one person reads it and everyone else listens. And in ancient times, when books had to be copied by hand and were scarce, people would memorize them. It was not at all uncommon for Christians to learn the entire Bible by heart. John Chrysostom, the famous bishop of Constantinople at the end of the fourth century, spent two years in a cave on a mountain doing this. The exercise ruined his health, but his sermons were always extremely good – hence the name 'Chrysostom', which means 'golden-mouthed'.

Such feats are not confined to ancient times. The English Unitarian John Biddle, who lived in the seventeenth century, memorized almost the whole of the New Testament in both English and Greek. Unfortunately, his incredible grasp of the Bible led him to conclude that the doctrine of the Trinity was not true, because he could not find it in the text. Since Anglican orthodoxy was more rigorously enforced in those days, he spent much of his life in prison. Evidently, a little learning can be a dangerous thing.

Surprisingly, it's not really all that difficult to learn a lengthy piece of text by heart; we just never have any reason to do it these days. All the same, these memory feats are hardly for everyone, and a religion that features a sizeable body of scripture must value not only literacy but also education. In the book of Acts, in the New Testament, the apostle Philip meets an Ethiopian official who, by a happy coincidence, is reading the Old Testament. He asks the man if he understands what he is reading, and the official replies, 'How can I, unless someone guides me?' It is a principle that has always been important to Christianity, and the religion has invariably revolved around not just the Bible but the commentators, theologians, preachers and others who have lived since – in other words, an enormous mass of writing. In the Middle Ages, for example, Western Christians would meditate not just on scripture but on the works of Augustine, probably the greatest of Christian writers, and his ideas would influence the way they understood the Bible and other works too. In the East, the Orthodox Church has always placed great emphasis on tradition, and while the Bible is the most important part of that tradition, the great writers of the past come a close second. Since at least the fifth century, members of the Eastern Christian churches have always tried to remain true to the religion of the 'Fathers'.

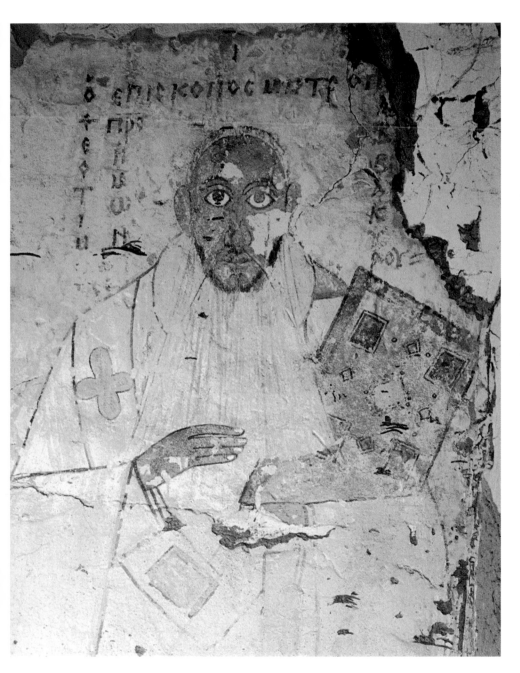

AN ICON OF ST JOHN CHRYSOSTOM, PATRIARCH OF CONSTANTINOPLE IN THE LATE FOURTH CENTURY. IN REALITY, JOHN — WHOSE NICKNAME MEANS 'GOLDEN MOUTH', IN HONOUR OF HIS BRILLIANT PREACHING — WAS SAID TO BE SHORT AND THIN, WITH A WIDE FOREHEAD, SMALL EYES AND A STRAGGLY BEARD, BUT STILL QUITE GOOD-LOOKING. THIS ICON WAS PAINTED IN THE SEVENTH OR EIGHTH CENTURY AT FARAS, THE CAPITAL OF THE ANCIENT NUBIAN KINGDOM OF NOBATIA.

Lighting the Dark Ages

All of this means books, education and learning, and throughout history Christians have gone to great lengths to secure all three. It's a concern that comes across most clearly at times when learning was not easy to come by – such as the Dark Ages, the rather negative name that is often given to the period between the fall of the Roman empire in the fifth century and the beginning of the 'high' Middle Ages in about the tenth or eleventh centuries. Of course, while there was indeed great political and spiritual confusion in this period, there were people of learning, just as there always had been. And it was Christianity that would play a central role in advancing that learning and laying the groundwork for the great educational establishments of the Middle Ages and beyond.

Take Benedict Biscop, for example, who pretty much single-handedly educated the north of England. Benedict was a nobleman from Northumbria, one of the most powerful Anglo-Saxon kingdoms in the seventh century, before these different, feuding states were united into one country. He gave up his position at the court, however, and chose a religious life – but he recognized that true religion could thrive only if it remained in touch with its historical roots. He travelled to Rome several times – a major undertaking in the Dark Ages – and each time he returned laden with relics, artwork and, most importantly, books. With these he established a large monastery at Wearmouth and Jarrow. As he lay dying, Benedict's final wish was that the library he had spent so many years putting together must not be split up. His successor not only honoured his wish, but doubled the collection.

Books were clearly very precious to the monks and scholars of the Dark Ages, and they strove to show this by making the books themselves beautiful things. A tradition arose of 'illumination', where the text is accompanied by pictures or patterns in the margins, and even the letters themselves are decorated. The practice was known in ancient Egypt, and in Rome shortly before the birth of Christ, but the Christians made it their own. In the West, it was the Irish who pioneered manuscript illumination, interweaving the text with elaborate patterns in striking colours. Probably the most famous example was the *Book of Kells*, which according to tradition was done by the great missionary Columba, who brought Christianity (and whiskey, of course) to what is now Scotland and (so we are told) calmed the Loch Ness Monster with a prayer and the sign of the cross.

Missionaries such as Columba took these traditions with them as they spread Christianity, and Irish illumination practices spread to the continent of Europe with men such as Columban (a different person from his almost-namesake). A rather terrifying character, he travelled through France and Italy, founding monasteries and causing chaos everywhere he went – because Irish Christianity was a little different from mainstream Catholicism by this stage, in flavour if not in doctrine. In centuries past, the Romans had always been rather scared of the Celts, whom they thought of as huge, hairy men covered in war paint; and things hadn't changed much. Columban and his monks were big, hearty men, who shaved the fronts of their heads and grew their hair long down their backs, as the pagan priests did, in a sort of early medieval mullet. And they brooked no nonsense, whether from their own monks or from local kings. The rules that Columban wrote for his monasteries are famous as some of the most severe of all time, prescribing, for example, six lashes of the whip for anyone who forgot to make the sign of the cross over their spoon or talked during dinner. However, his monasteries also continued the traditions of Irish illumination and calligraphy, the art of writing beautiful letters, and they mingled these traditions with those they found already on the continent – all done, presumably, in total silence, for fear of Columban and his whip.

Monasteries became, in part, art academies and studios, as the monks studied the art traditions that had developed and produced new works. Each monastery would have a *scriptorium,* or place devoted to the copying of books and production of new manuscripts. As a result, they were centres of learning, as people read and commented on the books that were being copied with such care, and then proceeded to write their thoughts in yet more books. At the same time, the monks recognized that learning wasn't just about endlessly copying books, but that it involved training people as well. Thus, monasteries became schools – the only centres of learning in existence for most of Europe. And Benedict Biscop, that indefatigable collector of books, is most remembered not for his library but for the fact that he took under his wing a seven-year-old boy who, along with many others like him, he housed, fed and educated at his monastery. That boy grew to become the Venerable Bede, the most learned man of his age. Bede seems to have spent more or less his entire life in the great library of Benedict Biscop, mulling on its contents, and he produced a stream of incredibly learned works on a variety of subjects, from how to write good Latin to how to calculate the date. Bede, incidentally, did not invent the modern method of counting the years from Christ's birth, but he did a lot to popularize the system.

While Bede was most famous in his day for his commentaries on the Bible, he has been celebrated since – and given the nickname 'Venerable' – for his work on history. His famous *Church History of the English* was not only the first book on English history, but the first to speak of 'the English' as a group. Until that time, the Anglo-Saxons were divided among various small kingdoms, including Bede's Northumbria, which were all completely autonomous, except when they went to war and one conquered another – which happened with almost monotonous frequency. Bede saw past these differences to a deeper unity of what he called the 'Angles'. Since most people in the country at this time thought of themselves as 'Saxons', it could be said that Bede not only invented the notion of 'Englishness' but gave it a name, and prevented the country from being called 'Saxland', which would have been a bit silly.

THE VENERABLE BEDE SETS TO WORK ON ONE OF HIS VOLUMINOUS BOOKS. FROM AN ILLUMINATED MANUSCRIPT, LATE TWELFTH CENTURY.

The flame of antiquity

What kind of thing were Bede and others like him teaching? On the one hand, of course, it was Christian doctrine, but there was far more to it than that. In its early centuries, Christianity had become closely intertwined with older classical learning, science and philosophy, until it was impossible to pull them apart. The process had been rather complex. The early church had had something of an ambiguous relationship with non-Christian philosophy, because philosophy in ancient times was a very wide-ranging subject, not like the relatively narrow academic discipline that it has become today. Philosophy covered what we would think of now as science, as well as ethics and religion; philosophers spoke about God and how to find him. We have already heard of Plato and Plotinus, and the notion that God can be found through the contemplation of beauty. Meanwhile, the philosophers of the Stoic school argued that true happiness could be found only in living a life of virtue, and they taught a rather severe morality. Many philosophers dedicated themselves to leading lives of contemplation, and they were more like monks than academics. Plato's Academy, for example, was not just a teaching institution but a place where people could search out immortal Beauty and Goodness – a cross between a university and a monastery. Another group, the Epicureans, believed that happiness lay not in virtue but in pleasure – but they argued that the best pleasures were the simplest, such as sitting on the grass, eating wholesome food and discussing philosophy. Their institution was called the Garden, where they would try to find this life of wholesome simplicity – a kind of ancient *Good Life*.

Evidently, the Christians were interested in many of the same things that the philosophers were, and some Christians saw philosophers as a potential threat. The great theologian Tertullian, for example, famously asked at the start of the third century, 'What has Athens to do with Jerusalem? What has the Academy to do with the church?' and he denounced philosophers as mere word merchants, compared with the Christians who actually lived good lives and knew God for themselves. Others, however, recognized that Christians might have a lot to learn from non-Christians. Gregory of Nyssa, the fourth-century theologian and mystic from what is modern-day Turkey, used an analogy from the book of Exodus: when Moses led the Israelites out of Egypt, they took with them all the treasure they could carry, and thus they plundered the Egyptians. In the same way, Christians could browse non-Christian learning, take all the best bits and Christianize them. So, for example, an important doctrine for Gregory was that God is incorporeal – a doctrine that he took not from the Bible but from Platonic philosophy. At the same time, however, he ordered his thought in an entirely Christian way – so that his God is not only the abstract and sublime goal of mystical contemplation, which the Platonic philosophers wrote about, but the loving creator who is shown to the world in Jesus Christ.

After the Roman empire became Christian, non-Christian learning became increasingly suspect – a process that reached its climax in 529, when the emperor Justinian I closed all the philosophical schools, including the ancient Academy of Plato

> 'Epicurus passed his life wholly in his garden: there he studied, there he exercised, there he taught his philosophy; and, indeed, no other sort of abode seems to contribute so much to both the tranquillity of mind and indolence of body, which he made his chief ends. The sweetness of air, the pleasantness of smell, the verdure of plants, the cleanness and lightness of food, the exercises of working or walking; but above all, the exemption from cares and solicitude, seem equally to favour and improve both contemplation and health, the enjoyment of sense and imagination, and thereby the quiet and ease both of the body and mind.'
>
> Sir William Temple,
> *Upon the Gardens
> of Epicurus*, 1685

> '*Since the definition of the terms 'existence' and 'substance', that is, 'person' and 'nature' – for both pairs mean the same thing and each is predicated of the same thing – remains confused and vague among those now counted wise, I have undertaken to elucidate and clarify them.*'
>
> Leontius of Byzantium,
> *Against the Nestorians and Eutychians*

in Athens. He closed them because they were pagan, not because he had some aversion to learning: Justinian I believed that Christian principles should govern the whole of life, and he enacted a series of decidedly robust legislations to ensure that they did so. For over a thousand years, there would be no education in the Christian world that was not explicitly and exclusively Christian. But that didn't mean that learning ceased to exist, or that the genius of the ancient philosophers was obscured by unthinking dogmatism. On the contrary, the ancient traditions were alive and well. They had simply become Christian. And the Christians didn't just plunder philosophy, unoriginally taking the best bits and plagiarizing them, as Gregory of Nyssa's metaphor might suggest; instead, they actively developed it into new and interesting directions.

For example, Plato's pupil Aristotle had pioneered the fields of logic and metaphysics with his notion of 'categories'. The idea was that things in the world could be divided into 'substances', 'qualities' that those substances possessed, 'relations' that existed between the substances and so on. Christian thinkers such as Tertullian (for all his hatred of philosophers) and Gregory of Nyssa built on this as they were talking of Christian doctrines. Indeed, Gregory's account of the Trinity revolves around a technical discussion of Aristotle's categories, a discussion that goes beyond Aristotle to consider how they apply to the divine. Similarly, in Justinian's day, a furious debate was raging in the Christian Middle East concerning how the divine and human elements of Christ relate to each other. As with all emotive subjects, the debate was sometimes unedifying; but it also produced a good deal of serious writing. Leontius of Byzantium, for example, represented the position that would eventually be recognized as orthodox, although he is not well known today. The reason may be that he argued for the orthodox understanding of Christ in an often incomprehensibly clever and technical way, using Aristotle's philosophy as the starting point of a long and remarkably difficult discussion of the nature of being, all developed as a sustained argument for his theology. If Aristotle could have been transported 900 years into the future to meet Leontius, he would no doubt have disagreed with much of what he said, but he would have recognized him as a fellow spirit: a philosopher in his own tradition.

The debates and controversies that were so important to people such as Leontius of Byzantium and other figures with exotic names, such as Theodore of Raithu, Philoxenus of Mabbug, Babai the Great and many more, are largely forgotten today, except by a few specialist scholars. And yet they, and other Middle Eastern Christians of that time and the following centuries, played a key role in the history of ideas. They translated the works of people such as Gregory of Nyssa, now regarded as the Church Fathers and weighty authorities, out of Greek and into Middle Eastern languages such as Syriac. Having done that, they turned their attention to the great Greek philosophers such as Plato and Aristotle themselves, who had so influenced Gregory and his contemporaries, and they translated *them* as well. Despite the fact that the pagan philosophical schools had closed, the study of classical philosophy continued, and indeed flourished. These scholars studied a mishmash of Plato, Aristotle, the Church Fathers and more recent writers such as Leontius, and they sought to find truth in them all. In the seventh century, however, the Muslims appeared and conquered most of the Middle East. Fortunately, they allowed Christians to live in their lands, recognizing that Christianity and Islam had a lot in common – although naturally they preferred it if the Christians converted to Islam. Now a dwindling force, the Christian philosophers continued to write and teach, although by this stage they tended to have Arabic-sounding names such as Hunayn Ibn Ishaq. But these Christians translated the works of Plato, Aristotle and others into Arabic, the language of the Muslims. It was in this way – via the Christians – that the Muslims learned about Greek philosophy, a process that would lead to the great Muslim philosophers of the Middle Ages – among them names such as Abu Yusuf al-Kindi, Alfarabi and the famous Abn Sina and Ibn Rushd, better known in the West as Avicenna and Averroes.

In fact, Christians of this time were interested in philosophy for its own sake, not just because of how it could be used to help theology. And this was true in western Europe as well as the Middle East. Five years before Justinian closed the Academy, there had been a scandal in Rome. The western half of the Roman empire had crumbled and Rome was now in barbarian hands, but much of the old Roman aristocracy was still in place, since the Ostragoths who ruled it recognized that the best people to help run the place were those who always had. One of these noblemen was a man named Boethius, who unwisely supported a friend who had made unflattering comments about Theodoric, the Ostragoth king. For his pains, Boethius was sentenced to death by clubbing. While in prison, however, Boethius wrote his famous *Consolations of Philosophy* – a curious book, since it is all about how Boethius is comforted by his Platonic and Stoic ideals, and it doesn't mention any Christian doctrines at all. This book would become the most read book of the Middle Ages, however; through it, the philosophy of antiquity was transmitted to the future. Boethius earned the title 'Schoolmaster of the West', and he would have the peculiar distinction of having his work translated by not one but two English monarchs – Alfred the Great and Elizabeth I.

Boethius's work was not for the casual reader, though. Apart from his *Consolations*, he produced a series of shorter essays on Christian doctrine, similarly based on a reworking of ancient philosophy; it has been remarked that his treatise on the Trinity, although only a few pages long, is one of the most difficult books ever written. More populist stuff was available from a man who lived a century later, in Visigothic Spain: Isidore, bishop of Seville. His *Etymologies* was essentially the first encyclopedia. Isidore conceived it as a compendium of all knowledge, scientific and otherwise, and raided the works of classical Roman scientists and philosophers for anything of interest. A generation later, and at the other end of the Christian world, there was John of Damascus, one of the most important Byzantine theologians – although Jerusalem, where he lived, was by this stage controlled by the Muslims. John's greatest book was called *The Fountain of Wisdom*, and it was intended to be an account of the whole of reality – a complete science, philosophy and theology, drawn from earlier authorities such as the Church Fathers and the philosophers. It was a remarkable achievement, and indeed the parts of *The Fountain of Wisdom* that deal

'Nothing is miserable unless you think it is, and any situation is happy if you can be content with it.'

Boethius,
The Consolation of Philosophy II

with logic and philosophy are a better introduction to ancient views on these subjects than many modern books. In its own day, it was influential not only on the Christian orient but on Muslim thinkers as well, who were impressed by the way John combined Christian theology and Aristotelian philosophy so perfectly that the seams never showed.

In ways like this, Christian writers preserved much of the learning of antiquity for the future – sometimes, as with Isidore, as fairly uncritical scrapbook compilers, and sometimes, as with Boethius or Leontius, as original developers of the tradition. Their endeavours laid the groundwork for the appearance of the universities in the Middle Ages and the explosion of learning that they would foster.

The giant and the Yorkshireman, and the first state education system

We've already seen how the monasteries of the early Middle Ages were as much centres of artistry and scholarship as they were spiritual retreats. Indeed, they offered the only decent education available. But their scholars were essentially amateurs: no fixed courses were available at monasteries, only facilities that monks could use if they so desired. Dedicated academic institutions had their origin in what would later become known as the 'Carolingian Renaissance', the result of the desire of one of the most significant figures in European history to educate the entire continent. On Christmas Day in the year 800, King Charles the Great of the Franks – or Charlemagne – had himself crowned emperor by Pope Leo III in the cathedral of St Peter's at Rome. The Franks were a people who had invaded roughly the area that is modern-day France – hence the name. But Charlemagne's domains stretched far beyond just that. He had spent many years conquering as much of Europe as he could get to, and his kingdom at this time consisted of not only France, but much of Spain, Italy, Germany, Hungary and Austria. He therefore, and not unreasonably, felt that he was the legitimate heir of the Roman empire in the West, and set about stamping his personal authority over the great empire he had forged.

Charlemagne was a towering figure, a patriotic Frank with a long moustache who always wore his national costume. According to legend, he was eight feet tall and in the habit of crushing horseshoes in his bare hands. But he was also committed to Christian learning and keen to promote it within his empire. To this end, he imported various scholars to his court, hoping to transform the informal military and political training that the court provided into something more substantial and structured. The most important of these scholars was a man named Alcuin, another Northumbrian

THE EMPEROR CHARLEMAGNE.
THE CROSS ON HIS CROWN EMPHASISES
HIS ROLE AS A CHRISTIAN RULER, BUT HIS
SWORD MAKES IT CLEAR WHERE HIS
POWER COMES FROM.
PAINTING BY ALBRECHT DURER, 1512.

like Bede. Alcuin had, like Benedict Biscop before him, already devoted much time and effort to travelling Europe and collecting books for his cathedral school in York. Now, transported to Charlemagne's capital at Aachen, it was his job to educate most of Europe – beginning with the mighty emperor himself and his family, who were all enrolled at the court school. It has to be said that Alcuin had limited success here since, despite his best efforts, Charlemagne never managed to learn to write. Perhaps he was too busy practising crushing things. Indeed, in contrast to Benedict Biscop, Charlemagne ordered in his will that his library should be sold and the money given to the poor – an order that was apparently ignored, since his son, King Louis the Pious, seems to have kept the books. Perhaps, being so pious, he donated the money to the poor anyway.

In any case, under Alcuin's influence, the king issued a series of edicts in the 780s which stipulated that monasteries had to provide for their members' intellectual nourishment as well as spiritual. One rule decreed that monasteries had to ensure that the *scriptorium* copied books in a clear, legible hand – a style of handwriting known as 'Carolingian minuscule', the ancestor of our modern lower-case alphabet (the upper-case letters came from the Romans).

Equally importantly, however, Charlemagne commanded that monasteries had to establish schools where all boys could be educated, not just those living at the monastery; these schools were generally separate buildings, next to the monasteries. In 797, Charlemagne ordered priests to establish schools in every community, where all children could be educated for free – asking the parents to donate only what they could afford. Alcuin is said to have put up a sign in Strasbourg urging visitors to the tavern to go to the school instead: 'Choose, traveller. If you want to drink you have to pay, but if you want to learn, you can have what you seek for nothing.'

Predictably, not everyone appreciated this meddling from above. Many regarded learning as a waste of time. Ratgar, the abbot of the huge monastery of Fulda in modern-day Germany, retorted that monks were better employed building churches than reading books, and he confiscated those that belonged to Rabanus Maurus, the head of Fulda's school. Rabanus had the last laugh, though, since he later became not only abbot himself but Archbishop of Mainz, and by his efforts to enact Charlemagne's legislation he is remembered as the 'teacher of Germany'. One of his books, *On Clerical Institutions*, was a three-volume collection of recommendations for the training of priests – who, in Rabanus's opinion, had to undergo a weighty course in all branches of knowledge, quite apart from their theological and spiritual training. Under the headship of Rabanus and others like him, monastery schools became impressive centres of academic excellence, the equivalent of modern universities. Gifted students might start training in one, then travel to another to complete their education under a particular teacher or with the aid of a famous library. And all this education was bilingual. Most people spoke local vernacular tongues as their first language, such as the ancestors of modern French or German, but they were trained to read and write Latin, the language of the Church Fathers. Yet many recognized the value of the vernacular tongues too. Lupus Servatus, head of the monastery school at Ferrières near Paris, was not content to inflict Latin on his monks: he also sent them to Prüm to learn German.

Meanwhile, Alcuin was writing textbooks to accompany the reforms. He had inherited the notion that there were seven parts to a complete education, which had developed in late antiquity. Alcuin, like other scholars of his time, knew about the seven liberal arts via a rather unlikely source – a wacky piece of science fiction by a peculiar and obscure Roman called Martianus Capella. In the early fifth century AD, he wrote something called *The Wedding of Philology and Mercury*, a fantastic tour de force in which the Roman gods set out to find a wife for the god Mercury, eventually settling on Philology ('love of words'). Philology travels through the sky to heaven for her celestial marriage – meeting along the way great names of the past – and as her wedding gift she is given seven handmaids, each of whom represents one of the seven liberal arts.

This bizarre book, a sort of cross between imaginative novel and moral fable, was remarkably popular for a thousand years, and improbably enough, despite its overtly pagan setting, it was the primary source for the usual medieval way of dividing up the sciences. The first three disciplines were grammar, rhetoric and dialectic – essentially, the skills of writing properly, speaking persuasively and thinking logically. Together, these were the study of language. They were followed by the four divisions of scientific study – arithmetic, geometry, astronomy and, perhaps surprisingly, music, since this was considered the science of expressing mathematical relationships in sound. Alcuin wrote textbooks on all of these, although only those on the first three survive. And he was followed by many more scholars, especially from Ireland; indeed, contemporaries complained of a kind of mass importation of philosophers from Ireland, and the system of the seven disciplines was known in places as 'the Irish method'. In the reign

> *'A love of learning arose in me almost from earliest childhood, and I did not despise what many people today speak of as a horrible waste of time. And if there had not been a lack of teachers… I could have satisfied my craving, for within your memory there has been a revival of learning, thanks to the efforts of the illustrious emperor Charles to whom letters owe an everlasting debt of gratitude.'*
>
> Lupus Servetus,
> Letter 1

of Charlemagne's grandson, King Charles the Bald, the palace school itself was put under the headship of an Irishman named Martin Hiberniensis.

The schools that sprang up throughout Europe, in cities, towns and villages, were not high-powered research institutes like the monasteries. They were meant to educate the common people in what was, in effect, the first national state education system. The teaching consisted of lecturing, or simply dictation, which the students were expected to note down as they sat on straw-covered floors – benches being a long way in the future. Some of the best teachers taught in the street – a measure of their popularity as well as of the meagre funds available to them. The pupils were taught the rudiments of grammar as well as social skills, the aim being to provide an education for the whole person. There was presumably a strong element of Christian doctrine, involving the study of the great Christian writers of the past, but little is really known of what was taught at this stage. This is because there was no formal curriculum, and what you learned at any school depended almost entirely on whoever was running it. However, large cities such as Chartres or Rheims did develop strong teaching traditions.

A trivial pursuit – the rise of the universities

After Charlemagne's death in 814, the renaissance he had started faltered. The empire passed, inevitably, into the hands of weaker rulers. His son, the dour Louis the Pious, who was said never to laugh once in his life, continued his father's educational and religious reforms but lacked the strength to control the factions of local rulers – not least his own sons, who on one occasion successfully deposed him and imprisoned him in a monastery, where he was probably much happier. After Louis's death, the sons carved up the empire, creating what would later become the different nations of modern Europe. Charles the Bald, who inherited most of France, was keen on learning. As we have seen, his palace school was especially notable for its large numbers of Irish teachers, and he also employed one of the most famous philosophers of the early Middle Ages, John 'Erigena', also from Ireland. On the whole, however, he and his brothers and most of their successors had more important things on their minds than the schools. But the traditions of learning that Alcuin and others like him had worked so hard to set up did endure, and they resurfaced in force 300 years later, in the eleventh century. Groups of scholars had begun to coalesce, primarily in Paris and Bologna, drawn together by mutual interest around the old schools. A major milestone was passed in 1079, when Pope Gregory VII legislated for the foundation of cathedral schools, to educate the clergy. Nine years later, the 'universitas' of Bologna, meaning the 'whole group' of scholars who had grown out of the old law school there, was officially recognized. In Paris, meanwhile, groups of scholars had gathered around different schools based around the Cathedral of Notre Dame, and on the left bank of the River Seine. As they grew, the groups merged, achieved a kind of critical mass and turned into the University of Paris. A new intellectual renaissance was occurring, which would prove more durable than the one Charlemagne had overseen.

'How pleasant life was when we sat among the writings of the wise, surrounded by a wealth of books and the worthy thoughts of the fathers, lacking nothing we needed for the religious life and the pursuit of knowledge!'

Alcuin, Letter 123
(to a former pupil)

Prmus prologus super genesim de
commendatione sacre scripture.

ad fine in hac temporali Uita tatu modo
et modo naturali sequedu si coparet
ad libros sacre scriptur...

A DISPUTATION AT THE SORBONNE IN PARIS. MOST STUDENTS WOULD LISTEN TO TWO HOURS OF LECTURES IN THE MORNING, FOLLOWED BY AN HOUR OF 'DISPUTATION' BEFORE LUNCH. THE SETTING LOOKS FORMAL, BUT THESE DEBATES COULD BE AS PASSIONATE — AND AS POPULAR — AS A SPORTING EVENT AT A MODERN UNIVERSITY. MANUSCRIPT ILLUMINATION FROM THE FIFTEENTH CENTURY.

These first true universities were decidedly informal affairs. There was no central authority or control, and they basically consisted of a number of schools and colleges, boarding houses and teaching halls. At Oxford, for example, founded shortly after Paris and in imitation of it, all the teaching happened in the church at the centre of the city, and the colleges evolved as students clubbed together in flats and houses, until eventually the teaching happened there instead. At Paris, meanwhile, some of the institutions within the university gained special prestige: the Sorbonne, for example, was founded in 1271 to house the poorest students, who often slept in the streets. Clearly, the old ideals of education for all, whatever their financial means, had long since perished; it was up to students or their families to pay their living costs and fees. The 'clerk of Oxford', who features in Chaucer's *Canterbury Tales*, with his ragged clothes and thin face, parodies the stereotype of the poverty-stricken medieval university scholar.

The curriculum was now more formal. Although there were not exactly degree courses as we would recognize them, students would attend lectures, and were first expected to master the three branches of language studies before moving on to the four branches of natural science. They would then be tested orally by the teachers before receiving a degree, or formal recognition of their mastery of these subjects, and being allowed to teach. The language and jargon became increasingly technical. The first three subjects were known as the 'three ways', or, in Latin, the *trivium*, while the four that followed were the *quadrivium*. And that, of course, is where we get the word 'trivia' – the stuff that every educated person ought to know.

While the origins of the *trivium* and the *quadrivium* lay in pagan antiquity, it hardly needs to be said that the medieval universities, and the subjects they offered, were completely Christian. The Catholic Church did not control the universities, although naturally it wanted to. The University of Paris was the battleground for a power struggle between the city authorities, the bishops and the scholars, until in 1231, the pope decreed that the universities themselves had the sole right to appoint teachers and conduct examinations. Indeed, in Bologna it was the students, not the teachers, who seized power, passed rules and administered the university finances – a situation that remained for centuries until modern times. However, the influence of the church remained very strong over the universities; many of the teachers were clerics of one kind or another. The University of Paris, in particular, was known for its strengths in teaching theology.

Also in the thirteenth century, there was a quiet revolution throughout the church with the appearance of the Franciscan and Dominican orders of friars who, unlike the more traditional monks, were dedicated to living lives of exemplary holiness, not in the cloister of a monastery but in the world, among ordinary people. Many friars found a natural home in the universities. Thomas Aquinas, one of the greatest thinkers of the thirteenth century and an alumnus of the University of Paris, was a Dominican friar. His colleague Bonaventure was a Franciscan, as was John Duns Scotus, at Oxford. At the new universities, these thinkers and others like them taught an understanding of the world built on the inheritance of antiquity, pagan and Christian alike.

Jumping into volcanoes – a Catholic education in the modern world

The medieval university, by providing an institution of learning and scholarship that was independent of any other authority, ecclesiastical or otherwise, supplied the impetus for education and learning to really take off and develop in new, creative ways. But although the educators were now formally distinct from the clerics, this did not mean that education ceased to be Christian. On the contrary, in modern times there has been a renewed emphasis on the ideal of Christian learning, especially the

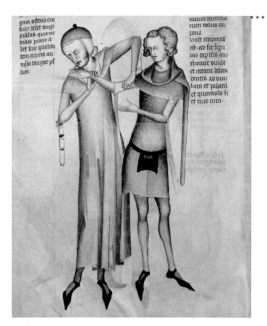

A BIZARRE WRESTLING MATCH? IN FACT, A YOUNG DOCTOR TAKING A STUDENT'S PULSE. PHYSICIANS TRAINED RATHER LIKE LAWYERS AND THEOLOGIANS — BY STUDYING UNDER ESTABLISHED MASTERS AND HOLDING DISPUTATIONS — BUT THEY ALSO DID DISSECTIONS. AS A RESULT, THEY KNEW QUITE A BIT ABOUT ANATOMY, BUT WERE LARGELY CLUELESS REGARDING THE SOURCES AND CAUSES OF ILLNESSES, WHICH WERE REGARDED AS DIVINE PUNISHMENTS. ILLUMINATION FROM MANUSCRIPT ILLUMINATION, 1345.

notion that education is a moral enterprise, one that should train the whole person, not simply the intellect.

One of the supreme examples of this modern approach to Christian education was that established by Ignatius Loyola. Born the year before Columbus discovered America, Ignatius grew up in and around the Spanish court and became a soldier. In 1521, however, he was in a battle when a cannonball fired directly at him passed, miraculously, between his legs, inflicting only relatively minor wounds. While he was laid up in hospital, he read books on the lives of the saints – the only reading matter available, and not his first choice – and unexpectedly became deeply interested in spirituality. Uncertain what to do with himself upon his discharge from hospital, he spent some time engaged in the traditional activity for those newly keen to aim for sainthood – trying to atone for his sins in a cave. But like John Chrysostom before him, he made himself ill. He then travelled on a pilgrimage to the Holy Land, but he was not allowed into Jerusalem by the Franciscans, who at that time ran the holy places. Discouraged, Ignatius returned to Spain and decided to educate himself from scratch, attending class in Barcelona with schoolboys, before moving to the universities of Salamanca and finally Paris to study theology. Here, in the 1530s, he gathered a group of like-minded friends around him who were also keen to regulate their spiritual lives. Pope Paul III recognized the potential value of the group, and they became the Society of Jesus.

The Society was not intended to be yet another order of monks; although its members were priests, they did not want to spend their time in a cloister. Ignatius's experience as a soldier led him to construct the Society along military lines, with himself – reluctantly – elected as its first 'general'. And the rules that he began to formulate for the Society over the following few years, based upon their shared experiences, were intended to help the members live a life of holiness and communion with God while serving him in the world in a variety of ways. The pope was keen that one of these ways should be mission, bringing the Christian message to those outside the church. Jesuits – as members of the Society became known – travelled the world. They brought Catholic Christianity to India, where a Christian church had been founded in very ancient times and which still survived, although out of communion with the West. They brought the Christian message back to China, where there had once been a thriving Christian church in late antiquity, but this had died out after some centuries. Now Catholicism returned, and it reached Japan too, brought there by Ignatius's friend Francis Xavier. Back home in Europe, the Jesuits were a powerful weapon in the Catholic Church's struggle against the forces of Protestantism, which was taking hold of much of the continent while the Society was formed. For Ignatius and the other Jesuits were very conscious of their status as *Catholic* Christians, and one of their dearest principles was loyalty to the Catholic Church, especially to the pope.

Yet one of the activities for which the Jesuits would become best known happened almost by accident. As large numbers of young men joined the Society, Ignatius recognized that they all had to be educated – after all, this was meant to be a Society of priests dedicated to spreading the Christian message, and preachers had to know

'As he was much given to reading worldly and fictitious books, usually called books of chivalry, when he felt better he asked to be given some of them to pass the time. But in that house none of those that he usually read could be found, so they gave him a Life of Christ and a book of the lives of the saints in Spanish. As he read over them many times, he became rather fond of what he found written there… While reading the life of Our Lord and of the saints, he stopped to think, reasoning within himself, 'What if I should do what St Francis did, what St Dominic did?''

Ignatius Loyola,
Autobiography 1

what they were talking about. A critical moment came in 1547, when Ignatius was asked to open a school for non-Jesuits. Thinking quickly, Ignatius realized that education was one of the best ways there was to preach the gospel. If his schools could offer the best education available, marrying the latest scholarship to a rigorous spiritual and theological training, he would not only spread the word of God but also swell the ranks of the Jesuits for the future. Ignatius therefore embraced the new educational programme enthusiastically.

By the time Ignatius died in 1556, there were thirty-five Jesuit schools throughout Europe. Like Alcuin before him, Ignatius believed that education should be available to everyone, regardless of financial standing, and he was lucky that the high level of donations the Jesuits received meant they could afford to make their schools free of charge. And the education on offer at these schools was no fundamentalist retreat from the wider world – on the contrary, the brilliance of Ignatius as an educator lay in the way he combined up-to-date learning with deeply rooted spiritual traditions. He had already composed his book of *Spiritual Exercises* for the use of members of the Society, a book that set out the rules and principles that were to govern the lives of its readers. Ignatius was tapping into a long-standing recognition among Christian thinkers that rules, if properly applied, are liberating rather than restricting. They can provide a system to help a person live a good life and order their thoughts towards God, if that is what they want to do. Ignatius's theological studies had taught him that, in this way, a person can lead a genuinely other-oriented life, fulfilling their human potential and becoming close to God. Ignatius now established a similar system in his schools, training his students not only in the latest discoveries and fashions of Renaissance humanism, but in living moral lives. He is said to have remarked, 'Give me a boy until he is seven, and he is mine for life' – meaning that the virtues that were instilled in the key years of education would remain with that person forever.

Little wonder, then, that the Jesuits were soon known as the educators of Europe. The clear and highly structured courses offered at their schools contrasted with those at the traditional universities, which still followed the old medieval system and taught the same medieval subjects. The Jesuit schools, by contrast, were up to speed on the new ideas of the Renaissance, and while they valued the 'scholastic' philosophy of medieval teachers such as Thomas Aquinas, they also taught the ideas of men such as Erasmus of Rotterdam, who were keen to establish new standards of scholarship to get back to the original texts of classical and early Christian authors, including that of the Bible.

The Jesuit enlightenment didn't stop in the schools. Ignatius believed that the search after truth in all spheres was a divinely sanctioned activity, and a disproportionately large number of Jesuits were at the cutting edge of science. To begin with, much Jesuit science consisted of writing commentaries on Aristotle, since the Jesuits strongly upheld the traditional authorities that the Catholic Church still recommended. But their faith in reason as a reliable tool of uncovering truth also meant that they pioneered new approaches in fields such as mathematics. Christian

IGNATIUS LOYOLA. PAINTING BY JACOPINO DEL CONTE, 1556.

Clavius, who taught at the Jesuit college in Rome, and who was the tutor of Matteo Ricci, was the leading mathematician of his day. Matteo Ricci himself, of course, whom we saw in more detail in chapter 1, was a one-man Enlightenment and the supreme demonstration of the quality of a Jesuit education.

To this was soon added an emphasis on exploration and observation. Many of their missionaries were also scientists, including astronomers who took the opportunity to record observations of celestial events that could not be seen from Europe. It was a Jesuit, John Baptist Riccioli, who published one of the first good maps of the moon in 1651; unlike his contemporary Johannes Hevelius, who thought the moon had oceans and life, Riccioli recognized it as a dry, dead world. Today, the names that they both gave to lunar features are still used.

Riccioli spent much time arguing against the Copernican theory that Earth revolves around the sun, as opposed to the other way around as had been taught in the Middle Ages. This was at the time a major talking point throughout Europe after the Catholic Church's condemnation of Copernicus's supporter Galileo in 1632. He was joined in this by a host of Jesuit names such as Malapert, Scheiner and Grandami. As loyal Catholics, the Jesuits were committed to defending the old Aristotelian cosmology, with Earth at the centre of the universe. They did this not simply by appealing to religious authority but by making scientific observations that they believed supported their theory. Although their arguments would soon be proved wrong, the Jesuit astronomers did contribute greatly to the advance of the science through their observations and calculations.

If anyone doubted the intellectual pre-eminence of the Jesuits, however, the existence of one man alone would have been enough to settle the matter. The splendidly named Athanasius Kircher was one of the most prominent scientists and thinkers of the seventeenth century, although the fact that many of his ideas sound rather strange, surreal or plain wrong to modern ears means that his name has been sidelined in favour of more mainstream characters such as Descartes or Halley. Born in Germany in 1602, Kircher became a Jesuit as a teenager and was educated at a number of their schools before going on to spend much of his life teaching at them, although he also enjoyed the patronage of the pope and a number of Catholic princes throughout Europe. Kircher threw himself into an improbably wide variety of interests: he climbed into the craters of erupting volcanoes to have a look at what was going on; he developed astronomical theories and wrote science fiction to explain them to a wide audience; he studied plague victims to try to understand how disease was transmitted (coming very close to the truth – that it was due to microscopic organisms); and his interest in music led him to build automatic organs

and even a machine for composing music. It was all in a day's work for an enterprising seventeenth-century man of letters.

The educational achievements of the Jesuits spread beyond Europe too. In fact, they helped to create the world's first completely literate society. Their bold experiment in social engineering was a huge success, but it ultimately perished and has been largely forgotten today. It took place in South America, where, in the colonial period, the Jesuits were very active in trying to improve the lot of the native people. Most of the time they were resented by the landowners, but they were given a free hand in Paraguay. The Jesuits gained control of this area (which included much of Argentina, Brazil and Bolivia too) in 1609 and determined to administer it as a completely free society, where the native people, the Guaraní, could live in liberty and enlightenment. They formed a number of 'Reductions' or communities of converted Guaraní, where they introduced the famous Jesuit education and did their best to spread Christianity and learning and help the people of Paraguay. These townships were quite substantial, with populations of up to 20,000, and while all this was officially just a mission that the Jesuits were conducting among the Guaraní with the permission of the king of Spain, in practice it was almost like a separate country. And the Jesuits' efforts were successful, in that civilization and culture flourished in the huge region. The idea was not to turn the Guaraní into carbon copies of Europeans but to help them realize the potential of their own culture; and, with the help of the Jesuits, they abolished the death penalty, established free services for the poor, built schools and hospitals and even shared all the fruits of their labour in common. For the first time in history, a society existed where everyone could read. It was all wonderfully utopian, and it lasted for nearly 150 years – when the dream was rudely shattered in 1750. The Spanish gave some of the Guaraní territory to the Portuguese, who wanted to take control of the Reductions in it; the Guaraní rebelled, lost the war, and the Jesuits were expelled for helping them.

Teaching the five-foot worm – the Protestant Enlightenment

If the Catholic Jesuits offered a model of how to combine state-of-the-art education with traditional Christian values, the Protestants were quick to rival them. Even as Ignatius Loyola and his friends were setting up their Society, Martin Luther was tearing down the old hegemony of the Catholic Church – a protest based, in part, on the new demands for more critical scholarship associated with the humanist movement. It was a desire to see knowledge put into the hands of ordinary people that led him to translate the Bible into German, as we saw in chapter 1. As the Reformation progressed, the momentum passed from Luther and the German-speaking nations to John Calvin, a rather thin, ascetic Frenchman and scholar who began as a humanist and turned into a noted supporter of the Protestant movement. Passing through Geneva in 1536, he was accosted by the local Protestants and asked to stay and help with their movement. Calvin remained in Geneva for the rest of his life (apart from a brief period of exile when some of the leading Genevans got sick of him), turning it into a model of Protestant faith and lifestyle.

JOHN CALVIN. LONG BEARDS AND FLAT CAPS WERE NOT STRICTLY MANDATORY FOR SIXTEENTH-CENTURY REFORMERS, BUT THEY DO SEEM TO BE HAVE BEEN THE PREVAILING FASHION.

Calvin is well known for his rather pessimistic evaluation of human nature and corresponding stress on the need for God if we are to achieve anything of value. He described the human being as a 'five-foot worm' (people in those days being apparently slightly shorter than today), and he believed that anything good that we manage to achieve is done not by us but by God working through us. In the hands of a lesser thinker, such ideas might have produced morbidity and paralysis – why do anything at all, if it's all down to God? But the workaholic Calvin certainly didn't think that people should sit back and let God do everything: on the contrary, it is through human effort that God works for the common good, and his concern is with the betterment of human beings.

One of Calvin's most important contributions to the city's life, therefore, was his reorganization of its education system. He was keen to set up a new Academy, but he was strapped for cash, so he went from house to house collecting funds for it personally. He was successful: a new Academy opened in Geneva in 1559 with free admittance and a curriculum that focused on science, the humanist study of the classics and theology. It was subsequently upgraded to a full university. Calvin also set up four schools to educate those who went on to the university; after his death, his successor at Geneva, Theodore Beza, made entry to these schools free as well. This was, in effect, the first free and integrated education system in modern times.

Why did Calvin and his colleagues concern themselves with such matters when there were theological tomes to write and Catholics to argue with? Like Ignatius Loyola, Calvin recognized, on the one hand, that this was an unparalleled way of spreading his beliefs. For example, one student from Scotland, John Knox, finished his studies at Geneva, returned home and helped establish the Calvinist church there. At the start, the Academy demanded a Calvinist confession of faith from students, but this requirement was dropped after a few years so that everyone, even Catholics, could join it. And on the other hand, Calvin saw that this was an exceptional way of helping people. Equipped with an education from Calvin's Academy, young people would not only be set up for whatever the modern world threw at them, they would also have imbibed principles of helping others and serving God, principles that would allow them to realize their full potential as human beings. And people flocked to the Academy: the intake was 900 students in its opening year, from all over Europe. Like the Jesuits, the Academy had a thoroughly international flavour, which not only gave breadth to its education but meant it had alumni throughout the known world.

While the Jesuits represented the new spirit of Catholic education, and the Academy of Geneva the Calvinist or Reformed response, the Lutherans were no less eager to get in on the act. After all, it was Luther himself who had helped kick-start a rise in literacy levels with his magnificent translation of the Bible. One of the key figures in the new Lutheran education was August Francke, who lived a century after Calvin and was educated in a strict and orthodox Lutheranism. Francke, however, rebelled to some degree against the faith in which he was brought up and joined the Pietists – a group who believed that personal commitment to Christ and living a good life were more important than what one believed, and who therefore tried to avoid the emphasis on correct doctrine that orthodox Lutherans and members of other Christian churches stressed. Indeed, for Francke, Christianity was not simply a set of beliefs to agree to: it was a life to be lived, a new life that would turn our world upside down and enable us to fulfil our potential as human beings.

In 1692, Francke joined the faculty at what would, two years later, become the new University of Halle. Here, he oversaw not only the establishment of the new university but a complete overhaul of the city's entire education system. Like Calvin, Francke recognized that the key to moulding a person lay in education, both what we would think of as primary and secondary education as well as at university. He therefore made particular efforts to integrate the whole education system in the city, employing students at the university to teach in the schools, for example; and he did everything he could to ensure that advancement was on the basis of merit, not birth or wealth. He was aided in the task by Christian Thomasius, a leading philosopher and legal theorist, who shared Francke's devout Lutheran ideals and beliefs in the value of education for training the whole person. Thomasius is remembered, in particular, for his insistence that there is a difference between law and morality – there is a sphere of private morality in which the law has no right to interfere. This was a new idea that had not been appreciated in the past; indeed, some Christian governments, such as that of Oliver Cromwell in England in the 1650s, had taken exactly the opposite line and criminalized those who committed even private sins. Thomasius's alternative view, however, would later become central to modern notions of the role of law and the nature of morality.

> 'Education is simply the soul of a society as it passes from one generation to another.'
>
> G.K. Chesterton, *The Observer*, 6 July 1924

Between them, Francke and Thomasius succeeded in making Halle the foremost German university. Indeed, it was in a sense the most *German* university then in existence, given Thomasius's dedication to teaching in German rather than the Latin that, even at this stage, was still commonly used in universities. This ideal of making learning accessible to everyone, in a language they could understand, was shared by another Christian thinker at Halle, the famous philosopher Christian Wolff. Wolff believed that the existence of God and the truth of Christianity could be proven with as much certainty as a mathematical theorem, a notion not commonly held even by Christians today. More sympathetically to modern minds, however, he was keen to escape the rather technical nature that philosophy had had to date: it consisted, at this time, of lots of remarkably clever men (mainly aristocrats) in big wigs writing very clever letters and essays to each other. Wolff, by contrast, wanted everyone to read his books, and he published them in German – with the rather unlikely result that books with titles such as *German Logic* or *Rational Thoughts on the Strengths of the Human Understanding* became bestsellers throughout Germany. Halle was perhaps the most important centre of the German Enlightenment, a movement that drew much of its strength from the Christian ideals of the Lutheran educators such as Francke and Thomasius.

CHAPTER 5

The Individual, Society and the World

A few months after her third election victory in 1987, the then British prime minister, Margaret Thatcher, commented, 'There is no such thing as society.' It was one of the more notorious statements from a public figure who was never shy to speak her mind. Many people regarded it as typical of the uncaring society that the modern Western world had become – one where people lead essentially solitary lives, unconnected to those around them. Of course, Thatcher was attacking what she regarded as the opposite problem – the tendency of many people to rely on society, or the state, to solve their problems for them. It was the age-old dilemma of how to balance the individual and society. How much should people take responsibility for themselves, and how much should they look out for other people? It's a problem that in the Western world has developed along lines defined, to a large extent, by Christianity.

From the fleshpots of Carthage to the garden of Milan – Christianity and the individual

In the year 387, a young man was sitting in anguish in a garden in Milan. He had been wrestling with problems of philosophy, religion and science for many years, and he could not find peace in any of the different answers he had investigated. Suddenly, he heard a voice from the next garden: 'Take up and read, take up and read.' In his overwrought state, he took it as a divine command, picked up a book of the letters of the apostle Paul and found what he had been looking for.

The conversion to Christianity of Augustine was one of the most important events in the history of Western thought. Augustine was destined to become the most important Christian writer of all time after the New Testament writers, but more than that, he was a major thinker whose thoughts covered a wide range of subjects. His understanding of Christianity would deeply influence all subsequent Western Christianity, but it would also deeply influence Western thought itself. Even today, in an increasingly post-Christian world, people are still thinking along the lines that Augustine first laid down.

In a way, the story of Augustine's conversion in that garden of Milan illustrates one of the most important things about Augustine's later influence. We know the story because Augustine told it himself, together with the explanation that the mysterious voice he heard was that of a child playing some game in the next garden. His *Confessions* was one of the first autobiographies ever written, an emotionally charged

St Augustine sits
wracked with anguish
in his garden in Milan.
Painting by Fra Angelico,
a Dominican friar,
1387–1455.

account of his life and the processes by which he became a Christian. The book takes the form of a prayer to God, but by choosing to cast this prayer as an account of his own life, Augustine was doing something radically new. He was recognizing that while God acts in the world, the most dramatic place he acts is within the soul of the individual believer (or soon-to-be believer, in his case). More than that, Augustine realized that there was something special about his own story. By narrating his spiritual journey and publishing it to the world, Augustine was acknowledging for the first time the importance of the *self*. The book was a huge and immediate success, although that may have had something to do with the fact that much of Augustine's musings on his spiritual journey revolved around the various sins he had committed, both at school as a boy and in Carthage as a young man.

The same basic approach comes out in Augustine's analysis of the nature of the mind, which forms much of his treatise *On the Trinity*. Augustine illustrates his teaching on the Trinity by comparing it to human nature. He suggests, for example, that just as the human soul contains the three faculties of memory, intelligence and will, so too God appears in three persons, the Father, Son and Holy Spirit. But the striking thing is that Augustine appeals here again to his experience of himself. When he speaks of the different mental faculties, he says that we know about them because we have experienced them ourselves; indeed, he speaks in the first person, pointing out that 'I', the person who is thinking about this matter, have experience of 'myself'. It makes a vivid contrast to earlier writings on human nature. Take, for example, Plato's *Phaedo*, which is presented as the discussion that Socrates holds with his friends before his own death. Appropriately, given the situation, Socrates talks about life after death and the nature of the soul, and he spends his final minutes demonstrating that there is a soul that lives after the death of the body, therefore his friends should not be upset at his own impending doom. But Plato does not represent Socrates as arguing from his own experience of what it is like to be a person. On the contrary, Socrates speaks in general terms about human nature as a whole.

Augustine's emphasis on his personal experience was closely bound up with his Christianity. As the title of his autobiography suggests, Augustine did not present an entirely positive view of his career. In fact, if his *Confessions* is to be trusted, he spent most of it racked with guilt for one thing or another. Augustine's writings reflected his terrible sense of his own sinfulness. At the same time, he had a correspondingly great sense of the grace of God in rescuing him from that sinfulness – as is illustrated by the devotional tone of the *Confessions*, presenting his life story as a thankful prayer to God.

RENÉ DESCARTES, LOOKING TYPICALLY DASHING. PAINTING BY FRANS HALS, C. 1640.

Augustine gave to Western thought a characteristic division that is not found as strongly elsewhere, for example in Asian philosophy. He clarified the distinction, fundamental to later philosophy and science, between the subjective and the objective, between *in here* and *out there*, between *me* and *others*. He gave it the basic conception of an interior, private life that is qualitatively different from the exterior, public one. In making this distinction, Augustine initiated the self-examining, introspective side of Christian spirituality. But more than this, in articulating more clearly than anyone before this fundamental difference between the self and the not-self, Augustine initiated the modern Western world view.

René Descartes, the most important philosopher of the seventeenth century and the man who, more than any other, ushered in modernity, made the distinction between the subjective and the objective central to his thought. Descartes explicitly divided the world into the physical and the mental, two quite distinct realms that may cooperate but can never really meet. Descartes was a Catholic, educated by the Jesuits, and his *Meditations*, in which he sets out the basic ideas of his philosophy, draws much of its language and ideas from Augustine. Like Augustine, Descartes presents his philosophical voyage as one of introspection, in which he dwells on his own nature and his own subjective experiences – indeed, to such an extent that he can doubt the existence of anything outside those experiences. But Descartes gave this approach a new, and modern, twist in his science. Descartes was not just a philosopher but a

certain things and acted in a certain way. It meant that you were part of a community – not simply a group of people who had something in common, but a group for whom the bonds between them were more important than anything that might set them apart. As the nineteenth-century Russian Christian poet, inventor and political thinker Alexis Khomiakov said, 'We know that when one of us falls, he falls alone; but no one is saved alone. He is saved in the Church, as a member of her and in union with all her other members.'

It is an idea that has always been central to Christianity, and which has formed part of the social impact of the religion. After all, if the faith transcends individual barriers, it also transcends barriers of nationality, race, gender and social standing. A striking statement of this notion was made by Peter Damian, a major figure of the eleventh century. Peter (who took the name 'Damian' in tribute to his brother, who paid for his education) was an earnest reformer who spent most of his time racing around Italy and beyond, dealing with clerical abuses at the behest of the papacy. What he really wanted was to be allowed to retire to his monastery, but unfortunately this never happened. Still, Peter did find the time to write a large number of letters, one of which was addressed to a certain 'Leo the hermit' and dealt with a very unusual problem: Leo, it seems, was a priest, and like many hermits he was in the habit of holding church services with no one else present. So what was he supposed to do when, according to the words laid down, he had to say things such as, 'The Lord be with you'? Who was he talking to? Was he supposed to say it to the bricks of his room? Peter answered that, if Leo was a Christian, he was never really alone. The whole church was with him in spirit. Wherever one Christian is, there too, spiritually, are all Christians. Therefore, Leo could quite properly say, 'The Lord be with you,' because he was addressing all Christians.

In modern times, an important representative of this general outlook is Desmond Tutu, the former Anglican Archbishop of Cape Town. His thought has sometimes been called 'ubuntu theology', after the African notion of community. Tutu insists that Christianity is all about community – about togetherness transcending barriers between different factions, a notion that he finds deeply embedded in traditional African values as well as in Christianity. It is only in peaceful community that people can become truly human, and it is for this reason that Tutu fought against the unjust system of apartheid in South Africa – never by fostering a bitter outlook towards those who oppressed black people, but always by looking to build bridges and include everyone.

It is this basic attitude that helped to give rise to the sense of connection with the past that we saw in chapter 1. Christians form a community to such a degree that past members can be just as important as present ones. And as we shall see in chapter 7, this notion of closeness between Christians has had important ramifications in Christian understandings of ethics and morality.

The musical onion – the world in harmony

It seems, then, that there has been a strong tradition within Christianity of *solidarity* – of emphasizing the links between people rather than the things that set them apart. And this ties in with what we saw in chapter 3 about Christians and the landscape. In the Middle Ages, the idea evolved of the spiritual and physical realms operating in close harmony – with human beings, who are both spiritual and physical, taking the middle point between them. In the twentieth century, the Christian writer C.S. Lewis described human beings as 'amphibious', which is a nice way of putting the same idea. Today, scientists tell us that it would take as many human beings to make a mass the size of the average star as it does atoms to make the average human being. We are halfway between the atoms and the stars; and to the medieval Christians, we were halfway between God and the devil. According to the Ptolemaic understanding of the world – named after the ancient astronomer Ptolemy – Earth was a sphere, around which the moon, sun and other planets revolved, each on its own plane. Beyond them was the plane of the fixed stars. The system was like a series of concentric glass spheres, or like the layers of an onion. Outside the outermost sphere was God,

6

'The Pythagoreans
devoted themselves
to mathematics and
admired the rigour of its
arguments, because of
all the studies that
people undertake, it is
the only one with proofs.
And they agreed that the
facts of harmonics are
due to numbers, and
thought that these and
their principles were in
general the causes of
existing things.'

Iamblichus,
*On the Mathematical and
Scientific Community,*
c. AD 300

surrounding the whole thing and keeping it in motion: it was his hand that moved the outermost sphere, which transmitted the motion to all the innermost layers. Right at the centre – as far from God as possible, but still surrounded by him – was hell, a sort of cavern at the centre of the earth. In the middle, poised halfway between heaven and hell, was the world of human beings.

Such a world view strikes us today as quaint. Few Christians today would believe that you could, in theory, travel to hell by digging, any more than they believe that the world is encased by a sort of snowstorm bubble, like something you see in souvenir shops. However, what is important about this world view is not the astronomical details but the principle underlying it, which is one of organic unity. All of these elements in the world system existed in a beautiful harmony, exemplified by the famous 'music of the spheres'. This idea went back to Pythagoras, the Greek philosopher, mystic and mathematician who lived in the sixth century BC. Pythagoras was a rather peculiar character about whom little is known; he saw himself as a sage, an almost religious figure, a status that was shown in his strange habit of wearing trousers instead of the draped sheet more usually fashionable at the time. Pythagoras started a sort of cult, whose members based their lives around the number mysticism that their founder taught. They believed that the world was essentially made of numbers, and that the study of mathematics therefore provided the key to understanding the world. In particular, the Pythagoreans were fascinated by the discovery that music seemed to be all about maths. The relations between different tones could be expressed as ratios. Music was therefore very important to them, and they believed that it was intrinsic to the world as well. They too believed that the universe consisted of a series of concentric spheres around Earth, which must be spaced apart from each other according to mathematically pleasing ratios. The Pythagoreans therefore believed that, as they rotated, the ratios between the spheres would produce a sort of cosmic music, inaudible to normal ears but pervading the world and accessible to the mystically inclined.

The notion of order and harmony was therefore central to ancient understandings of perfection and of how the world worked. The idea was enthusiastically taken up by the Christians. For example, Augustine had suggested that the ratios between different numbers are simply echoes of the perfection of God. Thus, by embodying these ratios in music, or in art, one can hope to reflect God's glory in a very real way. In the twelfth century, Thierry of Chartres took this idea to heart so strongly that other people accused him of turning theology into geometry!

The notion of harmony became even more prominent in the Renaissance. During this period, from approximately the fifteenth century to the early seventeenth, people consciously sought to revive ancient ideas. They combined them with the ideas they inherited from the Middle Ages to come up with a strange mixture of Christianity and mystical paganism. The Renaissance sages believed that everything in the universe was linked to everything else. In particular, they propounded the doctrine of the 'microcosm', according to which every human being is a kind of miniature version of the whole universe. This applies on the physical level – for example, the veins are equivalent to rivers, while the breath of the lungs is equivalent to the atmosphere. But more profoundly, it also applies spiritually. Renaissance philosophers claimed that, in order to know all things, we need only search within our own minds, for everything is reflected therein. Marsilio Ficino, the great Platonist philosopher and Christian preacher, taught that the human soul was the centre of the universe. The universe is so ordered that sympathetic resonances permeate through it, allowing us to understand everything by focusing only on ourselves.

Although Ficino and those like him were inspired by the mystical Platonic philosophy they knew was ultimately pagan in inspiration, they were also tapping into a more authentically Christian tradition. In earlier centuries, Christians in the Middle East had pioneered a kind of mysticism that focuses on the human soul and its depths. Ironically, the works of the most important of these mystics have been preserved under the wrong name, and no one knows who actually wrote them. He is known simply as 'Pseudo-Macarius', because his writings were attributed to Macarius, an ascetic who lived in fourth-century Egypt. In fact, the writings seem to come from Syria, and they reflect a kind of spirituality that was more common to that region than to Egypt. Pseudo-Macarius's spirituality revolves around what he calls the 'heart', the centre of human spirituality. At the time he was writing, many Christians, influenced by Plato, were emphasizing the distinction between the soul and the body. They believed that the soul is intrinsically spiritual, quite different from the body, and that it should, as far as possible, focus on God instead of on physical things. But Pseudo-Macarius, by speaking of the 'heart', emphasized that the soul cannot be understood apart from the body. Moreover, whereas Platonic Christians were interested in how God could be understood by the mind, thinking of the spiritual life in terms of the understanding, Pseudo-Macarius had a much more emotional approach. He recognized that spiritual progression involved the whole person, feelings as well as mind. Platonic Christians believed that the soul must essentially detach itself from the body and rise to find God, but Pseudo-Macarius taught that the soul must look within itself – within the whole person – to find God. It is within the heart of man that a constant battle rages between good and evil, and it is within the heart of man that God operates. For the heart has infinite depths, like a mansion with innumerable rooms, or a cavern with endless chambers. As Pseudo-Macarius put it in his 43rd homily:

The heart itself is just a small vessel, yet there also are dragons and there are lions; there are poisonous beasts and all the treasures of evil. And there are rough and uneven roads; there are precipices. But there is also God, also the angels, the life and the kingdom, the light and the Apostles, the treasures of grace – there are all things.

It was the ancient Greek philosopher Protagoras who said, 'Man is the measure of all things.' Quite what he meant by that is uncertain. But Christian mystics such as Pseudo-Macarius gave this thought a radical, new Christian twist, and it became an important idea in the Renaissance. Human beings are an integral part of the order and harmony that characterize the world, and that derive from God, who created and

> '*Contemplations of worlds enlarge the heart; thoughts of providence and judgement lift it up. Knowledge of incorporeal things raises the mind and presents it before the Holy Trinity.*'
>
> Evagrius Ponticus
> *To the Monks* 135–136,
> c. AD 390

JOHANNES KEPLER.
PAINTING BY HANS VON
AACHEN, BEFORE 1612.

sustains it. This Renaissance belief in harmony and connectedness pervading the universe is famously expressed by the speech of Ulysses in Act 1, Scene 3 of Shakespeare's *Troilus and Cressida*. We are told:

The heavens themselves, the planets and this centre
Observe degree, priority, and place,
Insisture, course, proportion, season, form,
Office, and custom in all line of order.
And therefore is the glorious planet Sol
In noble eminence enthron'd and spher'd
Amidst the other; whose med'cinable eye
Corrects the ill aspects of planets evil,
And posts, like the commandment of a king,
Sans check to good and bad.

This idea of universal harmony outlived the old medieval cosmology. One of the most important figures in the emergence of modern science was Johannes Kepler. Kepler, who lived in the late sixteenth century, did not have an especially happy life; he considered himself very ugly (although his hatred of bathing cannot have helped), and his cleverness made him a target for bullies as a child. His father abandoned him when he was a teenager, and his mother was imprisoned for witchcraft. Worst of all, he ended up as a poverty-stricken mathematics teacher. Nevertheless, it was while chalking some diagrams on the board in preparation for a class that Kepler had his great revelation. He was a supporter of the theories of Copernicus, according to which the sun was at the centre of the universe instead of Earth, and Earth and everything else revolved around it. This seemed to make nonsense of the old understanding of the universe, including the harmonious interaction of the celestial spheres. But Kepler noticed that if you drew a triangle with a circle within it and one outside it, the relation between the two circles was the same as the relation between the orbits of Jupiter and Saturn in the Copernican system. In other words, it looked as if the old ideals of geometrical simplicity and beautiful ratios could be preserved with this new way of thinking.

In fact, Kepler realized, if you put the sun at the centre instead of Earth, the system was actually geometrically more pleasing. Discrepancies in observations had led Ptolemy to add a couple of complications to his system. First, although each planet was attached to a crystal sphere that rotated around Earth, the planets also spun around smaller circles attached to those larger spheres. Second, and more disturbingly,

THE SOLAR SYSTEM AS COPERNICUS
IMAGINED IT — WITH EVERYTHING
REVOLVING AROUND THE SUN IN
CIRCLES. IN FACT, AS KEPLER KNEW,
THE ORBITS OF THE PLANETS AND
MOONS ALIKE ARE ELLIPTICAL.

the large spheres were not actually centred perfectly on Earth. Each one had a different centre, in a slightly different location somewhere inside Earth. So the earth was at the centre, but not at the exact centre of any of the planets' orbits. Although these complications were required to make the system match observations, they worried some people, because the system no longer seemed so neat. Kepler saw that once you allowed the sun to be at the centre, everything became much more elegant.

Kepler went further. In the old system, all the planets had revolved around Earth in circles. Copernicus had retained this idea in his system, having everything orbit the sun in perfect circles. But Kepler recognized that this was not accurate. In fact, everything orbits the sun in an ellipse – a sort of squashed circle. But isn't an ellipse a less pleasing shape than a circle? And what of the music of the spheres? Kepler answered that each ellipse was also a mathematically precise shape. As the planets move from one part of the ellipse to another, their speed alters – they move more quickly when they are close to the sun and more slowly when they are distant. And the differences in speed can be boiled down to simple ratios, which Kepler believed corresponded to intervals on the musical scale. In other words, instead of having a few glass spheres, each of which plays a single note, we now have a number of variable instruments, each of which plays a whole scale itself. Kepler actually wrote musical scores to demonstrate how this works. In his system, the planets are nothing other than a celestial choir, singing the praises of God in perfect harmony.

Scientists today regard Kepler as one of their great heroes for his pioneering work on astronomy. But they are rather embarrassed by the mystical side of his thought – all this stuff about the music of the spheres and the idea that all the planets are singing together in praise of God. But in Kepler's time there would have been nothing strange about this combination of mathematical science and Neoplatonic Christian mysticism. In fact, the modern distinction between 'faith' and 'reason', between religious fervour and hard-nosed, scientific sifting of evidence, had not yet developed in Kepler's time.

Taking it all on faith – Christians and reason

Christians have often been accused of 'blind faith'. The idea seems to be that they hold to a set of beliefs even when there is no evidence for them. Arguing with such people is impossible: show them reasons why God does not exist, for example, and they will simply brush them aside with a glib, 'Well, you just have to take it on faith.' Not only are they irrational, they are incredibly annoying to boot.

But this is something of a caricature. In fact, while there undoubtedly are and always have been Christians who take such a line, it has traditionally not only been a minority approach within Christianity but has been frowned upon by the mainstream. It is known as 'fideism', the idea that everything is to be believed simply on faith, irrespective of what evidence or reason tells us; and although its extreme form has never quite been regarded as heresy, it has never been a respectable Christian position. Perhaps the best exponent of this kind of Christianity was the Danish philosopher Søren Kierkegaard, a peculiar and rather unhappy and isolated figure of the early nineteenth century. Kierkegaard believed that life is essentially about choices that confront us whether we like it or not. We are forced to make decisions based on our immediate experience in the here-and-now, not on the basis of abstract reason. For example, do we lead a life of pleasure or of trying to help people? Whichever we choose, we do it not for calculated reasons but as a response to our current situation. Similarly, can we go beyond self-reliance to reliance on God? Kierkegaard believed that to do this we must make a 'leap of faith', which involves putting aside our rationalist worries and simply living in the light of God.

> 'Without risk there is no faith. Faith is precisely the contradiction between the infinite passion of the individual's inwardness and the objective uncertainty. If I am capable of grasping God objectively, I do not believe, but precisely because I cannot do this I must believe.'
>
> Søren Kierkegaard,
> *Concluding Unscientific Postscript*

Many people have found Kierkegaard's rather anguished philosophy of existence extremely attractive, even if they disagree with his Christian views, and he is today regarded as a seminal modern thinker and the godfather of 'existentialism', one of the most important intellectual movements of the twentieth century that similarly tried to analyse what it is like to exist in the universe and face the choices it throws at us. Many have also found Kierkegaard's fideism to be attractive, but of course it faces the charge of irrationality. If it is not rational to make the 'leap of faith', then why do it? More pertinently, why make one 'leap of faith' rather than another? Why place our faith in the Christian God rather than, say, the Muslim one? Arguments like these ensure that extreme fideism remains something of a minority position in mainstream Christianity.

Kierkegaard himself was not as extreme a fideist as some; he did not think that the 'leap of faith' was something opposed to reason, but something that one did when reason ran out, as it were. That is, reason can take us only so far, and after that one must rely on faith alone. He was criticizing the opposite to fideism, 'rationalism'. Those who take this approach argue that Christians should take nothing at all on faith: on the contrary, they should believe only what can be proved to be true. This way of thinking became popular in modern times, in the seventeenth and eighteenth centuries. Some rationalists were quite orthodox, such as the Cambridge Platonists, a group of philosophers at Cambridge University in the seventeenth century who argued that the rational and the spiritual are exactly the same thing. But others, having resolved to believe only what reason proved, came to the conclusion that many traditional Christian doctrines were not up to scratch; they therefore ditched notions such as the Trinity or Incarnation to end up with a rather stripped-down, anaemic version of Christianity known as deism. Deism was rather fashionable in the eighteenth century, but it gave way to its logical descendant, atheism.

What, then, is the authentically Christian approach? We can gather something of that if we consider the fact that fideism, as a philosophical position, actually predates Christianity. The Greek philosopher Socrates had stated that he knew nothing, except the fact *that* he knew nothing. His disciple, Plato, expressed a similarly questioning attitude by writing his works in dialogue form, in which different characters express different ideas and, often, no firm conclusion is reached. But those who inherited Plato's tradition became much more dogmatic, attributing definite doctrines to their master and continuing to teach them in a more well-defined and unwavering way. About a century after Plato's death, the head of his Academy, a man named Arcesilaus, became unhappy about the way things had been going. He wanted to get back to the questioning attitude of Socrates, and so he argued that human beings actually know nothing. In fact, he even denied that knew the one thing that Socrates claimed to know – the fact that he knew nothing! Arcesilaus was so committed to uncertainty that he doubted even that. But this kind of scepticism didn't seem very constructive. In particular, people pointed out, if we don't know anything, how can we do anything? Arcesilaus would have us all standing in a state of quivering uncertainty, never achieving anything at all.

So his successor at the Academy, Carneades, took this general approach in more interesting directions. He suggested that, while we can never know anything, and we can never really trust our senses to tell us the truth, there are certain kinds of things that *seem* true. For example, I cannot really doubt that I am sitting here at this table, if that's what I am doing. Carneades suggested that impressions like this are 'persuasive', and he listed various qualities that make some impressions more persuasive than others. So, although we cannot have certainty, we can still judge between statements and decide that some are more probably true than others. This gives us a framework of consistent beliefs by which we can order the world, and on the basis of that framework we can act reasonably.

It's somewhat ironic that the early Christians didn't like the kind of philosophy that went on at the Academy. When the great theologian Augustine of Hippo became a Christian, one of the first things he did was write a book attacking their ideas. He felt that this kind of philosophical uncertainty was opposed to Christianity, which is about the truth. If the truth could never be known, where did that leave Christianity? But in fact, the toned-down scepticism of philosophers such as Carneades was not only eminently sensible but bore a strong resemblance to the approach that Christians would later set out for their own faith.

That, at least, has been the Christian mainstream in modern times. It was rather different in the past. Augustine's belief that Christianity was a matter of truth – of certainty – was reflected in the belief, common to most Christians and pagan philosophers alike in the first few centuries of the church's history, that God's existence could be proved quite easily. In the Middle Ages, Christian thinkers pioneered increasingly ambitious attempts to demonstrate the truth of their religion rationally. Take, for example, Anselm, who was Archbishop of Canterbury in the late eleventh century. Anselm was not a very effective archbishop, being a rather sweet and otherworldly character whose reaction to political intrigue was to feel ill. That was not an advantage in medieval England and meant he spent much of his time being exiled by the king – although he harboured no ill feelings and, when told of the king's death, burst into tears. Fortunately, Anselm was able to pull himself together a little more when he was writing, and his works reflect an extremely tough philosophical mind (and one that was quite capable of being rude about *intellectual* opponents, such as his contemporary Roscelin). He believed that it was possible to prove God's existence in an almost mathematical way (the famous 'ontological proof', which seeks to show that God exists from an analysis of the meaning of the word 'God'), and moreover, that it was possible to prove the central doctrine of Christianity, that God became human and died to save humanity. In his *Why God Became Man*, Anselm set out to show this through the power of reason alone, without relying on the authority of scripture or the church – since his aim was to convince non-Christians, who would obviously not accept those authorities.

A more lasting attempt was made two and a half centuries later by Thomas Aquinas, a weighty thinker in more than one way – for he was, apparently, a hugely fat man. Nevertheless, he was probably the most brilliant thinker of the Middle Ages, and a man whose influence is still great even today (and not only because he invented the limerick, as we saw in chapter 2). In the nineteenth century, his theology was made *the* official theology of the Catholic Church, which meant that all Catholics were required to accept his views. In the 1960s, Aquinas lost this privileged status, but needless to say he remains an extremely powerful voice within Catholic thought. This 'official' status has meant that, within the Catholic Church in modern times, Aquinas has been alternately deified as having the answer to everything and denigrated as a ghastly, dead authority whose ideas are well past their sell-by date. The truth, of course, lies somewhere in between. Certainly, Aquinas represents the basic Catholic belief that God and the world are essentially in harmony with each other. What is true is true, and there is no clear dividing line between 'natural' truth and 'religious' truth. So methods of investigation that we might associate with non-religious activities, such as science and mathematics, can in theory be applied to what we might think of as religious spheres. For example, it is possible to prove the existence of God, as well as the fact that the search for God is the secret to living a fulfilling life. However, Aquinas did not believe that you can prove just anything like this, simply because reason is not infallible. Moreover, not everyone has the ability, the leisure or the inclination to spend their time in philosophical contemplation. Aquinas was always concerned about what Christianity meant for the ordinary person rather than for intellectuals in ivory towers – however much he may have been one of those intellectuals himself.

No matter how intellectual you may be, Aquinas said, you cannot hope to understand God, because he is so much higher than our intellects. You cannot rationally demonstrate that God is a Trinity, for example. For that, you need revelation. Fortunately, God has given us such revelation, in the form of the teachings of the Bible and the church. But why should we believe in these revelations? On the one hand, if

THOMAS AQUINAS WAS, BY ALL ACCOUNTS, EVEN FATTER THAN THIS MANUSCRIPT ILLUMINATION SUGGESTS.

they are real revelations from God, they must be true, since God would never lie. But Aquinas is on slightly shakier ground when it comes to showing that they *are* real revelations. He can't *prove* that they are true, for the reasons given above. But he can give arguments that suggest degrees of probability, even if they are not proof. And more, he can take the argument to his opponent. If, say, someone tries to argue that Jesus was not really God, then Aquinas can provide arguments against that position. For if it is really true that Jesus was God, then the statement 'Jesus was not God' is false, and a false statement is always disprovable, at least in theory.

So Aquinas gives a picture of reality where reason can reliably tell us a great deal, and he points the way to revelation to complete the account. In this way, he follows the famous principle of his predecessor Anselm of 'faith seeking understanding'. Faith and reason are both essential to theology, but faith is, in the end, more important.

In modern times, however, the role of reason in religious thinking has become rather more controversial. In the late eighteenth century, the German philosopher Immanuel Kant dealt what most people regarded as a fatal blow to the old approach when he argued that reason cannot reliably talk about things that lie outside our experience, such as religion. In other words, you cannot *prove* God's existence or anything like that – and Kant aimed a particular barrage at Anselm's 'ontological' argument for God. Officially, the Catholic Church has, since 1870, rejected this position, and it condemns the notion that God's existence cannot be proved by reason alone – but since then, many Christians have revised the old way of thinking. Instead of extreme rationalism or fideism, they suggest that reason can incline us towards a Christian viewpoint, without being able to prove it definitely. Perhaps the most prominent exponent of this approach today is the Oxford philosopher Richard Swinburne, who has made a conscious effort to create a philosophy that is a sort of 'Aquinas for today', in line with modern ideas about how reason and religion work. Swinburne insists that we cannot prove God's existence or anything of that nature, but he argues that there are a number of considerations that, if we think about them, make God more likely. For example, the fact that there is a world does not prove that it was created by God, but God might be a good explanation for its existence. The fact that Christian mystics report experiences of God does not prove that they have experienced him, but God is one good explanation for their experiences. And if we take these considerations together, as well as a number of others, the conclusion is that God's existence is actually more probable than not. Armed with this basic conclusion, Swinburne then goes on to argue that, given a probable God, it is also probable that he will exist in a loving community of three members (the Trinity), and that he will intervene in human history to save us (the Incarnation). Rational to the last, however, Swinburne accepts that these conclusions are rather less probable than God's existence in the first place. It is clear that Swinburne is keen to set his religious views on a common-sense footing, one that is not authoritarian or dogmatic, but thoughtfully persuasive. Carneades would probably have had a lot of sympathy for this programme.

Thomas Aquinas and Richard Swinburne are clearly very different thinkers (apart from anything else, Swinburne is quite thin) and disagree on a large number of points.

> 'The existence of the universe, its conformity to order, the existence of animals and men, men having great opportunities for co-operation in acquiring knowledge and moulding the universe, the pattern of history and the existence of some evidence of miracles, and finally the occurrence of religious experiences, are all such as we have reason to expect if there is a God, and less reason to expect otherwise.'

Richard Swinburne,
The Existence of God, 1979

But they do reflect a basic approach that has, historically, been common to mainstream Christianity, which is that religion is essentially reasonable. This expresses itself in Aquinas's work in the idea that rational philosophy can tackle Christian doctrine, and in Swinburne's in the use of common-sense 'probable' arguments. Other Christians have used other methods. For example, the seventeenth-century French mathematician Blaise Pascal – who in his youth had been an inveterate gambler – tried to show that Christianity is rational by making it into a wager. Either you believe in God or you don't. If you believe in him, you will gain the benefit of a happier life (since it will have meaning for you). What's more, if he exists, he will reward you after your death, whereas if he doesn't exist you will never know. If you don't believe in him, you are likely to lead a less happy life, and if it turns out that he exists after all, you could be in a lot of trouble. In other words, believing in God is a better bet than not believing in him. By making this argument, Pascal was not trying to persuade people to believe in God – on the contrary, he hated the way that some philosophers tried to argue God into existence, as if he were a mathematical theorem to be studied. Rather, Pascal wanted to show that believing in God is not irrational. For those who do choose to put their faith in him, it is a choice that makes sense.

It seems, then, that contrary to the common belief that faith and reason are intrinsically at odds, faith can sometimes be quite rational – or so, at least, Christians have argued. And more than this, Christianity has, historically, fostered a deeply rational world view. In antiquity and the Middle Ages, Christianity provided a holistic, structured, rational world view. It carried with it the twin notion that the world is essentially ordered, and that it can be understood rationally. The greatest exponent of this basic approach was Dante Alighieri, whom we saw in chapter 2. Dante's *The Divine Comedy* reflects the ordered, structured universe described by Thomas Aquinas, but it also reflects the faith in reason that he represented. In the poem, Dante is guided through hell and purgatory by the Roman poet Virgil, who represents the human power of reason and philosophy. Through natural philosophy, Dante travels from hell to purgatory, at which point Virgil is replaced by Beatrice, a young woman with whom Dante was in love. Finally, in heaven, his guide is Bernard of Clairvaux, the great theologian and mystic. The message is clear: using your brain will take you to the truth, and then the power of love and Christian holiness will take you within. Dante's work, as we saw in chapter 2, is a prime example of religious myth – of a grand story that tells us something about ourselves. In a way, the combination of grandiose myth and the use of philosophy in the same work explains much of the success of Christianity. The pagan religions that, in Europe, were displaced by Christianity also featured powerful myths, but they did not seek to provide a rational or comprehensive view of the world. Christianity, by maintaining the mythic element but combining it with the scientific and philosophical approaches that it inherited from the classical world, provided a much more satisfying world view. It was one that appealed to both the head and the heart at the same time.

In fact, the idea of the intrinsic rationality of the world was built into Christianity from the very beginning. The famous opening words of John's Gospel are, 'In the

'Let us say, 'Either God is or he is not.'... Let us weigh up the gain and loss involved in calling heads that God exists... Let us assess the two cases: if you win you win everything, if you lose you lose nothing. Do not hesitate then: wager that he does exist.'

Blaise Pascal,
Thoughts 418

vigiamammanon ma ozannio
comio traiscenta questi corpi leui
Ondella appiso oun pio sospiro
gluochio orioso uer me conquel senbiante
che maore fa soura figluol oeliro

beginning was the Word, and the Word was with God, and the Word was God.' The word for 'Word' here is 'Logos', a Greek word that could mean 'word', 'thought', 'rationality', 'principle' and a host of other things. It was a philosophical term used by the Stoics to describe the way that God runs the universe. The Logos, they thought, was the basic rationality of the world, like a great cosmic mind permeating through everything. In fact, the human ability to reason is nothing other than a sort of fragment of this cosmic Reason. By applying this term to Jesus at the start of his Gospel, John was making a bold statement about who he was.

And the idea of the Logos proved very popular among later Christians too. Take Justin Martyr, a writer of the second century who is often regarded as the first real Christian theologian after the New Testament period. Justin was a Platonist philosopher who converted to Christianity – according to his own account – after encountering a mysterious old man on a beach who urged him to read the Old Testament prophets. Although he became a Christian teacher, Justin always regarded himself as a philosopher, and he continued to wear the distinctive cloak that philosophers used as a kind of uniform. Justin evidently placed great faith in the power of reason to convince: he wrote two eloquent defences of Christianity addressed to the Roman emperor, in which he tried to convince his readers that Christians should not be indiscriminately tortured or executed, but listened to sympathetically. He also wrote a long dialogue with a Jewish philosopher named Trypho, in which rational discussion eventually proves the truth of Christianity. But Justin expressed this faith in reason most clearly in his use of the Logos idea. He often referred to Christ as the Logos, and for him the Logos was a kind of secondary god, one that permeates the world and sets it on a rational footing, as well as acting as intermediary between the world and God himself. Like the Stoics, Justin believed that every human being is rational because they share, to some degree, in this Logos.

So for Justin, and other early Christian philosophers like him, the world is intrinsically rational. Moreover, there is a basic affinity between the rationality of the world and human rationality. This notion would become fundamental to medieval Christendom.

From weather magic to the uselessness of books – questions and answers

This basic idea that Christianity is rational has meant that it has sometimes fostered quite a questioning approach to the world. We can see this idea of Christian rationality if we look at three people with distressingly similar names who all lived in the Middle Ages – a time when, if popular stereotypes are to be believed, religion discouraged rationalism and freethinking.

The first is Agobard of Lyons, who was one of those brilliant and rather earnest Carolingian scholars who, in the ninth century, set about dragging Europe out of the Dark Ages and setting it up for the high Middle Ages that were to come. Despite the place and time in which he lived, he was in some ways a very modern person. Spanish by birth, Agobard fled the Muslims in his native land to the realm of Charlemagne, where he became bishop of Lyons.

Lyons was a city of some dignity and standing – or at least it had been until the Saracen invasions of the eighth century. Agobard found himself ministering to a scared and anxious people, desperate to rebuild not only their city but also the sense of order that had once seemed so secure. The new empire of Charlemagne was helping to restore political order, and the people were safe from foreign attack; but they were also having to deal with the social instability that their new circumstances brought. Lyons's location, just to the east of what is now central France, placed it at a natural crossroads in the Carolingian world, and people of all nationalities flooded through its gates, bringing with them not only exotic trade but equally exotic philosophies.

To Agobard's exasperation, he found that many people of Lyons sought to regain a sense of order through superstition. In an age when political and social circumstances could change without notice on the fortunes of war, people tried

THE ZODIAC — THE CONSTELLATIONS
THROUGH WHICH THE SUN PASSES
EVERY YEAR. LIKE MOST ANCIENT
AND MEDIEVAL ZODIACS, THIS
ONE FEATURES THE TWELVE
CONSTELLATIONS THAT ARE STILL
FAMILIAR FROM NEWSPAPER
HOROSCOPES, FOR SOME REASON
MISSING OUT THE THIRTEENTH —
OPHIUCHUS, THE SERPENT-HOLDER.
ILLUMINATION, C. 1000.

instead to control nature itself. Lyons enjoyed something of a burgeoning industry in sorcerers who specialized in controlling the weather, something they were more than happy to attempt for a fee. Agobard was horrified that so much money was spent on these quacks when there were people starving in the streets – and indeed much of the anger in his attacks on superstitious practices came from his strong sense of social justice. But it also came from his fundamental sense of rationality. How, he argued, can there be magicians controlling the weather when we know that the weather is relatively predictable? The regularity of the weather shows that it is a natural phenomenon, not subject to our whims. Not content with setting out his arguments in writing, Agobard made a special point of searching out people who claimed to have seen magic in operation. He would visit them and try to show, by force of argument alone, that they had seen no such thing. It's easy to appreciate his annoyance with a superstitious age when he trenchantly comments, 'So much stupidity has already oppressed the wretched world that Christians now believe things so absurd that no one ever before could persuade the pagans to believe them.'

Part of Agobard's hostility to superstitious beliefs and practices like this, as well as others such as the old custom of cheering on the moon during a lunar eclipse, was due to the fact that they were pagan in origin, and a Christian bishop would be opposed to them on principle. Yet Agobard seems to have objected to them just as much because they offended his sense of what was rational, and in particular, the rationality of the world. Indeed, Agobard was perfectly willing to subject his own religion to this yardstick. For example, he rejected the use of icons or other holy images in worship, arguing that a picture has no soul or substantial reality.

Agobard represents the recognition that the world is orderly and can, at least in theory, be understood – a recognition that is matched by a sometimes impatient demand that people should turn their brains on for once and actually think about what they believe and do. Yet it is important to see that Agobard's rationalism was not incidental to his Christianity. His belief in God, and in the orderliness and comprehensibility of God's actions as revealed in the Bible, gave him a solid ground on which to base his sense of how the world worked and his criticism of irrational superstition. In so doing, he was simply part of a long tradition of Christian superstition-busting. Augustine, for example, wrote against the practice of astrology, using a variety of rationalist arguments that he had culled from various sources. For example, if one's birth time determines the course of one's life, why did the twins Esau and Jacob in the Bible turn out so differently? And if the astrologers argue that the few seconds' or minutes' difference between their births can account for such divergent careers, then how could one ever hope to get an accurate reading? After all, you would have to know the time of your birth to the absolute second to have any chance.

This emphasis on the role of reason in working out what was real remained strong throughout the Middle Ages. We can see this in our second, similarly named character, Peter Abelard, who was one of the best-known medieval philosophers. In the twelfth century, he was one of the most famous celebrities in Europe – philosopher, theologian, songwriter – in an age when the most brilliant debaters could enjoy a status not unlike top sportsmen today. He was also famous as an ill-starred lover and unwilling eunuch, after relatives of his lover Heloise decided he hadn't been treating her well enough and took drastic measures to ensure that she would be his lover no longer. Still, the swaggering figure that Abelard cut in the streets of Paris was matched by a genuine brilliance and, perhaps, arrogance, fostered by irritation at the relative dullness of his contemporaries and even his teachers. Abelard recognized that it was unsatisfactory to assume that what great authorities said was true, because they might disagree with each other. He even wrote a book, entitled *Yes and No*, to demonstrate this. It consists of passages from the Church Fathers, arranged so that they contradict each other. Abelard got into trouble for this, because he had not made it clear how the contradictions should be resolved – but of course he had done this deliberately, hoping to spur readers to think for themselves.

A contemporary of Abelard shared his distrust of blind reliance on authority and combined it with a desire to promote scientific learning. Adelard of Bath was an Englishman of the twelfth century who took the unusual step of travelling around the Mediterranean and into Muslim lands in search of learning. Needless to say, such an activity was decidedly controversial, given that this was exactly when noble and pious Europeans were heading off on the Crusades in the hope of killing lots of Muslims. Still, on his return home, Adelard devoted considerable time and effort to telling others what he had learned abroad, and he taught at a number of universities in France, where he helped to spread the sciences of astronomy and mathematics. One thing that struck him particularly from his travels was how much most people, whether Christian or Muslim, seemed content to be told what to think by higher

'*The key to wisdom is this – constant and frequent questioning… for by doubting we are led to question, and by questioning we arrive at the truth.*'

Peter Abelard,
Yes and No

authorities. As he pointed out to his friends in Europe, they believed what they did because they had read it in Christian books; but the people he met abroad believed different things that their Muslim authors had written. Who was right? Indeed, such was the respect given to authority, Adelard observed, that an enterprising writer could cover a few pieces of paper with any old rubbish, and people would believe it simply because it was written down. Adelard taught instead that God has given individuals the power to consider different claims rationally and to use their own judgment to discern between them. As he told his nephew, 'If you want to hear anything from me, you must both give and take reason.'

Fireworks and spectacles – order, alchemy and science

So Christianity provided the West with two basic notions: first, the ordered state of the universe, and second, its basic rationality and comprehensibility. Both of these were, of course, inherited from the classical world that came before, and given a Christian spin by figures such as Justin Martyr, Augustine and Thomas Aquinas. And this world view provided the kind of context in which modern science could begin to develop.

We can see this more clearly if we compare Western science with Asian, especially that of China. For much of its history, China was technologically in advance of Europe. For example, although Europe discovered iron before China, the Chinese had developed the technology of cast iron by the fifth century BC, before Europeans did. Much later, Europeans made a great deal of the three wonderful inventions of the Renaissance – the printing press, the compass and gunpowder – despite the fact that the Chinese had invented all of them first. There were, of course, many reasons for China's scientific prowess; but one of them was the fact that China possessed a stable, widely accepted and persuasive philosophy that sought to place the world on a comprehensible footing. This was the philosophy of Confucianism, which, by the time Matteo Ricci and the other Jesuits arrived in China in the late sixteenth century, had become neo-Confucianism, a comprehensive account of the principles that underlie the physical world. For centuries, Chinese philosophers had taught that the world is intrinsically harmonious. Running throughout the universe is something called *qi*, a life-giving force of unity that is present everywhere – rather like the Logos of early Christian thought. At the same time, however, there is a principle of duality – the famous *yin* and *yang*. *Yin* represents darkness, coldness and femininity, while *yang* is brightness, warmth and masculinity. The balance between these two opposites provides the variety within the universe, which is also expressed in the five *xing* or elements –

> **6**
> *'The greatest inventions were produced in the times of ignorance, as the use of the compass, gunpowder, and printing.'*
>
> Jonathan Swift,
> *The Battle of the Books*, 1710

THE ANCIENT CHINESE
PHILOSOPHER CONFUCIUS,
LOOKING QUITE JOLLY FOR
SUCH A CANNY POLITICAL
THEORIST. ANONYMOUS
CHINESE ARTIST.

fire, earth, metal, water and wood. The Chinese philosophers believed that these elements are not static but transform into each other, giving the universe a dynamism and sense of change. Just like the ancient Greek philosophers, the Chinese Confucian philosophers had the ideal of a philosophy that would fulfil the twin functions of explaining how the world works and satisfying the religious impulse. In the twelfth century, the philosopher Zhu Xi set out to explain everything systematically, in terms of qi and also another principle, li, which he believed was even more fundamental. Li, in Zhu Xi's thought, is simply 'principle' itself – it gives order to what would otherwise be a formless, chaotic world. And since everything that exists has some kind of form or order, Zhu Xi believed that li is everywhere, intrinsic to reality itself.

These ideas meant that many scientific practices developed in China long before they did in the West. For example, the earliest Chinese treatise on medicine, *The Pharmacopoeia of the Heavenly Husbandman*, dates from around the second century and sets out an ordered account of different herbs and other medicines, all in terms of their relation to *yin* and *yang*. In the centuries that followed, alchemy became an important discipline, as many physicians and scientists became obsessed with the search for eternal life. The search often backfired, perhaps partly because of the curious love they had for lead and mercury, neither of which is noted for its life-extending properties. Quite the reverse, in fact; and the emperor Aidi's attempts to prolong his life indefinitely led to his death by poisoning at the age of twenty-five. At least three Tang emperors are also thought to have died the same way. Indeed, such was the propensity of the alchemists to quaff nasty potions in the quest for eternal life that the resulting number of untimely deaths probably set Chinese science back by a considerable degree.

Nevertheless, Chinese science progressed. The alchemists developed sophisticated techniques in their work, such as sublimation and distillation, invented equipment to perform them and advanced knowledge of the chemicals they used. This progress was all driven by the basic ideal of tracing the nature of reality from the five elements back through *yin* and *yang* to *qi* – a sort of return to the pristine purity of the unity of reality. However, by the later Middle Ages, the practice of mixing elixirs had declined somewhat – perhaps as people realized what happened to most people who drank them – and alchemy 'internalized'. It became a kind of meditative practice, where the practitioner sought to retrace reality within their own soul rather than in a beaker. By the time that had happened, though, the alchemists had stumbled upon the formula for gunpowder, as early as the tenth century. First they used it for fun – making fireworks – and worthy engineering projects – blasting rocks out of the way. It wasn't long, however, before 'incendiary arrows' and 'fire lances' were being used on the enemy. By the thirteenth century, Chinese armies were firing blunderbusses at the invading Mongol hordes, and warfare would never be the same again. For the Mongols quickly worked out how to use the firearms themselves, and did so enthusiastically later on when invading the Muslim and Christian lands. In this way, the technology spread rapidly throughout the world.

It seems then that early science developed out of comprehensive philosophical world views. In the case of China, the philosophy of Confucianism presented a world that made sense, one in which harmony and order reigned. In the world of *qi*, *li*, *yin* and *yang*, systematic and increasingly elaborate experiments were possible. The alchemists didn't view their materials as a haphazard collection of unrelated stuff – just bits of lead, cinnabar, saltpetre and so on. They viewed them as different expressions of the operation and interaction of those fundamental principles that ordered the world. By manipulating them, alchemists could hope to manipulate those ordering principles themselves, create new substances and even extend their own lives. Of course, their attempts failed, but what they learned in the process was the start of science.

We can see the same thing happening in Europe and the Muslim lands in the Middle Ages. Here, the ordered world view was that inherited from antiquity – in Europe via the Christian tradition, and in the Muslim countries via the Islamic philosophers, who had themselves, as we saw earlier, inherited it from the Middle Eastern Christians. Just as in China, the understanding of the world's order that this involved led to the development of alchemy, the attempt to understand and manipulate the harmonious relations between elements of the world. One of the first European alchemists was a man named Artephius, who, according to his own testimony, had successfully distilled the elixir of life and lived for a thousand years – although, unaccountably, he doesn't seem to be around any more. The most famous was probably Raymond Lull, who lived in the fourteenth century and devoted himself to studying Arabic philosophy and alchemy. Indeed, he not only debated with Muslims first-hand, like Adelard of Bath, but he wrote theological works in Arabic – for Lull, as well as being an avid scholar of all things arcane and mysterious, was a Christian theologian. If the stories are true, then Lull lived a remarkable life: imprisoned by Edward II of England in the Tower of London, where he was forced to use his arts to create large quantities of gold (insisting, as he did so, that the king use it only to pay for the Crusades), he later escaped and was eventually killed by the Muslims at the relatively young age – for an alchemist – of 150. So, at least, we are assured.

Characters such as Artephius and Lull are certainly bizarre, and they were probably fairly peculiar even before their stories got elaborated by later credulous generations. But their work did lay many of the foundations of modern science. A more respectable figure was Roger Bacon (not to be confused with the later Sir Francis Bacon, the courtier of Elizabeth I and also an avid amateur scientist). Bacon was an eminent Franciscan who studied at Paris before settling at the University of Oxford; unfortunately, he seems to have suffered from that slight tendency to arrogance that also marked Peter Abelard. His vigorous demonstrations of just where other writers, such as Thomas Aquinas, went wrong did not win him many friends. He was also unfortunate to be working during a period when the Franciscan authorities banned their members from publishing any books without their approval; luckily, Pope Clement IV liked Bacon and allowed him to override the ban.

Bacon was an encyclopedic thinker, who touched on just about every subject common to the time. He wrote about God and about theology, of course; but for him these subjects merged into those of alchemy and science, subjects that he believed were extremely important but had been neglected by most of his contemporaries. He was an astronomer, and he made important suggestions for revising the calendar. He made a special study of optics and lenses, setting out the theory of how one might build a telescope or a microscope and inventing spectacles. His alchemical research led him to study the composition of different chemicals and how they can be altered by processes such as distillation. While he was at it, he also predicted steamships, self-propelled cars and aeroplanes – although unlike the more famous prognosticator Leonardo da Vinci nearly two centuries later, he doesn't seem to have actually designed any.

In his *On Experimental Science*, Bacon made a passionate plea for the use of experiment and observation in the natural sciences. He wrote:

There are two ways of acquiring knowledge, one through reason, the other by experiment. Argument reaches a conclusion and forces us to admit it, but it does not make us certain, or eradicate doubt so that the mind rests calm in the intuition of truth, unless it finds this certainty through experience... argument is not enough, but experience is.

> 'The strongest arguments prove nothing so long as the conclusions are not verified by experience. Experimental science is the queen of sciences and the goal of all speculation.'
>
> Roger Bacon,
> *Third Work*

In his book, Bacon argues that science is actually very useful – something that makes rather odd reading today, since we are familiar with all the technological benefits science has brought. Bacon's claim that science helps us to expose fraudulent magicians, for example, is unlikely to be necessary today – although the work of modern rationalists such as James Randi, who devote themselves to debunking the claims of psychics, telepaths and other paranormalists, shows that the spirit of Agobard of Lyons lives on. But it is in Bacon and others like him that we can see the beginnings of modern Western science. For these people, Christianity and investigation of the world went hand in hand, for everything was created by God and imbued with his order and harmony. Today, scientists often mark the beginnings of modern science with the work of Kepler and Galileo that we saw earlier. Certainly, that point did mark a radical departure from the past, as experimental science gathered pace and scientists began to overturn the received wisdom of antiquity. But there is also a continuity between those early modern scientists and their predecessors, a continuity that is shown by Kepler's own fascination with harmony and the divine order in the universe. Even Sir Isaac Newton, the greatest scientist of the seventeenth century, devoted much of his energy to alchemy and mystical studies. Similarly, the intellectual climate that made the emergence of modern science possible had its roots in the Middle Ages and the Christian world view that had developed then.

Chapter 6

A Way of Life

Some of the great Christian saints have, it must be said, engaged in what most people would consider to be extravagant or over-the-top behaviour. Take Simeon Stylites, who spent several decades of the fifth century standing on top of a pillar – a clever move, since it kept him away from the people beneath and their associated temptations but at the same time kept him in full view and made him extremely famous. Or consider Sister Mary Margaret Alacoque, a seventeenth-century nun who carved the name of Jesus on her breast. Dominicus Loricatus, an Italian monk of the eleventh century, wore iron armour under his monastic robes and was in the habit of whipping himself (with scourges in both hands) while reciting the entire book of Psalms. In fact, in one marathon session of self-flagellation, he managed to recite all 150 Psalms eight times (and had started on the ninth) before finally collapsing. We have already heard of John Chrysostom, who spent two years in a cave learning the Bible by heart and ruining his digestion; we could also mention the Desert Fathers of the fourth and fifth centuries, who spent many hours trying to deny the impulses of the body and focus instead on spiritual things. One of them once told a disciple, 'For twenty years I have never had as much bread, water, or sleep as I wanted. I weighed my bread, measured my water, and snatched a little sleep, leaning against a wall.'

Most of us would agree that this kind of behaviour seems morbid, a denial of the goodness of the body and the things that God provides to nourish it. It is easy to assume that people like this were perverted in some way, suffering from a fetishistic hatred of themselves. Or, taking a marginally more positive view of the situation, we could think that they forced themselves to endure a life of hardship because they thought it was the right thing to do, or because God commanded it, or because it was the only way to get to heaven. Something we rarely appreciate is that they often did it simply because they preferred it. Nicephorus of Chios described the life of the ascetic like this:

He remains always a victor, always glorified, always happy, always rich, always cheerful and joyful, even if he happens to fall into extreme poverty and into a great many adverse and grievous circumstances of this present life. For inasmuch as he hopes in Almighty God, he does not despair, he is not sorry, is not anxious, but expects help from above.

Francis of Assisi and an upside-down life

How could a life that seems so unpleasant be preferable to a normal one? The question was answered most famously by Francis of Assisi, probably the most beloved Christian leader of all time. Indeed, publishers today are still keen to produce books about him

THE ALLEGORY OF POVERTY — JESUS, IN THE CENTRE,
PRESIDES OVER THE MARRIAGE OF ST FRANCIS TO
POVERTY. THE ROLE OF THE HOBBIT IN THE FOREGROUND
IS UNCLEAR. FRESCO IN THE LOWER CHURCH OF THE
BASILICA SAN FRANCESCO IN ASSISI
BY GIOTTO DI BONDONE, C. 1266-1337.

because they know that they will always sell, such is his continuing popularity. Born in Italy in 1182, Francis was the son of a wealthy merchant and as a young man led a charmed life: well dressed, witty, popular with everyone and never short of money. But he began to feel unsatisfied with this life, a dissatisfaction that led him one day, while on pilgrimage to Rome, to swap clothes with a beggar and spend a day begging in rags. Francis found, paradoxically, that he was happier this way than he had ever been: it freed him of the pressures and cares of everyday society. He became so addicted to giving away his money that he started to give away his father's too, to the fury of his parent, who took him to court. Disowned by his family, and a figure of fun to the smart young set who had once hung on his every word, Francis left Assisi and devoted himself to poverty. He determined that he would own nothing apart from the simple clothes he stood up in. Having given away all his money, he even threw out his empty wallet.

To most of the well-off middle classes of Assisi, such a lifestyle was nothing short of insanity; but a few people were inspired. They recognized that Francis wasn't simply making himself miserable for the sake of it. On the contrary, they saw that he was opting out of the system of power and wealth that trapped them all. Francis therefore began to attract followers, who like him gave away all they had to the poor and resolved to live together with no property or home. And, despite the strictness of their rule, they found that they were indeed much happier than they had been in their former lives. They had no cares or responsibilities. They had nothing to get in the way of focusing on serving God and helping others, and they found that this new focus made them feel freer than they ever had before. Francis and his friends gave the lie to the common assumption that the more religious one is, the more dour or miserable one will become. Indeed, the little group was so happy and laughed so much that people called them 'God's jesters'.

Francis did not give up material wealth because he thought it was unimportant. On the contrary, it was because he recognized its power that he sought to escape from it. The thirteenth century may seem remote today, but in many ways it was not so unlike the modern world, which was beginning to evolve even as Francis was wondering what to do with his life. In the past, the medieval world had been one of stable hierarchies. The feudal system meant that everyone had a place in society and a role to play. Society was intrinsically local: there was little economic exchange between different towns. Instead, people worked for their local baron and exchanged goods with their neighbours. But all that was beginning to change. The century before Francis's birth had seen the Crusades, the series of wars against the Muslims, when huge numbers of people had headed off to the Middle East. Ships had been built for them and land

THE FAMOUS EXPLORER MARCO POLO LEAVES VENICE, PROBABLY ON HIS SECOND TRIP IN 1271, IN THIS PICTURE FROM A FOURTEENTH-CENTURY MANUSCRIPT. UPON HIS RETURN, THE BOOK HE WROTE ABOUT HIS TRAVELS TO THE COURT OF KUBLA KHAN INSPIRED MANY OTHERS TO SEARCH FOR ROUTES TO THE ORIENT — INCLUDING CHRISTOPHER COLUMBUS. BUT MANY OF HIS CONTEMPORARIES ACCUSED HIM OF MAKING IT ALL UP, AND EVEN TODAY THE RUMOUR PERSISTS THAT MARCO WAS NOTHING MORE THAN ONE OF THE GREATEST LIARS IN HISTORY. ON HIS DEATHBED, HOWEVER, MARCO INSISTED THAT HE HADN'T TOLD THE HALF OF THE WONDERS THAT HE SAW.

CUSTOMERS LINE UP TO BUY EXOTIC ORIENTAL SPICES FROM THE PERFUME SHOP IN THIS ROMANESQUE CAPITAL FROM THE TWELFTH CENTURY.

routes opened up. These ships and roads were still there when the soldiers returned, and people had a new sense of the wider world and the possibility of travel. They also had a taste for the exotic, as the Crusaders brought back goods and ideas from the East – everything from chess to spices. The ships that had once carried soldiers to war now began to fill up with cargo, and a trade network sprang up throughout Europe, connecting the continent to distant countries. Ports such as Venice and other north Italian cities became astonishingly rich as the produce of two continents flowed through them, and a new class of society came into being – the merchants, who instead of fitting into the neat feudal system existed alongside it and became increasingly powerful. They were the ancestors of the modern middle classes, a group who were powerful not because of birth or social status but because of the power of money. The world where people were who they were simply because of who they were was giving way to a new world, where people could make themselves into what they wanted to be. And increasingly, what they wanted to be was rich. Whereas the lord's manor or the church had once formed the focal point of every community, now it was the marketplace. Market towns swelled as people moved from the countryside to barter their goods, and they now expected to be paid not in labour but in hard cash. It was the beginning of our modern capitalist system.

This was the world that Francis – the spoilt son of a wealthy north Italian cloth merchant – sought to escape. He did not believe that the world of wealth and trade, of power and worldly influence, was something to hanker after. It did not free people – on the contrary, it enslaved them. Capitalism meant not the freedom of people to pursue wealth, but the freedom of wealth to ensnare people. And so he completely rejected the whole thing – the pursuit of worldly position, and even the possession of any material goods or wealth at all.

Is that a reasonable goal? After all, most of us hardly have the option of giving away everything we have and going to live on the

street. We have responsibilities to other people and also to ourselves. And yet there is something instinctively attractive about Francis's alternative. Perhaps the answer is to be found in one of the most misquoted verses of the Bible, 1 Timothy 6:10, which states that 'the love of money is a root of all kinds of evil'. What causes people to become trapped by a hostile system is not money itself, as the verse is usually misquoted, but the *love* of money. That can pollute even the most optimistic situation, as we can see by looking at an example from the history of the spread of Christianity itself.

Slaves and missals – Mvemba Nzinga and Congo

It was in the late fifteenth century – as Columbus was discovering America – that Portuguese explorers sailed down the west coast of Africa and made contact with a startling new civilization whose existence had previously been unsuspected by Europeans. Congo was, at this time, a country of considerable wealth and power. The capital, Mbanza Kongo, had a population of between 60,000 and 100,000, and it was ruled by a complex political system whereby the king was constrained in his decisions by a council of twelve advisers – four of whom had to be women.

The people of Congo received Christianity quite enthusiastically. Many of them regarded it as a sort of addition to the religion they had already. They believed in a wide range of gods and other supernatural spirits, so it didn't make too much difference to add one or two more. There was also the bonus that with Christianity came various other benefits of European culture – crops, tools and weapons – and legal and political systems. Many people in Congo admired the Portuguese systems of government and law, and they tried to introduce the ideas and practices into their own country to add stability to the existing system.

The most intriguing figure in all this was Mvemba Nzinga, who ruled Congo from 1506 to 1543 and stamped his authority and personality over the whole country. He was certainly a canny politician. He was a Christian, and to the Portuguese he seemed like a dream come true – a powerful African king who was also a sincere and devoted Catholic, one who spent his spare time reading theology books and who knew the Bible better than the Europeans did! Indeed, he was generally known by the name Afonso, which he took at his baptism. Afonso made Christianity the state religion of Congo and set about an ambitious church-building programme. But he recognized that Christianity could not simply supplant the local religion, and he took pains to present it as a development of traditional cults rather than something new. For example, he put the priest of the water cult in charge of looking after water for baptism. In this clever way of creating an authentically African Christianity, with its roots in African culture as well as in European thought, Afonso was simply following the initiative of Christian missionaries for centuries. Boniface, the English missionary who brought Christianity to the Germans in the eighth century, also used the customs of the locals to help convert them. They played a game in which they threw sticks called *kegels* at smaller sticks called *heides*. Boniface brought religion to the game: the *heides* were now to represent demons and knocking them down showed purity of spirit. Whether this made the game any more fun is, alas, unrecorded.

Afonso also recognized the power of Christianity to educate. Although Congo was a socially and culturally highly developed nation, it was technologically behind Portugal. In particular, it lacked the printing press. When the Portuguese sent the first printing press there, it caused something of a sensation; and missionaries and colonists could command enormous sums for any paper they cared to sell to the locals. Afonso saw that without a rapid modernization programme it would be hard for his country to interact with Portugal as an equal. He therefore took great pains to appropriate European learning for his people. He sent his sons to Portugal to be educated, with considerable success – one became bishop of Uttica in North Africa, and another professor of humanities at the University of Lisbon. At the same time, Afonso established new schools throughout Congo and forced the children of the nobility to attend them. It was a bold initiative, and one that was especially striking given that it was native-led. It was Afonso, king of Congo, who took the lead in spreading Christianity and education throughout his country. The attempt was rather like that of Mesrob Mashtotes, who, as we saw in chapter 1, brought not just Christianity but literacy and literature to his native Armenia in the fifth century.

Unfortunately, Afonso's efforts had less long-term effect than Mesrob's, because the Portuguese proved less high-minded than the Africans they were supposedly helping. Whereas Afonso was genuinely concerned for education and piety, the Portuguese were more interested in recouping the considerable costs they had incurred in exploring the African coast and sending missionaries and colonists to Congo. While they hoped to find gold and other valuable minerals in the area, they were most interested in slaves. The sugar industry was beginning to take root in the Atlantic islands and, later, in South America, and there was a massive demand for people to work on the plantations. Weight for weight, sugar was almost as valuable as gold, and the enormous profits the new crop promised outweighed any scruples the Portuguese might have had about commandeering labour from the new lands they had discovered. By 1516, despite Afonso's protests and attempts to regulate the new trade, 4,000 slaves were being removed from Congo every year. Such was the low cost of locals and the high cost of European paper and learning that the Portuguese could buy a slave with a single Catholic missal – a horribly ironic trade given the hopes of King Afonso to use Christian learning to help his people. And in the end, European contact ended the civilization of Congo just as surely as it ended the civilizations of the Aztecs and the Incas in the Americas. The economy of the country became increasingly dependent on the slave trade, but as other African nations opened their doors to the Europeans and started undercutting Congo's prices, the economy faltered. At the same time, the selling of firearms to local rulers undermined the central government of Congo, as the distribution of power became increasingly unbalanced. The country splintered into a mass of competing petty chieftaincies. Meanwhile, the population was being shipped away, and the country died. Less than a century and a half after

'I swear that such a sight would greatly astonish your highness. He says things so well phrased and so true that it seems to me that the Holy Spirit always speaks through him, for he does nothing but study, and many times he falls asleep over his books, and many times he forgets to eat and drink for talking of our Lord, and he is so absorbed by the things of the book that he forgets himself, and even when he is going to hold an audience and listen to the people, he speaks of nothing but God and the saints.'

Rui de Aguiar, writing to King Manuel of Portugal about King Afonso of Congo, 1516

Afonso's death in 1543, the cities over which he had ruled were deserted, patrolled only by elephants.

Had the Portuguese peddled a fake idol to Afonso and his countrymen? Had their religion promised them salvation with one hand and stolen their lives and liberty with the other? It was certainly Christians who did these things – at least, those who professed to be Christians. And yet it was not Christianity that was responsible for what happened. It was the sugar trade that ended the power of Congo, and the avaricious greed of the Portuguese traders and settlers. And more than this, King Afonso was powerless to stop them because his country relied on trade just as much as Portugal did. The king of Congo derived much of his status from the fact that he ruled over the trade system, and if he had managed to prevent the slave trade throughout his kingdom, the local governors would have rebelled against him. For all his Christian erudition, Afonso was part of a system that was based on acquisition and avarice, and though he tried to regulate or even stop the slave trade altogether, he also ensured that it operated in the more outlying regions of his territory, and he profited from the sales himself by imposing hefty taxes on them. Indeed, in the short term, the slave trade simply enhanced Congo's power and wealth among the African nations of the area, while the long-term decline of the country was partly due to the fact that other African nations started selling slaves more cheaply, undercutting Congo and helping to wreck its economy. It certainly wasn't merely a matter of evil Europeans exploiting the Africans, but one of Africans exploiting each other too. Perhaps Francis was wise, after all, to put himself as far from danger as possible by completely rejecting the whole system.

Christianity does not simply preach the importance of a moral life. It has always possessed a strong current of criticism of power, of wealth, of worldly desire. When that tradition has been forgotten, the result has been episodes such as the spoliation of Congo. But when it has been remembered, Christianity has fostered some of the most profound and appealing moral approaches that have ever been taught. It is a tradition that goes back to the teaching of Jesus himself.

Jesus and the back-to-front ethic

By deliberately living a life that was utterly at odds with conventional wisdom about what makes us happy, Francis was not just striking a blow against the materialist society in which he lived: he was also following what he believed was a core element of Christianity. One of the things that inspired him to give away all that he had was the moment when, sitting in church, he heard a reading of Mark 10:21, where Jesus tells a questioner, 'Go, sell what you own, and give the money to the poor.' It's a saying that has inspired many. There is a story of one of the Desert Fathers who owned nothing but a copy of the Gospels, but he gave it away to help the poor, saying, 'I have given away the book that told me to sell all I have and give to the poor.'

We are told that the young man to whom Jesus said this went away unhappy, because he was rich; and indeed there is some evidence that even some of the earliest Christians were not very happy with it. Matthew's Gospel, which is generally thought to be based partly on Mark's, seems to have been written for a wealthier readership. In Mark 12, we are told that Jesus saw a line of rich people putting money into the Temple treasury. When he saw a poor widow drop in two tiny coins, he told his disciples that she had given more than all the others – because although it was so little, it was all she had. Matthew, however, reading this story in Mark, decided not to put it in his Gospel! Again, in Luke 6, Jesus declares, 'Blessed are you who are poor, for yours is the kingdom of God.' Many scholars believe this represents an older form of the saying than the one that appears in Matthew – 'Blessed are the poor *in spirit*' – a worthy sentiment, no doubt, but not quite the same.

It seems that Matthew was keen to 'spiritualize' this kind of teaching. In his eyes, when Jesus talks about the poor being blessed, he doesn't mean the actual poor – people with no money. He means those who *feel* poor – those who are depressed or without hope, or who feel far from God. And in Matthew's version, Jesus goes on to bless those who mourn, those who are meek, those who are merciful and so on. That doesn't necessarily mean that Jesus didn't say these things, of course: merely that it was this kind of thing that Matthew wished to emphasize.

Nevertheless, the back-to-front thinking that appealed so much to Francis reappears throughout the Gospels, in Jesus' ethical teaching. Ethics is the art of trying to live right – indeed, of trying to work out what it is that makes a certain action or way of life *right* in the first place. It is clearly an issue of central concern to Christianity, as to other religions, and for Christianity, thinking on the issue begins with the teaching of Jesus – which is based, above all, on the principle of selflessness. Throughout the

> 'None of you can become my disciple if you do not give up all your possessions.'
>
> Luke 14:33

JESUS PREACHES
THE SERMON ON
THE MOUNT.
PAINTING BY
J. JAMES TISSOT,
1899–1900.

Gospels, Jesus takes every opportunity to overturn or oppose the natural human instinct to look after number one. Thus, according to Acts 20:35, Jesus told his followers, 'It is more blessed to give than to receive,' and Matthew 5–7 contains the famous Sermon on the Mount, in which Jesus teaches a morality that deliberately turns all received wisdom upside down. We are told, for example:

Do not resist an evildoer. But if anyone strikes you on the right cheek, turn the other also; and if anyone wants to sue you and take your coat, give your cloak as well; and if anyone forces you to go one mile, go also the second mile. Give to everyone who begs from you, and do not refuse anyone who wants to borrow from you.

Not all Christians have liked this teaching. Origen, the great third-century theologian, argued that this passage was not meant to be taken literally, his reasoning being that no one is ever struck on the right cheek, because if you slap someone you hit their left cheek with your right hand! Evidently, Origen was right-handed himself, and did not consider the possibility that one might use a backhand sort of stroke. According to the Gospels, Jesus' disciples were also reluctant to assimilate these ideas. Mark 10 tells the story of the brothers James and John who asked to sit by Jesus' side in heaven. The other disciples were not unnaturally annoyed at this, but Jesus told them, 'Whoever wishes to become great among you must be your servant, and whoever wishes to be first among you must be slave of all.'

Indeed, the teaching goes beyond how we live in relation to other people. Jesus was interested in ethics not for its own sake, but in how it relates to the kingdom of God, which is both here on earth and something that is coming in the future. In that kingdom, we are told, the normal worldly values are reversed. In Mark 10:25, we are told that it is easier for a camel to go through a needle's eye than for a rich man to enter the kingdom of God, while in Mark 10:31, Jesus declares, 'Many who are first will be last, and the last will be first.' Perhaps most ominously, in Mark 8 we are told, 'If any want to become my followers, let them deny themselves and take up their cross and follow me. For those who want to save their life will lose it, and those who lose their life for my sake, and for the sake of the gospel, will save it.'

The teaching of Jesus certainly contrasts with much ethical teaching in ancient times. There are, however, some points of contact. For example, one of the most famous sayings of Jesus is Matthew 7:12, from the Sermon on the Mount: 'In everything do to others as you would have them do to you; for this is the law and the prophets.' This teaching was known not only to Jewish teachers of the time but also to Greek philosophers. In *The Republic*, written nearly four centuries before the Christian Gospels, Plato had his characters discuss the nature of justice (or righteousness). When one of the characters suggests that it is just to help one's friends and harm one's enemies, Socrates argues in response that it can never be good to make somebody worse than they currently are; but this is what we would do if we were to harm our enemies. Therefore, it follows that we should try to do good to everyone, irrespective of whether they are our friends or not. He concludes:

> 'Presumably, to say
> that happiness is the
> chief good seems a
> platitude, and a clearer
> account of what it is is
> still desired. This might
> perhaps be given, if we
> could first ascertain the
> function of man. For just
> as a flute-player, a
> sculptor, or any artist,
> and, in general, for all
> things that have a
> function or an activity,
> the good and the 'well' is
> thought to reside in the
> function, so would it
> seem to be for man, if he
> has a function... If this
> is the case, and we state
> the function of man to
> be a certain kind of life,
> and this to be an activity
> or actions of the soul
> implying a rational
> principle, and the
> function of the good
> man to be the good and
> noble performance of
> these... human good
> turns out to be activity
> of soul exhibiting
> excellence.'
>
> Aristotle,
> *Nicomachean Ethics I*

So, if anyone tells us that it is righteous to give to everyone what he's owed, and if he understands by this that a righteous man should harm his enemies and help his friends, he isn't wise to say so. What he says isn't true, since we have realized that it is never righteous to harm anyone.

Again, Jesus' teaching that wealth and social position will not help you would have appealed to the Stoics, a very popular group of philosophers who were famed for their moral philosophy. They taught that happiness is exactly the same thing as virtue. So if you are virtuous you will be happy, irrespective of your material status. They therefore believed that, contrary to common sense, a good man who is being stretched on the rack is happier than a bad man who lives in a palace. It is goodness that makes us happy, not anything else. This is why today we still describe someone who is willing to put up with hardship as a 'stoic', and when someone who has lost something manages not to become upset, we call this a 'philosophical' attitude.

Still, some Stoics, perhaps realizing that this sort of thing was unlikely to catch on, modified it a little. They said that although things such as money and good looks are not what really make us happy, it's still better to have them than not. They could say this because of a fundamental notion in Greek ethics – that of *nature*. The Stoics believed that a thing – any thing – functions best when it is true to its nature. We might say that a car is designed to run on a certain kind of fuel and be driven in a certain way. If we pour the wrong kind of fuel into the tank and race about, grinding the gears, the car will get broken. Similarly, human beings by nature function best under certain conditions – when they get the right kind of food, the right exercise and so on.

The most famous statement of this kind of ethics was made by Aristotle, Plato's pupil and arguably the greatest philosopher of all time. His *Nicomachean Ethics*, one of the most important books ever written, is essentially an unpacking of this basic idea that human happiness lies in realizing human potential. To Aristotle, leading a *good* life was exactly the same sort of thing as leading a *healthy* life. There are certain ways to keep ourselves healthy, by eating, exercising and so on. If we do not do them, or if we do them too much, we will become ill, for health lies in moderation. Similarly, in any situation there is a right way to behave, which is established by reason. Acting in the right or virtuous way – this right way being worked out rationally – is Aristotle's definition of happiness, and it is important that in Greek the word for 'virtue' (*arete*) is the same as the word for 'excellence'. In acting virtuously, we become excellent human beings.

While Aristotle's ethical theories are complex and subtle and still studied today, some of his examples strike us as a little quaint. Take, for example, his description of the 'magnanimous' (literally, 'great-souled') man, who represents the virtue of, essentially, being great – avoiding the twin evils of being too humble and being vain. The great-souled man, we are told, is good and knows that he is good, because he is the man who deserves honour. He is brave and honourable, and he is likely to be aristocratic and rich, because we tend to revere such people – although, Aristotle assures us piously, that is less important than being virtuous. The great-souled man is generous, but he does not like to be given things, because it makes him seem inferior to whoever is doing the giving, and he hates to be in debt. He is not afraid to let people know what he thinks of them, good or bad, although he will tend not to admire anyone else, because that would suggest that they are greater than him. Most of all, the great-souled man is self-sufficient, looking out for number one and not letting his happiness depend on anyone else. We are told that he is likely to walk and talk slowly, with a sensible and deep voice, because he is so great himself that he is unlikely to be excited by anything else.

That, it seems, is the kind of person who was admired in classical Greek society, and indeed, such a person might well be admired by many people today. And the teaching of Jesus is certainly at odds with this kind of ideal. Aristotle's great-souled man is concerned above all with himself – after all, he's the greatest thing around, so what could be more important than himself? He is concerned to maintain that position of greatness, so he avoids being in debt to anyone else or doing anything that makes others seem superior to him. Jesus, by contrast, recommends thinking of others even before oneself: he commands his followers to give everything that is asked of them and then give more; and he tells them that those who are considered great in the world will be the least in the kingdom of God. The great-souled man is a typical Greek aristocrat, but God blesses the poor and the meek.

From the kingdom of God to how to use the bath – the Christian moralists

As the examples of Plato and Aristotle show, the philosophical examination of ethical issues was already well advanced when Christianity came on the scene, and it has remained a central subject of debate for philosophers ever since. Christians certainly can't claim to have invented ethics, but they have made a major contribution to it.

Some have seen Jesus as essentially a moral teacher, and they have tried to show how his teaching can be worked into a comprehensive ethical 'system'. A system of ethics tries to show not only *what* is right and what is wrong but *why* it is right or wrong. For example, the nineteenth-century philosopher and atheist Jeremy Bentham argued that actions are right or wrong depending on their consequences. So an action that brings about more good is morally preferable to one that brings about less. Moreover, Bentham claimed that the only way of measuring how much good or evil an action brings about is through looking at pleasure and pain. So, in any situation, the morally right action is the one that will cause the most pleasure and least pain, and the morally wrong action is the one that will cause the most pain and least pleasure. With these basic principles in place, Bentham could work out a whole system of ethics, showing why some actions are better than others, and how we can tell. Bentham's ethical theories had one especially famous consequence. When he died, in 1832, there was a great shortage of human bodies for medical students to practise on, because people were afraid of dissection: they believed that it would be impossible for them to be saved if their remains were not properly buried in the normal fashion. Bentham

BENTHAM, STILL IN HIS GLASS BOX, CONTEMPLATES ETERNITY. HIS REAL HEAD WAS REMOVED SHORTLY AFTER HIS DEATH AS IT WAS SIMPLY TOO HORRIFIC, AND REPLACED WITH A WAX REPLICA. THE ORIGINAL HEAD IS IN A GLASS CASE OF ITS OWN SOMEWHERE IN THE COLLEGE VAULTS.

had pointed out that leaving your body to medical science was far more beneficial than just burying it, so he did just that; and on an appropriately dark and stormy night after his death, he was publicly dissected in London. After that, his skeleton was dressed, stuffed and put in a glass case to create what was called the 'auto-icon' – because Bentham had suggested (with, perhaps, an element of wicked humour) that this was cheaper and therefore more beneficial than making a statue. Bentham can still be seen sitting in his glass box in a corridor at University College, London; and there are many students who, returning to their rooms in an inebriated state after dark, have had the nasty shock of stumbling across him.

Influenced by Bentham and others like him, some nineteenth-century Christian thinkers tried to set out an ethical system that was based on the teaching of Jesus. For example, the German academic Albrecht Ritschl, one of the leading theologians of the nineteenth century, argued that Christianity was essentially about living a good life. He believed that God could be known only through the life and teaching of Christ, but that 'knowledge' of God was not the same sort of thing as 'knowledge' of a scientific fact. In fact, he suggested that religion is not about 'facts' at all, but 'values'. 'Knowing' God through Christ is therefore a matter of following Christ's ethical teachings: it is a matter of making his values central to your life, as they were to his. Ritschl was interested not as much in God himself as in Jesus and his ethical teaching, and the effect that this has on human beings. The idea of Christian 'togetherness' that we saw in chapter 5 was important to Ritschl. He believed that the ethics of Jesus are worked out at the social level, rather than the individual level, and so he focused his attention on the church community and how its members interact with each other. In so doing, the ethics of Jesus were always paramount.

These ideas were taken to a more political dimension at the turn of the twentieth century by an American Baptist minister named Walter Rauschenbusch. As he ministered to the poorest members of New York society, in the area known as 'Hell's Kitchen', Rauschenbusch became concerned that Christianity should have a real impact on their lives. It should address their deprived social and economic circumstances. He therefore became the central figure of the Social Gospel movement, which became very popular in the early years of the twentieth century in America. Rauschenbusch believed that the ills of society could be traced back to greed and selfishness, to the ethic of individualism, of personal acquisition – exactly the same things that Francis of Assisi hated so much. In their place, Rauschenbusch tried to promote the ethics of Jesus, which are based around giving, not getting. They are based around a concern for society, not for the individual. In Jesus' world, Rauschenbusch believed, everyone is in it together. Like Ritschl, he believed that when

> '*Religious knowledge moves in independent value-judgements, which relate to man's attitude to the world, and call forth feelings of pleasure or pain, in which man either enjoys the dominion over the world vouchsafed him by God, or feels grievously the lack of God's help to that end.*'
>
> Albrecht Ritschl,
> *The Christian Doctrine of Justification and Reconciliation III*

Jesus talked about 'the kingdom of God', he meant a perfect society, the church, in which these ethical principles become a reality.

So in the hands of thinkers such as Ritschl and Rauschenbusch, Christianity has been a powerful influence in the construction of ethical theories, something that is normally the preserve of philosophers. In particular, Christianity is not just something to sit around thinking about, but something to go out and do; people like Rauschenbusch did not write books about the 'Social Gospel' because they thought it was interesting, but because they wanted to go out and actually help people. And they did achieve things too. Rauschenbusch himself was an influence on progressive politicians such as Woodrow Wilson, and he was also an inspiration to Martin Luther King Jr. We shall see some of the practical results of Christian ethics in the next chapter.

However, it might seem that there should be more to Christian ethics than simply an application of the teaching of Jesus. In a religious context, questions about morality inevitably involve questions about God. What does God have to do with all of this? After all, on the face of it, the ethic of love, as preached by Jesus, needn't necessarily have anything to do with God. Jesus could, after all, have been simply an enlightened human teacher.

It is often said that religion offers the only reliable framework for ethics. That is, we know that, say, murder is wrong because God tells us so. If there were no God, then there would be no reliable basis for morality. All we would have would be human concepts. This might suggest that the sentence, 'Murder is wrong', means nothing more than, 'Murder is generally considered socially unacceptable' or, 'We don't like murder.' And that seems too weak – too relativistic. Without divine commands to underpin morality, morality has no permanence and could be changed by human whim. Suppose you believed that morality is just a matter of social convention, and suppose that you then found yourself shipwrecked on a desert island with an extremely annoying companion. In the absence of any society or threat of punishment, would there be any reason not to whack him over the head with a piece of driftwood and chuck him into the sea?

Perhaps there would, and philosophers call the search for an explanation of what ethics *is* and *why* we should try to be ethical at all 'meta-ethics', meaning that it goes beyond finding ethical principles to stating what ethical principles actually are. Are they statements of fact? Are they expressions of taste? Are they commands? By appealing to the divine, many Christian thinkers have sought to find a way to answer these very difficult questions.

Thomas Aquinas, the most important Christian thinker of the thirteenth century,

> 'The championship of social justice is almost the only way left open to a Christian nowadays to gain the crown of martyrdom. Theological heretics are rarely persecuted now. The only rival of God is mammon, and it is only when his sacred name is blasphemed that men throw the Christians to the lions.'
>
> Walter Rauschenbusch,
> *Christianity and the Social Crisis*

devoted considerable thought to these matters. What he came up with was a combination of Aristotle's theory with Christian ideals – indeed, Aquinas was greatly influenced by Aristotle in all his writings, and he referred to him as simply 'the Philosopher'. Like Aristotle, Aquinas argued that human beings are built in such a way that they have a proper function. Just as an eye functions properly when it sees, or a tree functions properly when it grows, so too a human being functions properly when it contemplates God. Aristotle had also believed that a life of philosophical contemplation is best for human beings, and he had even said that, because this life involves using our minds, which are the most divine parts of us, it almost makes us divine ourselves. Aquinas, however, Christianized this by introducing the notion of divine law. If beings that God has created are to act properly, they must do so within a framework of God's own actions. God rules over the whole universe, and he is supremely rational. Therefore, when Aristotle says that the right action is the one that is in accord with reason, what he means is the one that is in accord with God. In other words, it is God who underpins the moral law. The moral law is the set of commands and prohibitions that God imposes on the world through his actions and plans. Because God is eternal – that is, not bound by time – the law is eternal.

At this point, there might seem to be a reasonable objection. If certain actions are morally good or bad simply because of God's say-so, then why does God say so? That is, suppose we say that murder is wrong because God forbids it. Well, could God have decided not to forbid it? Suppose he had instead commanded us to murder and forbidden us to help people. In that case, would murder be morally good and helping people morally wrong? If we say that good and evil are based solely on the commands of God, then we ought to say that they would – which seems odd. Moreover, it makes God seem arbitrary. The seventeenth-century Christian philosopher Gottfried Leibniz argued that this way of thinking makes God into an unpredictable tyrant, one whose whim is law without any justification other than that it *is* his whim. Instead, we should say that if God forbids murder, he must have a good reason to do so. In other words, murder must be wrong anyway, and God forbids it *because* it is wrong – instead of the other way round, that it is wrong because God forbids it.

But that seems awkward too, because now God is constrained by something outside him. And if it is not God who makes some things right and some things wrong, then who does? Aquinas's answer was that God's commands aren't simply arbitrary whims, and he showed this by combining the notion of divine law with that of natural law. Rational agents in the world, such as human beings, act with some end in view. That is, we don't just act on every whim, but we deliberate and plan our actions with the aim of achieving something definite. Moreover, when we do this, we aim for something good – or at least what we perceive as good. But God is the greatest good that there is. So if we are to act in the most rational way, we will always be acting in a way that brings us closer to God. This is why contemplation of God is the most perfect life there can be for human beings. Acting in accordance with God is the most natural plan and therefore the best. The laws that God lays down are those of nature. In actual fact, of course, people often do not act in a way that is in accordance with God's will.

> 'Now God, by his wisdom, is the creator of all things. He has the same relation to them as a person who makes does to things that his skill has made. Moreover, he governs all the acts and movements that are to be found in every single creature... Accordingly, the eternal law is nothing else than the model of divine wisdom, in that it directs all actions and movements.'
>
> Thomas Aquinas,
> *Summa Theologiae* I 190

That is partly because we do not have a perfect understanding of right and wrong, any more than we have a perfect scientific understanding of the world. What we do have is our own intellectual ability to understand right and wrong: our conscience. If we were presented with the moral truth as clearly as God understands it, and if our will power had not been corrupted by original sin, we would be unable to avoid wanting to follow that truth, because by nature we want what is good. But because our consciences are less clear, because they sometimes make mistakes, we can resist them if we want to. And because, in Aquinas's view, Adam's sin has spoilt us and made grace necessary for salvation, we often do want to.

So then, for Thomas Aquinas, morality is hard-coded into the world by God. It is not that God issues edicts simply as he sees fit. When Moses climbed the holy mountain to be given the Law, what he received was not just a set of rules that God had decided to impose on human beings. On the contrary, it was the manual for living a good, worthwhile, fulfilling life as a human being – an instruction manual direct from the manufacturer. God created the world, including human beings, and the moral law is part and parcel of that world. That is why the divine law is also the natural law.

Aquinas represents the kind of medieval world view we saw in chapter 5 – one where the whole of reality is seen in an organic, holistic way. There is, in his view, no contradiction between the natural and the divine spheres, but they flow seamlessly into each other. This is not to say that God and the world are the same thing, an idea that would have been abhorrent to Aquinas, but rather, they are not intrinsically opposed to each other. Put another way, faith and reason complement each other. The law that God reveals from on high is the same law that human reason – the conscience – can work out for itself, although, naturally, divine revelation is more reliable.

In modern times, many Christians have criticized this way of thinking. Perhaps the most famous is Karl Barth, one of the most important Christian writers of the twentieth century. Barth's theology revolved around the notion of revelation. He believed that it was a central principle of Christianity that God can be known only when God chooses to reveal himself. He hated the idea that people can come to know God, and therefore morality, through their own powers, whether through reason or anything else. So he rejected Aquinas's identification of the divine law with the natural law. In fact, Barth said that any attempt to set out an ethical system from reason alone was intrinsically sinful. It was the elevation of human principles to the position that God should have in our lives. That, in his eyes, was the central mistake of the nineteenth-century Christian thinkers, who tried to interpret Jesus' teaching as if it were simply a system of how to live correctly, without any reference to God. But, in fact, ethics makes sense only in the context of God. This is a more radical claim than the claim that God is the source of right and wrong, as Aquinas believed. That is a theoretical claim, one that we can establish at the level of theory and then, if we want, forget in practice, provided that we continue to do what is right. For Barth, by contrast, the notion of ethics make sense only if we actively think about God at every stage. In Matthew 19, the young man whom Jesus tells to sell all he has begins by asking Jesus how to live a good life. Jesus replies, 'Why do you ask me about what is good? There is

> **6**
> *'Faith is not concerned with a special realm, that of religion, say, but with real life in its totality, the outward as well as the inward questions, that which is bodily as well as that which is spiritual, the brightness as well as the gloom in our life. Faith is concerned with our being permitted to rely on God as regards ourselves and also as regards what moves us on behalf of others, of the whole of humanity; it is concerned with the whole of living and the whole of dying.'*
>
> Karl Barth,
> *Dogmatics in Outline*

only One who is good.' In other words, it's no good talking about how to live right if you don't talk about God at the same time. So Barth suggested that ethics is based on divine command. This does not mean that God lays down a series of rules at some point in history and then leaves us to get on with obeying them. Rather, the divine command is God himself, the divine will that underlies and overarches all things, and we obey it by following God – not just doing what he says, but aligning our will with his and coming to rely on him completely and without compromise. In the last resort, living morally is about a personal encounter with and commitment to God, not the intellectual reflection on a set of moral principles.

So Barth rejected the notion of ethical systems completely, because they are a humanizing of what should remain a divine command. In this, he was a little like Augustine. Augustine also believed that ethics is essentially about obeying the will of God, and he even went as far as to insist that God can legitimately order us to do things that we are incapable of doing. For example, in the Sermon on the Mount, Jesus tells us to live perfect lives; but none of us is actually capable of this. Augustine also represents the way in which the Christian notion of sin can be useful when talking about ethics. We saw earlier how the philosopher Jeremy Bentham argued that actions are right or wrong by virtue of their consequences. For Augustine, absolutely the opposite is the case. Actions are right or wrong by virtue of their *intentions*. If I try to deceive someone but fail, I am guilty of lying just as much as if I had succeeded. This is because, for Augustine, morality is all about the will. The essence of sin is the intention to disobey God, just as the essence of virtue is the intention to obey. So here we see the emphasis on not the action, or the ethical system, but the internal point of view of the individual. Augustine saw true evil as residing not in external actions but in the soul itself – not in the act of murder, for example, but in the hatred or lust for power that may motivate it. This sort of approach would be extremely influential within Christianity in later centuries.

Another theologian who had some problems with Aquinas-style ethical systems was Reinhold Niebuhr, who, like Rauschenbusch, was concerned to make Christianity politically and socially relevant to everyone, not just middle-class intellectuals. Like the nineteenth-century theologians, Niebuhr made the ethic of love, as taught by Jesus, the centre of his ethics, and he recognized that it represents a radical and often disturbing commentary on our normal way of thinking of the world and of right and wrong.

Like Rauschenbusch before him, Niebuhr argued that the ethic of love is revolutionary because it overrides the egotism that is so basic to most of our everyday lives. We set up defences between ourselves and others, and we act to try to secure our own interests. While we may help others, we still mentally distinguish between their interests and our own, and where possible we try to minimize harm to ourselves. It is a fence-building way of life, one that is based around ideals of power or wealth – the ideology of capitalism, in fact, the early version of which so repelled Francis of Assisi. But Jesus' ideal of love means ignoring all these divisions between 'mine' and 'yours'. It is based on the love of God for humanity – as Niebuhr put it, on 'vertical'

> 'The fact is that more men in our modern era are irreligious because religion has failed to make civilization ethical than because it has failed to maintain its intellectual respectability. For every person who disavows religion because some ancient and unrevised dogma outrages his intelligence, several become irreligious because the social impotence of religion outrages their conscience.'
>
> Reinhold Niebuhr,
> *Does Civilization Need Religion?*

relations between God and people, rather than 'horizontal' relations between people and other people. And the basic message of Christianity is that God enters into the human world unreservedly, breaking down the barriers between the creator and his creation. The ethic of love is therefore an ethic of removing barriers and entering into the concerns of the other person completely – and this is the right thing to do because it is what God does.

Niebuhr's main point, however, was that you can't turn this approach into an ethical 'system', which lays down certain rules. Such rules are just human constructs that inevitably fail to cover every eventuality, or which get outdated as society moves on. At the same time, of course, you have to have ethical principles of some kind. The ethic of love is a middle road between the extremes of authoritarianism and libertarianism. It offers a principle on which to base one's behaviour from situation to situation, but it does not dictate exactly how it should be applied in each situation. This idea is similar to that of Aristotle, except that instead of practical reason telling us how to act in each situation, we are led by love, which is inspired by God's love for the world.

Certainly, those Christians who have aimed to set out how the rule of love actually operates in day-to-day life have produced very interesting accounts, but they are not, perhaps, of lasting ethical value. One of the most interesting is that by Clement of Alexandria, who was a Christian teacher in the second century. Clement was an enormously erudite man, who went out of his way to try to overturn the common prejudice of the time that Christians were stupid – following a barbarous religion with watered-down moral teaching that had been plagiarized from the Greek philosophers. In fact, Clement filled his writings with so many quotations from classical writings that they are an important source for reconstructing the thought of those authors whose works have otherwise been lost. His *The Instructor* presents Christ as the moral teacher of humankind. In fact, the word he uses for 'instructor' (*paidagogos*) is that used for a child's tutor. The work gives a wide variety of ethical maxims for everyday life. We learn that Christians are allowed to make jokes and laugh, but not to excess and never over inappropriate subjects. They should not sleep on beds that are too soft, because that hinders digestion. Women can wear shoes, although they shouldn't have too many, but men can go barefoot or, if they prefer, wear slippers. And Christians should avoid the public bath where possible, but if they do go, they should not expect other people to pour the water over them.

Clement's teachings were, no doubt, very useful to the Christians of his day, who wanted to live a lifestyle that was better than the pagans; in particular, they wanted to avoid what they regarded as an unseemly obsession with bodily things. Clement therefore condemned laziness, gluttony, vanity and so on. Today, however, his teachings seem at best trite and at worst sanctimonious. But more than that, they are determined by the social mores of his day. It is not clear, for example, why lovemaking should be confined to the evening and not allowed in the morning, or why people should avoid sneezing or sitting with their legs crossed. In strictures like these, Clement appealed to what was 'seemly' – in other words, what was generally acceptable or desirable in his society, but not necessarily in ours. It is easy to laugh at

CLEMENT OF
ALEXANDRIA, IN A
TWELFTH-CENTURY
BYZANTINE FRESCO.
DESPITE HIS HALO,
CLEMENT WAS NEVER
OFFICIALLY MADE A
SAINT, PARTLY BECAUSE
SOME OF THE IDEAS IN
HIS WRITINGS WERE JUST
A BIT TOO RADICAL FOR
MORE CONSERVATIVE
TASTES.

the social mores of the past, and no doubt future societies will laugh at what we consider socially acceptable or unacceptable. It is a good argument, though, for Niebuhr's contention that it is dangerous to lay down supposedly permanent moral laws, because any attempt to do so will inevitably be influenced to some degree by temporary cultural assumptions.

Today, perhaps more than ever, the debate goes on over the role of ethics within the Christian message and how it is to be interpreted. In 1993, Pope John Paul II – himself a philosopher of no mean ability – issued an important encyclical, or letter to the whole Catholic Church, on the subject entitled *Veritatis Splendor* ('The splendour of truth'). In it, the pope condemned the kind of ethical theory associated with Niebuhr, according to which we cannot lay down definite rules but must apply the principle of love, taught by Jesus, on a situation-to-situation basis. At the same time, he condemned the attempt to build an ethical system on the basis of human reason alone. Instead, the pope supported the general position of Thomas Aquinas, that there is a fundamental ethical system built into the world, created by God; it is accessible to practical reason, just as the natural world is accessible to theoretical reason, but ethics only makes sense in the light of God, as Barth insisted. The Catholic Church teaches that ethics is a matter of truth, not of mere opinion or preference, and that this truth, like all truth, comes from God. Is the pope right? Such a question cannot be answered in a book like this. But no one who reads his thoughts on the matter, whatever their own religious views, can fail to recognize that there is a great deal of wisdom in what he says, just as there is in the words of many of the other thinkers we have looked at briefly here.

CHAPTER 7

Changing the World

From the earliest days, Christians have been concerned about the injustices of society. Take one of the first Christian writers, Justin Martyr, who wrote in defence of Christianity in the second century and who, in around 165, was beheaded for his pains. Justin not only defended Christians from the attacks and objections of others, but he took the fight to his opponents by criticizing their own practices. In particular, he seized upon the Roman practice of 'exposition' – the abandoning of unwanted babies on hillsides, so that they would either be found by a kind-hearted passer-by or die. Justin denounced exposition as a barbaric practice, and he warned his pagan readers that God commands everyone to lead a good life, and that he will punish or reward everyone according to their actions. Some philosophers, such as the Stoics, believed in fate, the idea that everything we do is predestined and determined. Justin vigorously rejected this idea, asserting instead that every person is responsible for their own actions. His accusations of immorality in society at large were taken up some decades later by the Roman Christian writer Tertullian, who harangued the leaders of the Roman empire not only for exposition but for the savagery of the gladiatorial games, human sacrifice and the common practice of political assassination.

A tale of two cities – subverting society

Of course, there wasn't much that people such as Justin and Tertullian could actually do about the injustices they perceived in society. They were too busy being persecuted themselves to be in a position to change anything. But paradoxically, Christians have sometimes found that they are more effective when they are not in a position of power. It is when Christianity is distinct from the dominant culture of a society, or its political leaders, that Christians can be a voice of dissent. It is a paradox that resonates with many of the Christian values we have seen in this book – the values of Francis of Assisi, embracing poverty as the key to a fuller life, or those of Shusaku Endo, seeing victory in defeat. Jesus himself, after all, was a voice of dissent in his own society, and died as a condemned criminal.

So some Christians have become quite subversive in their attempts to act on their principles. Take the case of Daniel and Philip Berrigan, two American brothers who were both Catholic priests and both leaders of the protest movement against the Vietnam War in the 1960s. In 1968, they were among the Catholic 'Catonsville Nine' who broke into a draft board in Catonsville in Maryland and burned the records. Daniel received three years in prison and Philip three and a half. Philip never gave up

the fight. Although he left the priesthood – marrying a former nun – he retained his strong Christian convictions, above all the firm belief that modern military weapons, especially nuclear weapons, are inherently evil and opposed to God's will. In 1973, he co-founded Jonah House, a simple, monastic-style community in Baltimore dedicated to spreading values of peace, and in 1980, he helped start the Plowshares Movement – a reference to Isaiah 2:4, which promises a future time of peace when 'they shall beat their swords into ploughshares, and their spears into pruning-hooks; nation shall not lift up sword against nation, neither shall they learn war any more'. The group's members break into military installations and attempt to disable nuclear weapons. Philip Berrigan died in late 2002, still preaching a message of peace and railing against the foreign policies of the Bush administration. His brother Daniel, still a Jesuit priest and prominent anti-war activist, writer and poet, presided over his last rites.

Needless to say, not everyone will approve of the Berrigans and their actions. It is a moot point whether or not Christians should break the law in acting on their principles. There is a rather notorious passage in Romans 13, where Paul tells his readers that they must obey the secular authorities at all times, because they are appointed by God. And yet it was those same authorities that were later to order Paul's own death. Clearly, Paul's words should be taken in their historical context – a time when Christians might potentially be regarded as politically subversive, and when it had not yet become clear how extreme the authorities might be in their actions against the Christians. In practice, most Christians have taken the view that civil obedience is a virtue, but that it may be overridden when the authorities act contrary to what is right.

The classic example is Nazi Germany, and many Christians were in the forefront of the fight against the policies of Hitler and his colleagues. This was despite the attempts of the Nazis to infiltrate their ideas through the existing church structure in Germany; indeed, Hitler remained a member of the Catholic Church until his death, at least in name. In 1934, the year that Hitler became Führer of Germany, many Christians formed the 'Confessing Church' to oppose the notion that Christians owed allegiance to anyone other than Christ. Karl Barth, a leading theologian and one of the prime movers behind the Confessing Church, stated that Christians must 'hold the Bible in one hand and the newspaper in the other'. The theologian Rudolf Bultmann, meanwhile, taught that civil disobedience had now become an actual virtue, and it was the duty of Christians to disobey all orders from the Third Reich, no matter how innocuous. Perhaps the most famous Christian to work against Hitler, however, was Dietrich Bonhoeffer. Like Barth and Bultmann, Bonhoeffer was an intellectual, academic theologian, who wrote at length on the problems of making Christianity

> 'Let every person be subject to the governing authorities; for there is no authority except from God, and those authorities that exist have been instituted by God. Therefore whoever resists authority resists what God has appointed, and those who resist will incur judgment.'
>
> Romans 13:1–2

DIETRICH BONHOEFFER, THE CONTROVERSIAL THEOLOGIAN AND ANTI-NAZI CONSPIRACIST, IN A VERY SHARP SUIT.

relevant to a modern world, which was learning to reject the old religious certainties. He had close links with many American theologians, and spent some time in America. In 1939, however, Bonhoeffer left America to return to Germany, stating that he could not stand on the sidelines while his country descended into evil and chaos. Instead, he chose to work for those who resisted the Nazi regime, acting as a liaison with foreign sympathizers and using his prominence in the international church as a cover. However, his activities were watched, and he was imprisoned. In April 1945, as the Red Army was closing in on Germany and Hitler had all but disappeared into madness in his bunker, Bonhoeffer and his co-conspirators were executed.

The experience of Christians such as Bonhoeffer who have stood up to tyrannous regimes reflects the understanding of the world put forward by the great theologian Augustine of Hippo. He lived in a time of transition and uncertainty, as the Roman empire, weakened by corruption and a collapsing political system, found itself beset on every side by hordes of fur-clad warriors from the howling northern wastes. The sacking of Rome by the Visigoths in 410 was, to Augustine's generation, something like the terrorist attacks of 11 September 2001 on the United States – a clear symbol that something fundamental had changed in the world order. It was pointed out by many that this had happened not long after Rome had abandoned its traditional gods for the upstart faith of Christianity.

Augustine wrote his famous *City of God* – one of the most influential books of all time – initially as a response to this problem; but like many authors Augustine had a tendency to overrun his word limit. The project got rather out of hand, and two decades later the indefatigable bishop found that he had written a landmark work in religious thought and political science. Despite the forbidding size and scope of the book, Augustine's basic thesis was quite simple. Humanity is divided into two 'cities' – the earthly city and the heavenly city. Augustine traces their origin to Cain and Abel, the sons of Adam and Eve. Cain killed Abel, and, according to the Old Testament, went on to found a city. For Augustine, this symbolizes the fact that worldliness – the ideal of living within the world, in safety and security – is associated with sin. The heavenly city, by contrast, is a spiritual reality only, and its inhabitants may mix with the populace of the earthly city but their hearts do not lie there. It is almost as if a subversive society, apparently rootless and with no political or social power, were mingled throughout a city.

It is striking that Augustine, influential bishop in a Christian empire, should have set out a vision of the world that puts the heavenly city and the earthly city at odds, and that teaches that political and spiritual power are quite distinct. But of course, to Augustine, both cities are ultimately part of God's plan, and his providence underlies everything that they do. That is why, despite the antagonism of the two cities, the story is ultimately about the city of God, and it is why the book takes that city as its title.

Spin-doctoring and law-making – taking the lead

In the century before Augustine began his short essay on the fall of Rome, Christians had found themselves dealing with a situation that seemed, on the face of it, the exact opposite of what he would describe. After the conversion of Emperor Constantine, Christianity was transformed almost overnight from a forbidden religion, whose practitioners might be arrested or executed, to the favoured faith of the empire. Now the Christians had serious influence over mainstream society. One of the most significant Christian figures who used this new influence to try to change things was the famous bishop Ambrose of Milan.

Ambrose began his career as a lawyer and politician. The son of the prefect of Gallia, he received a splendid education at Rome and quickly rose to become governor of Aemilia-Liguria, which he ruled from Milan. In 374, however, Auxentius, the popular bishop of Milan, died. Crowds gathered at his basilica, and Ambrose joined them as a precaution in case things got out of hand. Unexpectedly, however, a child began shouting, 'Ambrose for bishop!' The crowd took up the cry, and Ambrose, despite having no particular experience in working for the church, found himself elected bishop of Milan. This was the sort of thing that could happen in those days, when it was quite possible to be baptized as a Christian, ordained as a priest and consecrated as a bishop all in the course of one – presumably incredibly long – church service.

Despite the slight irregularity of his election, Ambrose was a very dedicated bishop. After a sabbatical to read up on theology, he set about consolidating the faith throughout Milan and the surrounding region, embarking on an ambitious church-building programme. At the same time, he was determined to lead as holy a life as he could. He was austere and self-denying, even melting down church treasures in order to help the poor. At the same time, he retained the canny political senses he had developed in his secular career. One notable piece of spin-doctoring occurred at the opening of a splendid new cathedral, the Basilica Ambrosiana. Apparently moved by a divine whisper, Ambrose strode through the grounds of the new building and instructed his men to dig at a particular spot. There, before the crowds, they uncovered two skeletons, which the bishop proclaimed (despite having no particular evidence) to be the remains of two Christian martyrs from an earlier century. To acclamations from the crowd, the relics were carried inside and reburied under Ambrose's altar. It was

> 'Why are you disturbed? I will never willingly desert you, although if force is used, I cannot resist it. I can grieve, weep, and groan. Against weapons, soldiers, Goths, my tears are my weapons, for these are a priest's defence. I ought not, I cannot resist in any other way. But to flee and abandon the church is not my way.'
>
> Ambrose of Milan, 'Sermon against Auxentius', to his congregation

AMBROSE OF MILAN,
OOZING AUTHORITY
WITH HIS MAGNIFICENT
ROBES AND BISHOP'S
STAFF, PREVENTS THE
BRUTAL, SKULKING
EMPEROR THEODOSIUS
FROM COMING INTO
CHURCH. PAINTING BY
ANTHONY VAN DYCK,
C. 1619.

clear to everyone that God had blessed the cathedral, Ambrose and the orthodox understanding of Christianity that he promoted.

Ambrose was certainly a clever man. Augustine, who was greatly inspired by listening to him preach, remarked that he was so brilliant, he could even read without moving his lips! In those days, speed reading had not yet been invented, and often people read aloud, even in private, which meant it took a lot longer to read a book than most people take today. His own books were filled with ethical exhortations: Ambrose believed the thing that showed Christianity to be superior to paganism was the lives that Christians led, and he repeatedly implored his readers to lead good lives. In person, Ambrose was enormously charismatic, a brilliant speaker and one who was not afraid to use strong-arm tactics to achieve what he thought was right. Milan and not Rome, by this time, was the usual residence of the emperor of the western half of the Roman empire, and as bishop of the city, Ambrose had his ear. He acted as a sort of unofficial uncle and adviser to the young and rather weak Emperor Gratian, and later to Theodosius the Great, a powerful ruler who not only reunited – briefly – the two halves of the Roman empire but made Christianity its official religion. Together, Theodosius and Ambrose formed a rather uneasy partnership – two strong, charismatic men who recognized each other's power and its potential usefulness but were not willing to compromise on their own ideals. The most famous clash between them occurred in 390, after a rebellion at the city of Thessalonica. Enraged, Theodosius ordered a massacre, in which up to 7,000 people died. Ambrose, aghast at the atrocity, refused to let the emperor enter his church. We are told that he said, 'It seems, Emperor, that you have not thought about your guilt in that great massacre. But now your anger is over, do you not realize how great your crime was? You must not be dazzled by the splendour of the purple that you wear… How could you lift in prayer hands which are stained with the blood of such an unjust massacre? Go away, and do not add to your guilt by committing a second crime.'

The emperor, horrified, confessed his guilt to the bishop, who imposed on him a month of public penance for his crime. After the penance was over, they were reconciled, and Ambrose once again received Theodosius into his church. No doubt Theodosius was well aware that bowing to the accusation of a popular bishop and admitting his guilt might well enhance his own popularity; but, equally, Ambrose was a brave man to speak to the mighty and intemperate emperor in such a way. Some decades earlier, in the time of Constantine and his immediate successors, it had seemed that the state wanted to have authority over the church, as if the church were a sort of 'department of religion'. But now, Ambrose represented a new notion, that the church might claim authority over the state. It was not a civil or political authority but a moral one, born of the idea that right and wrong are determined by the commands of God and that these commands apply equally to all people, even to the emperor in his splendid purple robes.

Not only was the church coming to have authority over the state, but it was also having a radical effect on society. People were beginning to have a sense of social responsibility. In the past, Greeks and Romans alike had idealized the 'city' as the basic unit of human society, and they had regarded the 'citizens' as making up that society. Philanthropists and other wealthy individuals or families would make donations to their city, perhaps to pay for buildings or amenities. Official welfare, where it existed, was distributed according to citizenship, rather than actual need. For example, the Roman empire operated something called the 'annona' system, which shipped food from areas with a surplus to those with a deficit and distributed it to the people. It was a huge endeavour – every year, 5 million pounds of pork was collected from Italy, and 18,400 tons of grain from North Africa. This was why Egypt was so important to the Romans, because it essentially fed the rest of the empire. But people had the right to receive the distributed food if (and only if) they were 'citizens' of the city that was doing the distributing – it had nothing to do with need. No doubt the poverty-stricken benefited from the annona, but so did everyone else. And, it seems, there were plenty of poor people in the Roman empire – not simply the destitute and the hungry, but the equivalent of the lower working classes, who may have had a roof over their heads but lived hand to mouth and were very vulnerable to economic change. In an age where, apart from the annona, there was virtually no state assistance or welfare provision to the economically disadvantaged, people like this could easily become homeless and hungry. Moreover, the cult of the 'citizen' meant that foreigners had no place in the ideal image of the 'city'. Depending on 'the kindness of strangers', as Blanche DuBois did in the play *A Streetcar Named Desire*, would not get you very far in classical Greece or Rome.

The Christians, however, helped to turn this whole system around. For them, humanity was not divided between 'citizens' and 'non-citizens', it was divided between rich and poor. And 'poor', in this context, meant not only the destitute, but those vulnerable to poverty – traditionally, widows and orphans – as well as foreigners and other strangers. Christians believed that it was their duty to try to help these people. We have already seen Jesus' command in Matthew 19:21 to sell everything and give to the poor, and the tradition went back to the Old Testament too. Job 29:11–16 states:

When the ear heard, it commended me, and when the eye saw, it approved; because I delivered the poor who cried, and the orphan who had no helper. The blessing of the wretched came upon me, and I caused the widow's heart to sing for joy. I put on righteousness, and it clothed me; my justice was like a robe and a turban. I was eyes to the blind, and feet to the lame. I was a father to the needy, and I championed the cause of the stranger.

This ideal was deeply inspirational to the early Christians. In the middle of the fourth

'*The poor are our brothers and sisters… people in the world who need love, who need care, who have to be wanted.*'

Mother Teresa of Calcutta,
in *Time* magazine,
29 December 1975

century, Basil the Great, soon to become bishop of Caesarea in Cappadocia (in modern-day Turkey), preached a scorching sermon entitled 'Against the Rich', in which he railed at wealthy landowners who refused to share with the starving:

You miserable people! How will you answer the Great Judge? You cover your bare walls with tapestries, and do not clothe the naked. You adorn your horses with the most rich and expensive trappings, and despise your brother who wears rags. You allow the corn in your granaries to rot or be eaten by vermin, and you do not even bother to glance at those who have no bread. You hoard your wealth, and do not bother to look upon those who are worn and oppressed by necessity! You will say to me: 'How am I doing wrong if I hoard what belongs to me?' And I ask you: 'What are the things that you think belong to you? From whom did you receive them? You act like someone who goes to a theatre, and having sat in the seats that others might have taken, tries to stop everyone else from coming in, taking for himself what should have been used by everyone.' And so it is with the rich, who having been the first to gain what should be common to all, keep it for themselves and hold onto it. If everyone took only what he needed, and gave the rest to those in need, there would be neither rich nor poor.

There was, at the time, a famine in Cappadocia, and by preaching in this way, Basil was not only standing up for the starving people of his city but casting himself in the role of Old Testament prophet, taking the great and the good to task over social justice – just as Ambrose did with the emperor. He was successful: the rich did open their storehouses to the poor, and Basil himself did the same thing. He set up food distribution centres, and as bishop, he established a famous institution known as the 'Basileus' – a sort of hostel and hospital in one for the poor, hungry and foreigners. In fact, it was a particularly well-known example of a Christian institution that was springing up all over the empire in the fourth century – the *xenodocheion* ('house for strangers') or *ptocheion* ('place for the poor'). These buildings, which had no real equivalent in the pre-Christian period, were remarkably successful – in fact, by the end of the fourth century, one of the church's major roles was that of a public welfare system. In 362, the emperor Julian the Apostate (so called because he rejected Christianity and tried to make the empire revert to paganism) ordered the establishment of pagan *xenodocheia* on the model of the Christian ones. He thought it shocking that the Christians should be so much better at charity than the pagans.

In fact, of course, not only were the Christians leading the practice of charity, they were largely responsible for the new notion that it was a good thing to do in the first place. By thinking in terms of helping 'the poor', Christians were making society broader and more inclusive than it had been in classical times. In place of the old ideal of the 'city' and its 'citizens', society was now broadened to include everyone, even the most outcast. This more holistic notion was the basis for the medieval view of society, where everyone, no matter how great or how lowly, had a place.

And the church, especially its bishops, played a key role in that society. Not only was the bishop increasingly regarded as the person whose main job it was to protect the poor and the weak, but he had a vital judicial function too. The emperor Constantine set up the 'episcopal audience', whereby the local bishop acted as a judge in dealing with lawsuits and other disputes. People could agree to have the bishop arbitrate in their problem, but they had to accept his decision as final. It was, of course, a canny move on Constantine's part, since it not only gained him prestige among the bishops but helped unclog the legal system by shifting some of its responsibilities elsewhere. It was a great success – bishops found that much of their time was spent dealing with local legal problems, and they proved so good at it that many people converted to Christianity simply to be able to use the service. It was, of course, free, since no lawyers were involved – and lawyers in ancient times were just as expensive as they are today.

This Christianizing of society and the law would have great results later. It was one of the underlying principles of the radical reorganization of the Roman law that the Byzantine emperor Justinian oversaw in the sixth century. In the past, Roman law had operated on a case-by-case basis, made up of various precedents, judgments, imperial commands and other laws, resulting in a confused mass of legal material. In his *Corpus Juris Civilis*, Justinian aimed to reorganize the whole thing and set it on some simple principles. Part of the *Corpus*, the *Institutes*, stated that, 'The precepts of the law are these: to live honestly, to injure no one, and to give every man his due,' and the body of the text sought to apply this consistently to everyone. This system was the 'Roman Law' that would later become central to modern European legal systems. And it was based upon the notion that there are certain natural laws that God has established in the world, which operate universally, among high and low alike. These ideas would become deeply entrenched in the Western mind. Today, most Western countries – with the exception of Britain – have legal systems that derive their laws from a set of basic principles. Documents as important as the American Declaration of Independence or the European Charter of Human Rights can therefore be traced back to the ideas of the Christian legal system of Justinian.

A similar reorganization of the law on fundamental principles occurred two centuries later, in the Christian empire of Charlemagne that we looked at in chapter 4. Just as in the Byzantine empire, the legal system was a mass of ad hoc legislation; but Charlemagne had the additional headache that the different peoples he ruled over all had their own legal traditions. Saxons, for example, obeyed Saxon law, and they'd be damned if they were going to bow to some strange foreign laws from the Franks. Agobard, the energetic and rationalist bishop of Lyons, was especially pained by the situation. Lyons, being something of a crossroads of the empire, had several sizeable populations from different areas, and since they all doggedly followed their own laws,

'Conscious of its spiritual and moral heritage, the [European] Union is founded on the indivisible, universal values of human dignity, freedom, equality and solidarity; it is based on the principles of democracy and the rule of law. It places the individual at the heart of its activities, by establishing the citizenship of the Union and by creating an area of freedom, security and justice.'

Charter of Fundamental Rights of the European Union

nobody really knew what was happening. A person could commit a crime under one law, be prosecuted under another and convicted under a third, and then get away scot-free because nobody knew which one to enforce.

Charlemagne began by having all this morass of legal traditions written down, since many of the tribes preserved their laws only orally. He then set about issuing imperial decrees that could underlie or override these local laws throughout the empire. These 'capitularies' addressed what he considered the most important legal issues to resolve, and they always replaced any other laws on the subject that different people had. In this way, Charlemagne hoped to preserve a sense of ethnicity and continuity throughout his empire, keeping age-old traditions that had stood people in good stead, but also to have uniformity and clarity. The Capitulary of the Missi of 802 set out Charlemagne's purpose in his lawgiving: 'Everyone shall live entirely in accordance with God's commands, justly and under a just rule, and everyone shall be ordered to live in harmony with his colleagues in his job or profession.'

> '*Our task is, with the aid of divine piety, to defend the holy church of Christ with arms... Your task, most holy father, is to lift up your hands to God, like Moses, to aid our troops.*'
>
> Charlemagne,
> in a letter to
> Pope Leo III, AD 796

Conquistadors and missionaries

It looks like, if Augustine was right to analyse human society in terms of the heavenly and the earthly cities, the interplay between them is pretty complex. After all, what happens when the earthly city – when the political powers that be – are meant to be

'The Spaniards have shown not the slightest consideration for these people, treating them (and I speak from first-hand experience, having been there from the outset) not as brute animals – indeed, I would to God they had done and had shown them the consideration they afford their animals – so much as piles of dung in the middle of the road… One fact in all this is widely known and beyond dispute, for even the tyrannical murderers themselves acknowledge the truth of it: the indigenous peoples never did the Europeans any harm whatever; on the contrary, they believed them to have descended from the heavens, at least until they or their fellow citizens had tasted, at the hands of these oppressors, a diet of robbery, murder, violence, and all other manner of trials and tribulations.'

Bartolome de Las Casas,
History of the Indies

Christian? And what happens when other Christians start to speak out against them? One place where Christianity has been a powerful force within society, both as an authority and as a more subversive element, is South America.

One of the most well-known priests among the first Europeans in the New World was Bartolomeo de Olmedo, who accompanied the expedition of Hernán Cortés to Central America. Cortés's journey had been commissioned by the Spanish governor of Cuba, but the governor grew alarmed at the scale of Cortés's preparations and tried to stop him. Cortés was therefore technically a man on the run when he and his troops discovered the mighty civilization of the Aztecs, and rather than return to Cuba, he felt that he had little choice but to conquer the people he found and settle there. Olmedo did his best to act as a restraining force on the expedition – he opposed the massacres that Cortés ordered, and he also criticized his attempts to impose Christianity on the Aztecs by tearing down their idols and replacing them with Christian symbols. Olmedo felt it was better to persuade the Aztecs by setting a good example, until they felt moved to tear down the idols themselves. Unfortunately, Olmedo's influence came to little, and the Aztecs were roundly defeated by a combination of Cortés's forces, native groups who allied themselves with them against the Aztecs – who had been suppressing them for years – and the smallpox which the Europeans unwittingly brought with them. Cortés himself, despite being little more than a mercenary adventurer, ended his days in wealthy and lauded retirement in Spain.

Although the conquistadors and the Spanish settlers often treated the native Americans cruelly, the priests and missionaries who accompanied them tended to be much more humane. Indeed, many of them were revered by the natives. There was a strong tradition in their religion of suffering pain in the service of the gods, and they were naturally impressed by the ascetic and self-denying lifestyles of many of the missionaries, especially the friars. Moreover, many of the friars defended the natives and preached on their behalf to the settlers. On Christmas Day in 1511 in Hispaniola, the Dominican Antonio de Montesimos told the settlers that as Christians they were bound to love the Amerindians as themselves, for they were human beings just like them. Montesimos was a passionate campaigner for the rights of the Amerindians, although his attempts to persuade the king of Spain to stop the abuses came to nothing. He ended his days in Puerto Rico, which he largely converted to Christianity.

The contrast between the settlers and conquistadors, who sought to impose themselves on the New World and plunder it for all the wealth they could, and the Christian clerics, who showed genuine concern for the peoples of the lands they were exploring, came out most strongly in the life of Bartolome de Las Casas – the first in a long line of Christians in South America who were concerned about social justice. Las Casas's life revolved around the New World from his earliest years. When he was a teenager, his father, a soldier, accompanied Christopher Columbus on his first voyage of discovery to the Americas. He made his fortune there and was able to send Bartolome to the prestigious University of Salamanca, where he studied divinity and law. In 1498, Las Casas accompanied Columbus on his third voyage of discovery, and in 1502, he travelled with the conquistador Gonzalo Fernández de Oviedo and settled in Hispaniola, hoping to make his fortune like his father. However, he soon became concerned at the plight of the native slaves that the European settlers kept there, and he released all of his own. He spent the rest of his life – nearly fifty years – campaigning on their behalf.

In 1510, Las Casas became the first priest to be ordained in the Americas. The year after, he accompanied the expedition to conquer Cuba. Here, he witnessed further cruelties against the natives: Hatuey, the chief who led the resistance to the invaders, was captured and sentenced to be burned alive. Las Casas pleaded for him to be spared but was overruled. Hatuey was given the chance to convert to Christianity so that he might go to heaven after his death. According to Las Casas's account, Hatuey refused on the grounds that he did not wish to share eternity with white men.

Las Casas returned to Spain in 1516 to plead for the Amerindians. He was concerned not about the institution of slavery itself but the way the slaves were treated – not only were their lands stolen by the Europeans, but under the system known as *repartimiento*, the Spanish landowners had sole responsibility for what went on in their own territories. It was, in effect, a feudal system, one that was open to abuse depending on who the landowners were; and many forced the natives to work for negligible wages and under the lash.

The regent of Spain, Cardinal Francisco Jiménez y Cisneros, was impressed by Las Casas's pleas, appointed him protector of the Amerindians and commissioned him to return to America and set up a better-run colony in Santo Domingo. The mission failed owing to the natives' distrust of settlers. Las Casas, discouraged by his failure, joined the Dominicans.

However, he never stopped campaigning on behalf of the Amerindians. He wrote a number of books describing their suffering under the Spanish in such lurid terms that the English used them as anti-Spanish propaganda. He proposed the importation of Africans to the Americas to work instead of the natives, believing that Africans were hardier. Ironically, then, Las Casas's efforts on behalf of the Amerindians were a contributing factor in the development of the black slave trade. However, Las Casas

wanted all workers in the Americas to be properly looked after and paid. He was just as opposed to cruelty to Africans as he was to cruelty to Americans.

In 1540, he went back to Spain, and was a major force behind the new laws of 1542 that protected the Amerindians' rights. He returned to America to help enforce the laws – a difficult task, since most people simply ignored them. While there, he was made bishop of Chiapas. In 1547, Las Casas returned to Spain once more, never to return to the Americas. He continued the campaign, though, scoring a significant success with a conference at Vallodolid in 1550, at which he eloquently defended the rights of the Amerindians. This was, in effect, the first conference on human rights ever held.

A century later, Las Casas's ideals were continued by, above all, the Jesuits, who worked hard on behalf of the native peoples of South America – most spectacularly, as we have seen in chapter 4, in Paraguay. One of the most prominent Jesuits at the time was the Portuguese-born Antonio Vieira. Vieira grew up in Brazil, where he became a Jesuit priest, one of those incredible Jesuits of learning and brilliance who populated the seventeenth century. He spent much time in Portugal as a diplomat, politician, military mastermind, preacher and writer, where he argued that all citizens should pay taxes equally, and preached against the excesses of the Inquisition. But he also spent years travelling Brazil, living with the natives, translating the catechism into their languages and preaching the Christian message of peace and love. When he wasn't doing that, he was infuriating the Brazilian slave owners by campaigning for the rights of the slaves. Vieira was one of the leading lights of the seventeenth-century Catholic Church, but his ideals made him a lot of enemies, in both Brazil and Portugal. He died in some disgrace in Brazil in 1697, but he has since been revered as one of the most important and admirable figures in Portuguese history.

Sleeping fish and red bishops – Christians in modern Latin America

A modern heir to the principles of Las Casas and those like him is Samuel Ruiz García, who like Las Casas also served as bishop in Chiapas – in a diocese now named after the city of San Cristóbal de Las Casas in southern Mexico. García became Catholic bishop of the city, and the cathedral founded by Las Casas himself, in 1959 and served in the post for forty years, during which time he championed human rights issues in a wide variety of ways. He was, in particular, concerned about the plight of the indigenous people of southern Mexico, commenting that, before he became a bishop, he had been like a sleeping fish – his eyes were open, but he did not see. Like many well-off Mexicans, he viewed the indigenous people as essentially passive, there to be helped and educated, but unlikely to make any useful cultural or religious contributions of their own. After his appointment, however, he spent considerable time with the people, and found that *they* were opening *his* eyes, not the other way around. A group of indigenous wise men challenged him by asking if his God was interested just in souls, or in bodies too. Well over two-thirds of all Mexicans live below the poverty line, and the plight of the indigenous peoples in the south is especially dire. García dedicated his ministry to raising awareness of their situation and campaigning for better conditions. He did this in partnership with secular groups in the region, although he condemned those that advocated the use of violence in the struggle. Samuel Ruiz García has always insisted that the church does not simply contain poor people, or have a particular mission to the poor. The poor are actually its mission. It exists to serve the poor, and its poorest members are, paradoxically, its most important. In his case, his interest has been in indigenous peoples around the world, not just in Mexico, and he has worked tirelessly to provide them with material help as well as spiritual.

García's work on their behalf has certainly not gone unnoticed by the people. In 1994, the indigenous people of Chiapas rose up in armed rebellion against the new

THE DIMINUTIVE BUT
CHARISMATIC 'RED BISHOP',
DOM HÉLDER CÂMARA.

North American Free Trade Agreement, which they felt threatened their livelihoods and looked likely to plunge them even further into poverty. They asked García to moderate their negotiations with the government. In 2000, UNESCO awarded him the Simon Bolivar Prize, which is given every two years to those judged to have made an outstanding contribution to the dignity and freedom of peoples around the world, and which has formerly been given to such figures as Nelson Mandela.

There has been a whole host of priests and bishops like Samuel Ruiz García, who have identified with and worked on behalf of the poor in Latin America. One of the most famous throughout the world was Hélder Câmara, who in 1931, as he celebrated his first Mass at the age of twenty-two, tried to preach in the most elegant and learned words he knew. One of his teachers told him to stop being foolish – that from now on he was to speak for simple and humble people. As priest, bishop and, later, archbishop of Olinda and Recife in Brazil, he spent his life doing just that. Câmara was desperately concerned about human rights and spoke out against oppression throughout the world, especially that of the rich nations against the poor ones. The arms trade and destruction of the environment were, in his eyes, all part of the same problem, and he bitterly attacked the Brazilian government for its human rights abuses, earning their hatred. Not only did he spend nine years officially not existing, with all references to him in the media forbidden, but there were assassination attempts made against him. Many of the assassins sent against him could not bring themselves to kill him and instead confessed all and asked his forgiveness. The government nicknamed him 'the Red Bishop'. Câmara commented once, 'When I give food to the poor, they call me a saint. When I ask why the poor have no food, they call me a Communist.'

To the people, the physically tiny bishop was known simply as Dom Hélder. He identified with their simplicity to such a degree as to share it: as archbishop, he renounced the palace that went with the post and lived instead in a single back room of the church, furnished with little more than a table, a sink and a hammock. Instead of using an official car, he hitchhiked around the city.

Like Mahatma Gandhi in India, he was deeply committed to peaceful protest and the repudiation of violence and he organized the movement Justice and Peace Action to promote these ideals. The movement was made up in part of what were known as 'Abrahamic minorities' – small groups at the local level that were committed to observing and understanding the plight of the poor and helping them in their own areas. These groups transcended the Catholic Church to include members from all faith traditions, including humanists and atheists. Dom Hélder was nominated four times for the Nobel Peace Prize, and when he died in 1999, the Brazilian president declared three days of national mourning.

OSCAR ROMERO,
PHOTOGRAPHED IN
1979.

A similar campaigner for human rights, who was certainly not honoured by an official mourning period, was Oscar Arnulfo Romero, the enormously popular Catholic Archbishop of San Salvadore, the capital of El Salvador. Through his brave words and acts on behalf of his people, Romero himself became a victim of the violence he denounced – assassinated while saying Mass in March 1980.

El Salvador was, at the time, not a pleasant place to be. One of the smallest and least powerful of the Central American nations, the country had suffered political instability for years, being ruled by various military juntas since the 1930s. The 1970s saw not only a repressive right-wing military government but the rise of popular left-wing terrorism in protest against it. Political assassinations and 'disappearances' were rife, a situation that did not change with the seizing of power in 1979 by yet another military-sponsored junta. The country degenerated into what was, in effect, civil war. By 1980, 3,000 people were dying every month.

Oscar Arnulfo Romero was appointed archbishop of San Salvadore in 1977. He owed his appointment largely to the fact that he was seen as a rather insipid figure, a good theologian but hardly one who was likely to cause a fuss. Just a couple of weeks after his appointment, however, one of his priests, Rutilio Grande, was murdered. Grande, a close friend of Romero, had spoken out on behalf of the poor peasants against the landowners. Romero drove out to the country church in which his friend's body was lying, where he met the poverty-stricken congregation and vowed to continue the fight that Grande had begun. From that day on, Romero enraged the authorities by consistently denouncing their policies and pleading for the lot of the people. He set up a permanent commission to defend human rights in El Salvador, and he wrote to President Carter of the United States, pleading with him to stop sending money and weapons to the El Salvador government. Several of his fellow bishops denounced him to Rome as a rabble-rousing demagogue. But Romero's political activities were the direct result of his Christian faith. He was a deeply devout man, who would often be spotted slipping out of meetings to go to the chapel to pray. But like Samuel Ruiz García, he believed that understanding the lot of the poor is the key to understanding Christianity. Rather than thinking of the church in terms of bishops and priests, we should recognize that the bulk of its membership is ordinary people. And the poor are not just there to be passively helped – things can change for the better only when they are allowed to take control themselves. Romero believed that the task of the church is to challenge sin in the world around it, which must involve attacking institutions that perpetuate sin. To ignore that sin is to be complicit in it and take the sin into the church itself.

Every week, Romero made radio broadcasts in which he condemned the use of

> 'I am bound, as a pastor, by divine command to give my life for those whom I love, and that is all Salvadoreans, even those who are going to kill me.'
>
> Oscar Romero,
> in a newspaper interview
> two weeks before his death

terror and government death squads and called on soldiers to disobey immoral orders. His radio station became the most listened-to in the country, and his cathedral was invariably crowded by those who came to hear him preach. In a state where those who opposed the government were liable to be assassinated at any time, Romero became increasingly aware that his own death was likely. But he recognized that his Christian faith would not allow him to compromise and would, on the contrary, vindicate him. On one famous occasion, he stated, 'I must tell you, as a Christian, I do not believe in death without resurrection. If I am killed, I shall arise in the Salvadoran people.' On 24 March 1980, he preached a sermon on 1 Corinthians 15, where Paul states that before the body can be raised it must die, like a grain of wheat being planted in the ground. He told the congregation that those who dedicate their lives to the service of the poor are like that grain of wheat and are promised a bountiful harvest. Finishing the sermon, Romero stepped up to the altar to say Mass and was shot through the heart by a sniper. Such was his popularity that his assassination sparked an armed insurrection by the people, and the war continued until peace was finally established in 1992. Over the preceding twelve years, the US government, fearful of the possibility of a socialist regime taking power in El Salvador, had donated $6 billion to the government's war chest – despite their knowledge of how the money was spent.

Pope John Paul II has visited Oscar Romero's tomb on more than one occasion, and the process of his beatification – making him officially 'Blessed', one step below a saint – is under way.

Figures such as Samuel Ruiz García, Dom Hélder and Oscar Arnulfo Romero are modern representatives of a tradition that is as old as South American Christianity itself. Ever since the first missionaries came over with the conquistadors, the people of the continent embraced Catholicism, and the church, in turn, played a major role in their lives. The centrality of the Catholic Church to South American culture means that it has been at the heart of the revolutions and other social upheavals of the continent, and this in turn has had a major impact on how the church sees itself in that part of the world. The work of these Catholic figures helped to give rise to what became known as 'liberation theology', named after the 1971 book by the most famous theorist of the movement, Gustavo Gutiérrez. Gutiérrez and others like him argued passionately that theology should focus not on doctrine – as it had tended to do, historically, in the West – but on practice. How we behave is at least as important as what we believe. Moreover, they argued that the church's mission is primarily to the poor, and that God himself sides with the poor. They sought, in other words, to take seriously the teachings of Jesus on the poor that we saw in the last chapter.

To many, liberation theology was Marxism disguised as Christianity; but the

> '*The Gospel is proclaimed to the poor by means of concrete deeds. When Jesus made human beings see and walk and hear and, in short, gave them life, he was giving an example for that time and mandate to the Christian community throughout history... There is no authentic evangelization that is not accompanied by action on behalf of the poor.*'
>
> Gustavo Gutiérrez,
> *A Theology of Liberation*

liberation theologians insisted that, although they looked for God's help in this world rather than in the hereafter, their focus was always on *God* as the agent of salvation. True Marxism, by contrast, focuses only on material things and the agency of human beings alone. Throughout the 1970s, liberation theology made a great impact on Christianity throughout the world. In 1975, Pope Paul VI issued his apostolic exhortation *Evangelii Nuntiandi* on the importance of preaching the Christian message to those outside the church. In it, he devoted considerable space to the issue of liberation theology, welcoming the new emphasis on helping people's material situation as well as their spiritual welfare but arguing that the two go hand in hand. The pope taught that it is the love of God that inspires the church to help the oppressed, just as it is the love of God that inspires the church to preach the good news. Without that inspiration of God's love, and without keeping God in view as the final goal, any purely human endeavour to achieve social change and improvement will be ultimately doomed.

Christians and racial inequality

The ideals of liberation theology influenced similar movements in other parts of the world. In North America, for example, they took the form of the movement known as 'black theology'. The movement was born, in part, from the civil rights revolutions of the 1960s, a period of great change that owed an enormous amount to Christianity.

Christianity, in fact, had been central to African-American culture for many decades. The slaves of North America brought their ancestral religions with them to America, and for a long time, the slave owners were reluctant to encourage their conversion to Christianity – they were worried that if their slaves became Christians, they might have to let them go. It was eventually decided, however, that it was perfectly all right to have a Christian slave, and by the end of the nineteenth century, the religion was firmly entrenched in black communities across America. But Christianity did not mean quite the same thing to these people as it did to most white people. For one thing, it was often mingled with elements of the old African religions, producing exotic cults such as that of Voodoo, most often associated with the New Orleans area but widespread throughout the southern United States in the early decades of the twentieth century. Equally important was Christianity's emphasis on liberation. To the black slaves, and their twentieth-century descendants whose lives were little better, the Christian message represented the hope of future happiness. Gospel and spiritual songs from the period are dominated by biblical imagery of

THE ONLY KNOWN PHOTO OF THE TEXAN SINGER BLIND WILLIE JOHNSON. JOHNSON DIED IN 1947 AFTER HIS HOUSE CAUGHT FIRE. HE SURVIVED THE FIRE, BUT THE WATER USED TO PUT IT OUT LEFT HIS MATTRESS SODDEN, AND AFTER SLEEPING ON IT HE CAUGHT PNEUMONIA AND DIED.

heaven or the kingdom of God. Take the work of, for example, Blind Willie Johnson, a popular but rather scary character whose records combined stunning slide-guitar work with false-bass singing that sounds like the devil himself is trying to scare you into repenting of your sins. A glance at a list of his songs, released in the 1920s and 30s, reveals titles such as 'Bye and Bye I'm going to see the King', 'God moves on the Water', 'Trouble Will Soon Be Over', and 'Keep Your Lamp Trimmed and Burning'. Many of these songs not only look forward to the coming of God's kingdom but exhort the listeners to moral behaviour, reminding them that they shall reap what they sow – something that might apply to white people as well as black. Of course, in order to have their work recorded, singers such as Blind Willie Johnson had to keep the message fairly coded, but it was quite clear all the same: things are miserable now, but one day God will sort it out, and then the tables will be turned. Although the songs suggest that one must wait until heaven for this to happen, there is always the underlying hint that it might happen in this world too.

These were the days of 'Jim Crow', when black and white Americans were segregated in most areas of life, particularly in the South. Some churches tried to resist the colour bar. For example, the Pentecostal movement, which began in California in the early years of the twentieth century, prided itself on overcoming racial barriers and welcoming mixed congregations. For the most part, however, black and white churches were quite separate. There was a sense, then, in which black Christianity had developed separately from white Christianity. If black people were Christians – and, by the twentieth century, Christianity was deeply ingrained in American black culture – what they believed was *their* religion, not something that had been imposed on them. To these people, the Bible told the story of a God who sided with the oppressed – who led the Hebrews out of slavery in Egypt and who suffered with an oppressed people, dying with them, only to rise again and offer the promise of resurrection to others. Little wonder that the figure of Moses crops up again and again in black spiritual songs: 'Moses stood on the Red Sea shore, smoting at the water with a two by four. Well, if I could, I surely would, stand on the rock where Moses stood!'

This is the context in which Martin Luther King Jr grew up. The son and grandson of pastors of the Ebenezer Baptist Church in Atlanta, Georgia, King was an outstanding student at the black schools of his city and went on to study theology in Pennsylvania, where he found himself mixing with mostly white students. He was

awarded a doctorate from Boston University before returning to the South to become pastor of the Dexter Avenue Baptist Church in Montgomery, Alabama.

It was an upbringing that gave King a remarkably wide Christian background. On the one hand, his childhood in Georgia and his pastorate in Alabama meant that his roots were in the Christian world of the black South, with its emphasis on the hope of divine salvation. But on the other, his education at liberal east-coast colleges – an education that most southern black pastors would not have had – immersed him in the world of traditional liberal Christianity, of European-dominated theology and intellectual issues. Even as a child, King found himself questioning many of the beliefs that his family held unreservedly. He felt that the relatively liberal education he had received in Europe-based theology helped to bring a sense of critical reflection to his basic Christian belief in social justice and activism. At the same time, he recognized a strong element of politics even in the academic theology he was learning. For example, he discovered the work of Reinhold Niebuhr, whom we met in the last chapter, and absorbed his insistence on Christianity's need to address social injustice.

That dedication to social activism had been instilled in King from his earliest years. His grandfather had been a leading light in the establishment of the National Association for the Advancement of Colored People (the NAACP). And his father, Martin Luther King Sr, had believed that his ministry must be focused on the here-and-now needs of his congregation rather than otherworldly spirituality. He not only used church resources to help the poor but campaigned vigorously for black rights. King Jr, by the time he was working in Alabama, was also on the executive committee of the NAACP, and he helped to organize a huge, year-long boycott of Alabama's buses, in protest against the rules that segregated black and white people on them – a protest that was successful in having the segregation laws pronounced unconstitutional. King quickly became one of the most prominent figures of the civil rights movement, and in 1958, he became president of the Southern Christian Leadership Conference.

Over the following ten years, King established himself as one of the most widely-recognized people in America, and he gained a global following for his eloquent defence of human rights – something he summed up in his notion of 'somebodiness': that everyone, no matter what their race or background, is 'somebody' of worth. Inspired by Mahatma Gandhi in India, King was convinced that protestors had to use nonviolent means to achieve their goals. In this, he differed from the more militant activists for equal rights, such as the Nation of Islam, which campaigned for a separate black state. Its charismatic spokesman, Malcolm X, left the Nation of Islam to found his own movement, the Muslim Mosque, and instead called for a more inclusive ideal, preaching that the values of Islam might transcend racial boundaries. However, Malcolm continued to argue that only through empowered resistance could black people achieve equality, a notion that was reflected in the Black Power movement spearheaded by Stokely Carmichael. But while he worked with and respected both Malcolm X and Carmichael, Martin Luther King Jr argued that the Black Power movement represented a distortion of the true values of equality and nonviolence. He believed that it threatened to exacerbate the divisions between the races. Moreover, it was opposed to the renunciation of power that, as we saw in the last chapter, has been a vital thread running through Christianity from the teaching of Jesus onwards. King believed that turning the other cheek would, in the long run, prove far more powerful and effective than the proactive self-defence advocated by Malcolm X. It would not only liberate blacks from their unequal social status but liberate whites from their unjust outlook too, by demonstrating the dignity and worth of black people.

In this way, King preached racial integration and harmony. In his famous 'I have a dream' speech, delivered to a huge crowd of nonviolent protestors in Washington in 1963, he described his dream of a nation where the differences of the past were put aside and the descendants of slaves and of slave owners alike might live in harmony. That year, he was *Time* magazine's Man of the Year, and in 1964, he received the Nobel Peace Prize – but he donated the money to the civil rights movement.

In 1968, Martin Luther King Jr was shot while standing on a hotel balcony in Memphis. Riots erupted across the United States, resulting in 20,000 arrests. The governor of Alabama, stating that King had been an enemy of the United States, refused to attend his funeral; but 50,000 others walked in the funeral procession, including the four presidential candidates for that year, among them Richard Nixon. But King's body was carried on a farm cart, reflecting his concerns for – and identification with – the poor. Today, the United States celebrates Martin Luther King Jr Day every January. He is the only individual, apart from Christopher Columbus, to have a US national holiday named after him.

The struggle of Martin Luther King Jr for black rights parallels the struggle of many of the South American Catholics for the poor and indigenous people of that continent. And South American liberation theology is mirrored in the work of one of the most influential American black Christian writers, James Cone. Like King, Cone grew up within the black Christian community in the southern United States – in his case, in Arkansas – but later discovered European-style liberal theology when he went to university. He tried to use the critical tools this education gave him to express more clearly the ideals of freedom that he experienced in his background, a programme that produced his book *Black Theology and Black Power*, published in 1969. In this and his subsequent works, Cone tried to re-establish a connection with black Americans' African roots, to draw inspiration from their traditional culture in understanding modern black Christianity. From this perspective, 'white Christianity', where that acts to suppress the black voice, is actually a heresy, a distorted Christianity that has sold out to the culture of power. Instead, Cone argued that God sides – and identifies – with the oppressed to such an extent that we can talk about God's 'blackness'. Where the black Christian slaves had looked to the God who liberated the Hebrews and thought of Christ's suffering on the cross as God's identification with his suffering people, Cone urges people to come to grips with the fact that Christ himself was not white, and that the resurrection of this tortured member of an ethnic minority brings with it the hope of salvation to black people everywhere. For Cone, 'blackness' transcends the physical fact of being a black person and represents suffering groups or those who identify with such groups. Of course, God is not literally black, any more than he is white, but when we talk of him as 'black', we express the fact that he sides with the oppressed and works for their freedom. Similarly, people of any race can share in this 'blackness' if they do the same.

> 'There can be no Christian theology that is not identified unreservedly with those who are humiliated and abused. In fact, theology ceases to be a theology of the gospel when it fails to arise out of the community of the oppressed.'
>
> James Cone,
> *A Black Theology of Liberation*

A RALLY AGAINST APARTHEID, HELD BY STUDENTS AT WITWATERSRAND UNIVERSITY, JOHANNESBURG IN 1989, IS BROKEN UP BY POLICE WITH TEAR GAS.

Another country that has had a less than perfect record in race relations in modern times is South Africa, and here again Christians played a prominent role in the fight against apartheid. The apartheid system evolved in the 1940s and 50s, when the South African government enacted a series of laws categorizing everyone as black, white or 'coloured' (everyone else), and tried to keep them all segregated as far as possible. Black people were assigned to large reservations within the country, known as 'homelands', the idea being that they retained rights in these homelands, such as the right to vote, but lost them in the rest of the country. Protests and demonstrations against the system were dealt with through the declaration of 'states of emergency', under which even nonviolent protestors could be locked up indefinitely and often tortured. It was an abuse of human rights that led the United Nations to impose increasingly severe sanctions on the country throughout the 1970s and 80s. The economic pressure of these sanctions helped to bring about the dismantling of the apartheid system, and in 1994, the first elections in which everyone could vote equally were held, resulting in the election of the black rights activist Nelson Mandela to the position of president.

Christians were reacting against apartheid as early as 1955, when the Anglican priest Trevor Huddleston published *Naught for Your Comfort*, bitterly attacking the system. As a white man opposing racism by whites, Huddleston made a great impact both within South Africa and globally, and he was expelled from the country. He continued to work for the underprivileged, and as bishop of Stepney in London fought for the rights of Asian immigrants, but he never stopped fighting apartheid, becoming president of the Anti-Apartheid Movement and eventually returning to Johannesburg to a rapturous welcome in 1991.

Sadly, not all Christians regarded apartheid as wrong, and indeed the Dutch Reformed Church taught that segregation of the races was part of God's plan for humanity. Even so, some from within this church spoke out, the most prominent being another white cleric, Christiaan Frederick Beyers Naudé. He believed that apartheid was wrong and was not sanctioned by the Bible, a belief that was shared by the World Council of Churches. The Dutch Reformed Church withdrew from the council and expelled Beyers Naudé, who set up a Christian Institute to promote Christian unity among the races. The organization became increasingly militant, and its members were subject to investigation or having their passports confiscated, but it succeeded in its aims of raising awareness of the plight of black South Africans around the world.

However, perhaps the most famous Christian in the struggle for equal rights during the apartheid period was Desmond Tutu, probably the best-known and most respected non-Catholic Christian priest in the world. He was inspired, in part, by Trevor Huddleston, whom he met as a child and who he later said had shown him and many others that not all white men were bad. Tutu made his name in the 1970s and 80s as a rising star of black Christianity in South Africa, becoming the first black General Secretary of the South African Council of Churches in 1978 (a post in which he was succeeded by Beyers Naudé), and the first black Archbishop of Cape Town in 1986. Like Martin Luther King Jr, he became something of a focus for the equal rights movement, and like him, he made nonviolent protest central to his policy (something that Nelson Mandela did not do). Tutu's Christian faith has been as central to his outlook as it was to King. We saw in chapter 5 that his 'ubuntu theology' revolved around inclusivity and the overcoming of barriers between people – a faith that rested on the insight that just because white people were oppressing black people did not make all white people the enemy. On the contrary, Tutu's theology was all about breaking down barriers and embracing everyone, irrespective of who they might be – an outlook utterly at odds with the barrier-building of apartheid. Time and again, he has reminded his people that it is always wrong to hate, no matter what the circumstances. In 1984, Desmond Tutu was awarded the Nobel Peace Prize for his role as a central figure in the struggle against apartheid.

Christians and slavery

In earlier times, Christians had also been vociferous in stamping out the even greater injustice of slavery. The early church had been a little ambivalent about this issue – hardly surprising, given that the ancient world operated on the basis of slavery and could hardly have survived its eradication. In the New Testament, Paul's letter to Philemon, admonishing his reader to be merciful to a Christian slave, seems implicitly to condone the practice – while 1 Peter 2 instructs slaves to be submissive to their masters. Essentially, it seems that it hadn't really occurred to the New Testament authors to oppose slavery in principle. What they did insist upon was the fact that attachment to Christ overrides all social distinctions such as that between master and slave, and requires the good treatment of all people, whether slave or not. Thus, in his letter to the Galatians, Paul declared, 'For as many of you as have been baptized in Christ, have put on Christ. There is neither Jew nor Greek; there is neither bond nor free; there is neither male nor female. For you are all one in Christ Jesus.' In fact, Christianity was popular among slaves and other lower classes. For example, nearly all the people Paul greets in his letter to the Romans appear to be slaves. Unlike philosophers and aristocrats, the Christians did not despise those who worked with their hands. Paul was a tent-maker by profession, and Jesus himself had been an artisan, possibly a carpenter. And as the years passed, many more Christians became concerned for the lot of slaves. The act of freeing all one's slaves became increasingly common. One wealthy Christian woman named Melania paid for the freedom of so many at the start of the fifth century that she lost count of them all. And St Patrick, a Roman Briton who was enslaved by the Irish, to whom he brought Christianity, spoke out vehemently against the practice.

After the fall of the Roman empire in the West, slavery continued in the new barbarian kingdoms, which were the ancestors of modern Europe. But as the continent became increasingly Christian, the practice slowly dwindled. One figure in the gradual eradication of slavery was Bathilde, an Anglo-Saxon slave who was captured by Danish raiders and ended up in the palace of the Frankish kings. In fact, by the age of nineteen she had married King Clovis, and after his death she became regent of Francia, ruling for her young son. Despite the rapid elevation in her fortunes, Bathilde did not forget what it had been like to be a slave and did everything she could to stamp the practice out within her territories. Although existing slaves were not freed – something that would have destabilized society too much – it was illegal to acquire any more, and any slaves entering the kingdom were instantly freed. At the same time, she bought as many existing slaves as possible and freed them.

Slavery had virtually completely died out in Europe by the Middle Ages, since more or less everyone was now Christian and it was by this time felt impossible to have a Christian slave. The only exceptions were some Muslim slaves, captured during the Crusades; although there were plenty of Christian slaves in Muslim lands too, so the injustice went both ways. Thomas Aquinas, however, argued that slavery was a sin, opposed to natural justice. A number of organizations were founded to help those who

> *'This is the custom of the Roman Christians of Gaul: they send holy and able men to the Franks and other heathen with so many thousand gold coins to ransom baptised captives.'*
>
> St Patrick,
> 'Letter to Coroticus'

had been enslaved by the Muslims, such as the Order of Our Lady of Ransom, or Mercedarians – many of whom voluntarily became slaves themselves to minister to other slaves in the Muslim lands. Those Mercedarians who managed to remain free paid, over the years, for the freedom of hundreds of thousands of slaves.

One figure who did an enormous amount for slaves in early modern times was Vincent de Paul, who lived in the early seventeenth century and seems to have dedicated himself to helping the less fortunate with an almost frightening zeal. Born of a poor family in France, Vincent succeeded in gaining a good education – but as a young man, the ship he was travelling on was captured by Muslim pirates, and he spent some years as a slave in Algiers. Fortunately, he converted his master to Christianity, and together they escaped. Vincent became a spiritual director and tutor, but he also began taking a keen interest in the poor, setting up societies to help them. He was especially concerned for prisoners condemned to row in ships in horrible conditions, and he spent a considerable amount of time with them – not hard, since he was at the time employed by the minister in charge of them. Meanwhile, he founded the Daughters of Charity, a society of women who organized charity work among the poor in the countryside, as well as the Congregation of the Priests of the Mission, dedicated to spreading the gospel in the countryside. He founded hospices for the dying and more organizations to do good among the poor and needy in Paris. Vincent became famous and increasingly popular: he had the ear of Cardinal Richelieu himself, the ruler of Paris in the name of Louis XIII. But perhaps unsurprisingly, given his own experience as a slave, he was most concerned for the Christian slaves in North Africa. He sent many of his priests there, to preach and to try to improve their terrible conditions, and they succeeded in ransoming over a thousand.

Still, as we have seen, slavery reappeared with the exploration, in early modern times, of the Americas and Africa. The Americas opened up vast areas to cultivate, and Africa provided large numbers of people to cultivate them. It began in the 1430s, when the Spanish occupied the Canary Islands and enslaved their population. Pope Eugene IV immediately issued a papal bull condemning the action and ordering it to be reversed under pain of excommunication, but his orders were ignored. His successors, Pius II and Sixtus IV, repeated the order, to similarly minimal effect. The pope was simply not as powerful as he had once been, and the lure of vast profits in the new worlds that were being opened up was not going to help. Settlers began to enslave the Amerindians, and many justified it by arguing that these other races were not really humans but some inferior kind of creature. That was certainly not the official line from Rome: Pope Paul III declared that the Amerindians definitely were human beings and that neither they nor anyone else could be enslaved – but once again the pleas fell on deaf ears. In 1639, as the black slave trade accelerated, Pope Urban VIII decreed that this applied to Africans as well and that all African slaves should be freed and compensated for their captivity. The Jesuits tried to enforce this papal bull in Brazil and were expelled from Sao Paulo and attacked by mobs for their pains.

Some good was, nevertheless, achieved. The Catholic Church produced the *Code*

'They have deprived the natives of their property or turned it to their own use, and have subjected some of the inhabitants of said islands to perpetual slavery... We... exhort, through the sprinkling of the blood of Jesus Christ shed for their sins, one and all, temporal princes, lords, captains, armed men, barons, soldiers, nobles, communities and all others of every kind among the Christian faithful of whatever state, grade or condition, that they themselves desist from the aforementioned deeds, cause those subject to them to desist from them, and restrain them rigorously.'

Pope Eugene IV,
Sicut Dudum, 1435

A SLAVE MARKET IN
RICHMOND, VIRGINIA.
WOOD ENGRAVING,
AFTER A DRAWING BY
EDMOND MORIN,
1861.

Noir and *Código Negro Español*, codes intended to regulate and help the lives of slaves in the Americas, even if they could not be freed. And, of course, there was no slavery in the idealistic world of Paraguay, overseen by the Jesuits. But slavery became increasingly central to the economy of the southern part of North America in particular, and all the European nations with colonies in the New World relied upon it. However, as slavery became more entrenched, opposition to it began to grow. Britain played a central role in the transatlantic slave trade, with many Africans passing through ports such as Bristol, and it was among the British that opposition to slavery became especially prominent. A well-known Puritan theologian, Richard Baxter, was opposing the slave trade as early as the 1660s – although he also wanted to reunite all Christian churches while professing not to believe in bishops, so he was clearly not going to get very far. In America, meanwhile, a number of Christian groups were stridently opposed to slavery. The first were the Mennonites, an Anabaptist – or extreme Protestant – group who believed in pacifism, religious freedom, tolerance and living a simple life. In their settlement of Germantown, Pennsylvania, they published a pamphlet arguing that the colour of someone's skin should make no difference to their right to liberty. The slave owners of the region scoffed at their naivety. The Quakers, meanwhile, agreed with the Mennonites, and in 1696, they declared that any Quaker found trading in slaves would be expelled from their order. As the years passed, the Quakers became more and more opposed to slavery, to the extent of relocating their settlements from the southern states where it was more entrenched.

These people were, in many ways, Christian extremists, and their views were not those of the mainstream. That began to change in the eighteenth century. A Quaker in Philadelphia named Anthony Benezet devoted himself to opposing slavery, and in 1772, he wrote *Some Historical Account of Guinea*, which described the condition of slaves in graphic and horrific terms. It was widely read, and the movement gained ground. In particular, it was read by John Wesley, one of the leading religious figures of the day – an extraordinary preacher and leader of a growing 'Methodist' movement within the Church of England. Wesley was already deeply opposed to slavery, having been to Georgia as a young man and seen it first-hand, but Benezet's book helped to motivate him to speak out against it. In 1774, he published an eloquent *Thoughts upon Slavery*, which admonished the slave owners in unambiguous tones:

Are you a man*? Then you should have an* human *heart. But have you indeed? What is your heart made of? Is there no such principle as Compassion there? Do you never* feel *another's pain? Have you no Sympathy? No sense of human woe? No pity for the miserable?… Do you feel no relenting now? If you do not, you must go on, till the measure of your iniquities is full. Then will the Great GOD deal with* You*, as you have dealt with* them*, and require all their blood at your hands.*

As the years passed, the abolition movement gradually lost its rather dubious association with Quakers, Methodists and other marginals, and it was increasingly embraced by Christians within the Church of England and other mainstream denominations. An Anglican priest named James Ramsay became opposed to the practice while working in St Kitt's, in the Caribbean. He welcomed black people to his church and did his best to improve their lot – for which he was boycotted by the white landowners and eventually forced to return to England. Here, he wrote his influential

Essay on the Treatment and Conversion of African Slaves in the British Sugar Colonies, published in 1784. Many people listened to what Ramsay had to say, including a friend with the splendid name of Beilby Porteus, another priest who rose to become chaplain to the king and then bishop of Chester. Porteus preached against the maltreatment of slaves in the colonies and did his best, as a member of the House of Lords, to legislate in their favour.

The most famous of the abolitionists, however, was William Wilberforce, a precocious and talented Member of Parliament who looked into the issue of slavery in the 1780s and became horrified at what the evidence told him. In 1789, he presented his Abolition Bill to the House of Commons in what was said to have been the best speech ever made to Parliament. In the gallery, we are told, traders and merchants who had come to listen hung their heads in shame at Wilberforce's denunciation of their cruelty. But his opponents used the traditional parliamentary tactics of delay and amendation, and when the Bill was finally passed in 1792, it allowed only for the 'gradual' abolition of the slave trade. It quickly became clear that the process was going to be very gradual indeed; and while Wilberforce had enjoyed great public support before, the public tired of the cause. He continued to campaign, but he also spent time writing works of popular theology. Strangely, it was war with Napoleon that helped him, finally, to gain what he wanted. Napoleon was opposed to abolition, and so the British public, patriotic as ever, were suddenly all for it. In 1807, Parliament finally voted overwhelmingly to end the slave trade. There were still slaves in the colonies, however, and Wilberforce continued to campaign on their behalf. It was not until 1833 that Parliament eventually abolished the whole thing. Wilberforce, satisfied at last, died three days later.

CHAPTER 8

What Will Christianity Do for Us?

t seems that Christianity has had quite an impact on the world. But what is the situation today? It is unlikely that Christianity will again be the prime mover behind literacy and education, at least in the Western world. And the days when philosophy was the handmaid to theology, when a Christian world view provided the incubation chamber for the emergence of modern science, are certainly long gone.

Yet Christianity remains a potent force across the world. Approximately a third of the world's population are estimated to be Christians, of one kind or another. What might Christianity do for the world in the years to come?

The Wizard's maps and a shifting centre of gravity

An old man with a long, grey beard and pointy hat stands on a stepladder in the town square, haranguing the crowds. Is he some kind of lunatic? No – or at least, perhaps not. He's the Wizard, regarded by critics as a 'living work of art' and officially recognized as 'national wizard' by the prime minister of New Zealand. Despite having been born and raised in England, the Wizard has successfully become one of New Zealand's most recognizable and beloved figures, and his lectures – delivered outside the cathedral in Christchurch – are always popular attractions.

When not preaching his idiosyncratic politics or casting rain spells (something that would no doubt infuriate Agobard of Lyons), the Wizard is devoted – and, indeed, charged by the government – to devising 'a new and improved universe which puts New Zealand on top of the world both physically and metaphysically'. The most well-known manifestation of this is his world maps, which subvert traditional symbolism and expectation by the simple method of being printed upside down, with the south at the top. On this scheme, all the recognizable landmasses disappear, to be replaced by an unfamiliar world, one that seems to have a lot more sea, and which is dominated by areas such as South America and the Philippines. New Zealand, naturally, comes out on top.

Something like that is happening to Christianity today. Over the past century, its centre of gravity has been slowly but undeniably shifting, until the southern hemisphere has overtaken the northern in importance. The religion originated in the Middle East and flourished in Europe and, later, North America. But it is now waning in those areas. Islam has long been the dominant religion in the Middle East, and Europe is becoming increasingly secularized. Christianity remains very strong in North America – but the religion is gathering pace in the southern hemisphere, especially in Africa. A century ago, 9 per cent of the continent was Christian; today it

A baptism in Durban, South Africa. Every Sunday at dawn, priests from the Zion Church in the Khayelitsha township baptise new converts in the sea. The charismatic, Pentecostalist style of worship of this large, black church is typical of the distinctively 'African' Christianity that is already reaching out from Africa to communities around the world.

is 46 per cent. As the religion grows and spreads, its character changes. We have seen examples throughout this book of Christians adapting their faith to match their situation and cultural background, and nowhere has that been more striking than in Africa. In many ways, the African church hearkens back to the early church far more than in other continents. Whereas Christians elsewhere are divided between conservative and liberal, most African churches tend to be theologically conservative – holding to the traditional doctrines, rather than trying to reinterpret or abandon them to fit a modern world view. At the same time, they have integrated Christianity into a traditional African world view, one where the supernatural plays a major role.

It is sometimes supposed that Christianity in Africa is simply a hangover of the imperialist age, something that got imported and pasted over the indigenous culture. We have already seen that the situation is not so simplistic – that there was Christianity in Ethiopia, for example, over 1,500 years ago; and in Congo it was indigenous people such as King Afonso who were enthusiastic about Christianity and

sought to promote it. And the nature of African Christianity today also gives the lie to the notion that it is simply a European import that doesn't belong there. Christianity in Africa is, typically, authentically African, combining the world view and culture of traditional African religions with the new beliefs of Christianity. In some parts of Africa, over 10 per cent of the population still practise old, indigenous religions, and that has a huge influence over how newer religions such as Islam and Christianity are perceived and how they manifest themselves. And this means that a different kind of Christianity is developing and becoming dominant. In the West, many Christian theologians have sought to find a new way of thinking of Christianity – a non-supernatural way – in the belief that the old ways are no longer appropriate; but in Africa, they are not only surviving but thriving. Similar changes are taking place in South America, where the old domination of the Catholic Church is no longer as assured as it once was. As in Africa, Protestantism, and in particular the energetic, celebratory style of Pentecostalism, is becoming more and more popular.

'There is always something new coming out of Africa.'

Pliny the Elder,
Natural History 8, c. AD 77

And as the churches in the developing nations become more vibrant, and those in Europe less, so the former are increasingly dictating the future of Christianity. The largest Anglican Church in the world, for example, is the one in Nigeria; and this means that the African members of the Anglican communion are more and more able to exercise influence over the Anglican church as a whole. That has been especially noticeable in recent debates over the church's attitude to homosexuality, and the liberal approach of many European and American Christians has sometimes been overruled by the much more hard-line, conservative attitude of many Africans.

And the people who are filling the churches of Africa are different from the faithful of the old world. In particular, they tend to be a lot poorer. This means that

African Christianity is not only doctrinally conservative and open to notions of the supernatural, but it is especially concerned with this-world issues, with issues of poverty and justice. We have already seen the role that African Christianity played in opposing apartheid in South Africa, and Christian leaders in Africa continue to take a prominent role in opposing what they regard as abuses of power or injustice. Pius Ncube, for example, is the Roman Catholic Archbishop of Bulawayo, the second largest city in Zimbabwe. He is one of the few public figures in the country to take a consistent and vocal stand against the policies of Robert Mugabe, the controversial Zimbabwean president. Throughout the 1980s and 90s, Mugabe's rule oversaw a decided erosion of human rights: his political opponents were silenced or even killed, creating an effective one-party state. In particular, Mugabe's attempts to confiscate land from white farmers and give it to black ones has received international condemnation, as did his prosecution of his predecessor for 'unnatural sex acts' – Mugabe's term for homosexuality. But Mugabe refuses to accept that his policies have led to food shortages and starvation in Zimbabwe, and bitterly attacks Western governments that impose sanctions on his regime.

He also dismisses the condemnations from church leaders, including Desmond Tutu in South Africa ('an angry, embittered little bishop') and his own Pius Ncube ('another Tutu who thinks he is holy, but he is telling lies every day'). Ncube was educated by the Jesuits in Zimbabwe when it was still called Rhodesia, after the English colonialist Cecil Rhodes. He returned to the country in the 1970s and has repeatedly called for Robert Mugabe to stand down, accusing him of wrecking the country's economy and not caring whether his people live or die. Naturally, Ncube lives a dangerous life as a result, with government spies sitting in his church taking notes during his sermons and sometimes warning him to stick to purely 'religious' subjects. Much of the rest of the Catholic Church in Zimbabwe has failed to speak out against the government, and as a result, Ncube has become something of a marginalized figure; but the priests in his own archdiocese have loyally stood by him.

In 1960, the British prime minister Harold Macmillan said in Cape Town, 'The wind of change is blowing through the continent.' He was referring to the new post-colonial situation in Africa, as former colonies regained their independence. Today, the wind of change continues to blow, as many African countries, just like Zimbabwe, continue to struggle with the legacy of the imperialist era. At the same time, major problems such as the Aids epidemic, endemic poverty and national debt remain to be solved. In these uncertain times, the growth and vitality of the Christian churches throughout Africa can hardly fail to play a major role in the years to come. Figures such as Desmond Tutu, Pius Ncube or Janani Luwum (the archbishop of Uganda, whose stand against the dictator Idi Amin saw him arrested and murdered in 1977) represent the growing voice that Christianity will undoubtedly continue to have in African society and politics in the years to come.

Back to the future with the Catholic Church

There are more Roman Catholics in the world than there are Muslims. Despite the continuing growth of Islam, that situation looks unlikely to change, for the Catholic Church remains strong in South America and throughout Africa, and even in Europe and North America it is still an important institution. What contribution will the Catholic Church make to the twenty-first century?

That question may well have been answered forty years ago in one of the most important religious events of recent times – the Second Vatican Council. The Council was called by Pope John XIII within three months of his taking office in 1959, and was intended as a sort of extension and modification to the First Vatican Council, which had taken place in 1870. At that council, Pope Pius IX had sought to oppose modern tendencies in thought, such as liberalism and modern science, and had condemned them as wholeheartedly as he could, while also declaring his own pronouncements to be infallible. Vatican I had never technically ended, and so Vatican II was, in theory, simply a new session of the same council, but in reality it was quite different. Where Vatican I had been an entrenchment of traditional Catholicism against the modern world, Vatican II was an embracing of the modern world. The liturgy was changed to make it more open, less of a mystery performed by priests and watched by the people. And a new era of tolerance was inaugurated to those outside the Catholic Church. The council described the Orthodox Church in glowing terms, as its Eastern counterpart, and also opened the way for increased dialogue with Protestants. And this went beyond the borders of Christendom. The council affirmed the ties of Christianity to Judaism, and denounced any kind of persecution of the Jews that may have been committed in the name of Christianity. The positive aspects of Islam were also commended, and the council spoke of the similarities in doctrine and in ethics that Muslims and Christians share. These religions' shared devotion to God make them natural allies, and the council affirmed that it is a duty of all religious people, not just Christians, to love and respect all people, whoever they might be.

Stirring words, and ones that the Catholic Church is still unpacking. The more open and ecumenical direction of Vatican II has not been wholeheartedly embraced within the church, and Pope John Paul II, though he would, of course, never oppose a

‘One is the community of all peoples, one their origin, for God made the whole human race to live over the face of the earth. One also is their final goal, God. His providence, his manifestations of goodness, his saving design extend to all men, until that time when the elect will be united in the Holy City, the city ablaze with the glory of God, where the nations will walk in his light.’

Vatican II, *Nostra Aetate*, October 28 1965

recent ecumenical council and frequently quotes from its teachings, has in general taken a more conservative approach than it might suggest. In this he has, perhaps, been influenced more by the growing Catholic Church of the southern hemisphere than by the old heartlands of the north. But it does mean that many of the lessons of Vatican II still remain to be fully applied.

The decades since Vatican II have not, it must be admitted, seen unambiguous rapprochement between Christianity and other religions, especially Islam. On the contrary, those countries where Christianity and Islam both exist in large numbers, such as Nigeria and the Philippines, have seen increased tension and violence. Perhaps in the years to come the more unifying spirit of Vatican II will become more powerful in these regions. The council was, after all, the first Catholic council to welcome delegates from throughout the world, not simply Europe. Just as African Christianity has been invigorated by returning to an earlier Christian viewpoint, one of supernatural forces, miraculous healing and concern for the poor, so too European Catholicism may find a renewal in the teaching of the major council of the twentieth century. If it does, however, that will be a renewal largely for Europe and North America. African Catholicism is, in character, more in tune with Vatican I than with Vatican II.

Beards, basketballs and human rights

A cosmopolitan city such as London attracts all kinds of people. It has been said that there are more Kiwis in London than in any town in New Zealand itself, other than Auckland. Among the more unexpected groups, however, are six Franciscan friars from New York City who have set up home in Canning Town. Needless to say, a group of Americans who walk around in long, brown cloaks and sandals and sport bushy beards took some time to fit into East London society. But they believe they have been called to minister to that community, and that is precisely what they do, in whatever way seems to work. One of the friars, Brother Nicholas, is a basketball fan, so he has set up basketball coaching sessions with the local children, to give them something positive to do. The lessons get the kids to cooperate and respect others, and, the friars hope, strengthen the community. Even though there is no overtly Christian teaching at events such as this, the friars are disseminating their Christian values among those around them.

While the local media has picked up on the 'slam-dunk monks' (who are, of course, friars and not monks at all), there is a lot of this sort of thing going on quietly, behind

'Blessed is the man who supports his neighbour during his frailty to the extent that he would want to be supported by him, if he falls into an exactly similar situation.'

Francis of Assisi, *The Admonitions* 18

WHAT HAS CHRISTIANITY EVER DONE FOR US?

the scenes. Elsewhere in London, there is a group of Maltese Franciscans, who minister to the Maltese community in the city. That involves 'religious' ministry, such as holding Masses, but it also involves a lot of pastoral work, especially to people in hospital. The friars often become very close to the long-term patients they visit and offer close support – for sometimes, simply being there as a shoulder to lean on is enough.

Franciscan friars may look rather odd to most people today, in their medieval-style outfits, but they are still there, and they are doing an enormous amount of work behind the scenes. It is not just the Franciscans, of course. Christians throughout the world are continuing to work for justice and to alleviate the lot of the poor or the suffering. For example, one organization that seeks to tackle poverty at its source is Christian Aid, a charity set up by the churches of the UK and Ireland in 1945. Christian Aid is one of the highest-profile charities in Britain, raising large sums of money that are sent abroad, where local activists decide how best to spend them. Although the organization is not politically motivated, it does campaign against what it regards as the root causes of poverty and other injustices, which often involves taking a political stance. And the charity therefore speaks out against abuses by anyone, from the Burmese government to British American Tobacco.

Another area where Christianity may well have a benign influence in the future is human rights, particularly those of women. In recent years, there has been well-publicized controversy within the Christian world over the ordination of women. The first female priests in the Church of England were ordained in 1994, leading to a cooling of relations with the Roman Catholic Church and the Orthodox Church, both of which refuse to countenance the possibility. However, historically, Christianity has done much to emphasize the rights and dignity of women. In Galatians 3:28, Paul states that in Christ there is no male and female; in 1 Corinthians 7, meanwhile, he instructs husbands and wives to have mutual care for each other. There is no getting around Paul's basically male-dominated view of things, with his belief that the husband should have authority over the wife; but the authority he advocates is a respectful authority, one that cares for the needs of both partners, not a domineering authority. This is reflected in the early Christian prohibition on divorce, a rule that largely protected women from finding themselves cast out of the home – for divorce in the ancient world was essentially a male prerogative.

The idea that a woman is best protected by ensuring that her husband looks after her properly is perhaps not one that sits well with modern society, but the ideal of safeguarding women's rights is. As we have seen, much of the concern with rights that has such prominence in Western society today derives from its Christian heritage and the notion that individuals matter. Movements such as women's rights or animal rights have certainly gone beyond that Christian heritage, but they would probably not exist without it – at least not in the form that they currently take. As we saw in chapter 4, the distinction between private and public morality goes back to Christian Thomasius, the Lutheran philosopher who was one of the leading lights at Halle University at the end of the seventeenth century. In other words, the belief that individuals have the right to privacy, to their own space, to freedom, to pursue what they like as long as they do not infringe the rights of others, has its roots in the Protestant devotion to the individual and his or her own value in the eyes of God. It is an approach fundamentally different from that of some other cultures, such as Islamic culture, where religious and moral values are seen as permeating throughout society, without this emphasis on the individual's rights. Similarly, though Islam does not prescribe the restrictions on women's freedoms it is often caricatured as doing, it is true that some Muslim countries impose rather strange laws on them (such as banning them from driving in Saudi Arabia, for example), and some have taken such approaches to abhorrent excess – most notably, the Taliban regime in Afghanistan. In a future in which Islam and Christianity seem destined to continue to struggle for headway, particularly in Africa and South-East Asia, it is likely that their very different approaches to the roles of the individual and society will come more to the fore. Whether that encounter takes the route of Vatican II or a more antagonistic character, this is an area where Christianity's heritage will play a huge role, and where Christian values could continue to be extremely influential.

All of this again ties back to what we have seen throughout this book – the paradoxical power of Christianity when it runs counter to the dominant culture. In chapter 2, we saw how in works such as *Silence* the Japanese Christian author Shusaku Endo has explored the idea that, in Christianity, success might be the flip side of failure. Similarly, in chapter 6, we saw the counterintuitive teaching of Jesus, Francis of Assisi and others, that happiness can perhaps be found by rejecting the things that society normally regards as essential – even intrinsic – to happiness. In the same way, Christianity can sometimes be most influential, and do the most good, when it has something of an underground character. As we have seen in this book, Christianity has influenced the modern world in a huge number of ways. Sometimes it has done so as the dominant ideology. Literacy and education in the West, for example, owe a great debt to the Christian rule of people such as Justinian and Charlemagne. But sometimes it has done so from a position of relative weakness – such as the political activism of people such as Hélder Câmara or Janani Luwum. Some people have even argued that Christianity is better off in the latter role, and that the conversion of Constantine in the fourth century was one of the worst things that ever happened to the church, because it put it into a position of power and therefore caused it to sell out. That, of course, is a caricature of the truth. But it does remain the case that power has never been an unambiguously good thing from the church's point of view. While being in authority gives the church the means to act for the good, often being out of authority gives it more of a motivation. Perhaps, as the twenty-first century progresses, the church will once again take on board the teaching of Augustine from the fifth century. There are two cities in the world, the earthly city and the heavenly city. The two may share the same space; they may even, sometimes, be indistinguishable. But the heavenly city has its focus beyond the earthly, and it is more enduring. For the story of the world is the story of the City of God, and one way or another, it is God's providence that determines how things will pan out.

Index

Picture Acknowledgments

Picture research by Zooid Pictures Limited.

p. 2–3 Yann Arthus-Bertrand/Corbis UK Ltd.
p. 4 AKG – Images
p. 9 AKG – Images
p. 11 Erich Lessing /AKG – Images
p. 13 AKG – Images
p. 14 O. Alamany & E. Vicens/Corbis UK Ltd.
p. 16 Bo Zaunders/Corbis UK Ltd.
p. 17 Charles & Josette Lenars/Corbis UK Ltd.
p. 18 AKG – Images
p. 22–23 Viennaphoto/Alamy
p. 26 AKG – Images
p. 29 Tony Kyriacou/Rex Features
p. 30 AKG – Images
p. 32 AKG – Images
p. 35 Joseph Martin /AKG – Images
p. 37 Erich Lessing /AKG – Images
p. 38 Erich Lessing/AKG – Images
p. 42 New Line/Everett/Rex Features
p. 45 AKG – Images
p. 47 Robert Johnson, photo booth self-portrait, early 1930s/(c) 1986 Delta Haze Corporation. All Rights Reserved. Used By Permission
p. 53 Bettmann/Corbis UK Ltd.
p. 56 Lion Hudson/David Townsend
p. 58 Rex Features
p. 60 Bridgeman Art Library
p. 63 Corbis UK Ltd.
p. 68 AKG – London
p. 70 Mary Evans Picture Library
p. 73 Vanni Archive/Corbis UK Ltd.
p. 74 Adam Woolfitt/Corbis UK Ltd.
p. 75 Dean Conger/Corbis UK Ltd.
p. 77 Robert Holmes/Corbis UK Ltd.
p. 78 Christie's Images/Corbis UK Ltd.
p. 79 Peter Harholdt/Corbis UK Ltd.
p. 81 Paul A. Souders/Corbis UK Ltd.
p. 82–83 Peter Guttman/Corbis UK Ltd.
p. 85 Roger Wood/Corbis UK Ltd.
p. 86 AKG – Images
p. 88 British Library/AKG – Images
p. 93 Germanisches Nationalmuseum, Nuremberg, Germany/Bridgeman Art Library
p. 96 AKG – Images
p. 97 Gianni Dagli Orti/Corbis UK Ltd.
p. 99 AKG – Images
p. 101 Gilles Mermet /AKG – Images
p. 102 AKG — Images
p. 106 Musee d'Art Thomas Henry, Cherbourg, France/Bridgeman Art Library
p. 107 Erich Lessing /AKG – Images
p. 110 Lisa Trocchi; Gallo Images/Corbis UK Ltd.
p. 114 AKG – Images
p. 115 Images.com/Corbis UK Ltd.
p. 117 AKG – Images
p. 119 Erich Lessing /AKG – Images
p. 122 British Library/AKG – Images
p. 124 Erich Lessing/AKG – Images
p. 127 Mary Evans Picture Library
p. 131 Werner Forman/Corbis UK Ltd.
p. 132 Stefan Diller/AKG – Images
p. 134 Mary Evans Picture Library
p. 134–135 Gianni Dagli Orti/Corbis UK Ltd.
p. 138 Corbis UK Ltd.
p. 140 Mary Evans Picture Library
p. 143 University College London
p. 144 Corbis UK Ltd.
p. 150 Archivo Iconografico, S.A./Corbis UK Ltd.
p. 153 Bettmann/Corbis UK Ltd.
p. 154 WEIMAR ARCHIVE/Mary Evans Picture Library
p. 156 National Gallery Collection. By kind permission of the Trustees of the National Gallery, London/Corbis UK Ltd.
p. 161 AKG – Images
p. 163 AKG – Images
p. 164 Janet Jarman/Corbis/Corbis UK Ltd.
p. 166 PELLETIER MICHELINE SYGMA/Corbis UK Ltd.
p. 167 Leif Skoogfors/Corbis UK Ltd.
p. 169 Frank Driggs Collection//Redferns Music Picture Library
p. 170–171 Bettmann/Corbis UK Ltd.
p. 174 Reuters/Corbis UK Ltd.
p. 178 AKG – Images
p. 182–183 Alex Webb/Magnum Photos
p. 184 Reuters/Corbis UK Ltd.
p. 187 Simon Roberts/NB Pictures

Lion Hudson
Commissioning editor: Morag Reeve
Project editors: Laura Derico, Catherine Giddings
Proof-reader: Jenni Dutton
Jacket designer: Jonathan Roberts
Book designer: Nicholas Rous
Production manager: Kylie Ord